Paulo Freire's
Philosophy of
Education

ALSO AVAILABLE FROM CONTINUUM

On Critical Pedagogy, Henry A.Giroux
Education for Critical Consciousness, Paulo Freire
Paulo Freire, Daniel Schugurensky
Pedagogy of the Heart, Paulo Freire
Pedagogy of Hope, Paulo Freire
Pedagogy of the Oppressed, Paulo Freire
Pedagogy, Oppression and Transformation in a 'Post-Critical' Climate, Edited by Andrew O'Shea and Maeve O'Brien

Paulo Freire's Philosophy of Education

Origins, Developments, Impacts and Legacies

JONES IRWIN

continuum

Continuum International Publishing Group

The Tower Building	80 Maiden Lane
11 York Road	Suite 704
London SE1 7NX	New York NY 10038

www.continuumbooks.com

© Jones Irwin 2012

All rights reserved. No part of this publication may be reproduced or transmitted in any form or by any means, electronic or mechanical, including photocopying, recording, or any information storage or retrieval system, without prior permission in writing from the publishers.

Jones Irwin has asserted his right under the Copyright, Designs and Patents Act, 1988, to be identified as Author of this work.

British Library Cataloguing-in-Publication Data
A catalogue record for this book is available from the British Library.

ISBN: HB: 978–1–4411–4500–0
PB: 978–1–4411–8931–8

Library of Congress Cataloging-in-Publication Data
Irwin, Jones.
   Paulo Freire's philosophy of education : origins, developments, impacts and legacies / Jones Irwin.
      p. cm.
   Summary: "A critique of Freire's thinking, the influence of his work and ways in which his theories may be developed into the future" – Provided by publisher.
   Includes bibliographical references and index.
   ISBN 978-1-4411-8931-8 (pbk.) – ISBN 978-1-4411-4500-0 () – ISBN 978-0-8264-2638-3 ()
1. Freire, Paulo, 1921-1997–
   Criticism and interpretation. 2. Education--Philosophy. 3. Critical pedagogy. I. Title.
LB880.F732I78 2012
370.1–dc23

2011040416

Typeset by Fakenham Prepress Solutions Ltd., Fakenham NR21 8NN
Printed and bound in India

For my mother Úna and my father Leslie

CONTENTS

ACKNOWLEDGEMENTS

At St. Patrick's College, Drumcondra, I have a supportive set of colleagues and friends, and I would like to especially thank the respective groups in Human Development and the Education Department. At an institutional level, Mary Shine-Thompson has been a wonderful advocate for imaginative work in the intersection between the humanities and education. With regard specifically to my work on Freire, both Andy Burke and Joe Dunne were extraordinarily supportive from the time I began to teach philosophy of education in 2001. Without them, my understanding and love of Freire's work would never have developed as it has. Philomena Donnelly has been a great friend and co-worker on our elective and in seeking for deeper change amidst the traditionalism of the Irish education system, and I have really enjoyed working with both Philomena and Brian Ruane on our new (Freirean!) Ethics course. As Head of Education, Fionnuala Waldron has (as have Mark Morgan and John Canavan before her) been a facilitator of progressive work. Similarly, the students over the past ten years in Philosophy of Education and Human Development, both at undergraduate and postgraduate level (on the MA and Ed.D. programmes), have inspired me to new understandings of the possibilities of Freire's corpus of work. I sincerely thank them for their honesty of endeavour, integrity and sense of fun. In terms of the publication process, Continuum have been supportive from the moment they received my initial proposal, and I would like to thank Alison Baker and Rosie Pattinson, Nicholas Church and Kim Storry.

My partner Melissa has been a constant source of love and humour, and our children, Eloïse, Jeremy and Gregory make everything possible, with what Freire likes to call their 'bohemian' laughter and happiness. Little Calvagh Cullinane has provided me with the joys of the new experience of being an uncle, Judy and Mike are great confidantes, and Patrick, Mary and Zöe in Spain keep the continentalist spirit alive. I would also like to remember my late grandparents, Jones and Margaret Irwin in Sligo, and Patrick and Judy Mc Grath in Cork, whose sustaining love has been on my mind throughout the writing of this work.

I would like to dedicate this book to my parents, Leslie and Úna Irwin, who have, from day one, encouraged and balanced me in my sometimes obsessive pursuit of philosophy. I owe them more than words can ever say.

Jones Irwin, Dublin, August 2011

INTRODUCTION

From life to philosophy: exploring Freire's biography

The intimate connections between life and philosophy are nowhere more apparent than through an exploration of Paulo Freire's work. Throughout this text, in seeking to explicate Paulo Freire's philosophy of education, I will return to examples drawn from the detail of Freire's 'life'. This recourse to insights from Freire's existence, so as to help in an understanding of his thinking, is hardly an imposed method foreign to the tendencies of his work. On the contrary, this symbiosis between life and philosophy is everywhere manifest in Freire's texts, early to late. It involves less a kind of edifying approach which would supplement his theories with more down-to-earth experience, and more an integral commitment of his overall philosophical vision. From the very beginning, Freire's texts develop organically from existential and political situations, often of acute terror and vulnerability, such as that of the military coup in Brazil in 1964. Freire's philosophy is thus fundamentally a philosophy of life and politics, in a way that often more supposedly practical philosophies could never be. His writing evolves from a sometimes fraught but oftentimes celebratory understanding of the possibilities of living, both the immense dangers but also the intense joys of human relationship and community. As Nietzsche declared, 'I love only what a person has written with his blood' (quoted in Derrida, 1978, p. 328) and Freire is, in this sense, very much a writer in the Nietzschean tenor.

'A land of contrasts and a pedagogy of contradiction'

As one of Freire's greatest commentators, Carlos Alberto Torres, has noted, in 'A Land of Contrasts and a Pedagogy of Contradiction', much of the verve and tension of Freire's thinking derives from the specifics of his Brazilian upbringing and socio-cultural context (Torres, 1994): 'Brazil is a land of contrasts. Land of wonderful Rio de Janeiro, with the beautiful sights of the Corcovado mountain and its splendid world-class beaches, but also land of the Amazonian Indians, harassed, haunted, and murdered in their own dominion by gold prospectors and entrepreneurs of many sorts' (Torres, 1994, p. ix). Freire's early texts, for example, resound with the echoes and moods of the political and educational conflicts of the early 1960s in Brazil, conflicts which will lead to Freire's enforced exile. While his most famous text *Pedagogy of the Oppressed* (Freire, 1996a) tends to opt for a more universalist-humanist perspective, it is clear, as we will see from a reading of *Education as The Practice of Freedom* (Freire, 2005a), that Freire developed these ideas and concepts very much out of the crucible of a Brazilian society struggling with the damaging legacy of Portuguese colonialism, and with its own complex internal politics.

Freire's own upbringing in Recife and Jaboatão in Northeastern Brazil (he was born in 1921) had already exposed him to the reality of poverty and oppression, as this was one of the poorest regions of the world. Freire's own relatively affluent family were thrown into disarray by the premature death of his father when Freire was just 13, and he only entered the *ginásio* (or high school) when he was 16, while his classmates were aged 11 or 12 (Gadotti, 1994, p. 3). This no doubt contributed to his 'great difficulty in assimilating any kind of formal education' (Gadotti, 1994, p. 3), a factor perhaps contributing to his uncommon sensitivity to the weaknesses of traditional education. His mother's strong religious faith was also central to Freire's formation, and he always remained a Catholic philosopher, although hardly orthodox. He consistently challenged and criticized what he saw as the oppression perpetrated by the traditionalist church, advocating instead what he termed the 'prophetic church' (Gadotti, 1994, p. 4), in a manner which drew him close to the Liberation Theology movements of Latin America (Gutierrez, 2001; Torres, 1993). His first wife Elza was also a constant source of inspiration to Freire, who acknowledges her 'solidarity' (Gadotti, 1994, p. 5) throughout the difficult years of imprisonment and exile, right up until her death in 1986. His second wife, Ana Maria Araújo Freire, also features as a key interlocutor and reader of his later work (Freire, 2004) and we can thus foreground the significance of inter-personal relationships in the intellectual formation of Freire. We shall see how this inter-personal dimension also influences how Freire writes and indeed the very form of his texts as his work develops, with increasing recourse to the dialogue form and the epistolary text.

Freire's critique of traditional Christianity, and traditionalist education, draws its sustenance from an extraordinary array of philosophical sources, what Elias refers to as a theoretical 'eclecticism' (Elias, 1994). But Marx's thinking, and especially the early Marx, is a constant recourse throughout Freire's texts, and we shall see how the former's 'Theses On Feuerbach' (Marx, 1992a) may be seen as paradigmatic in the development of Freire's criticisms of traditionalist or essentialist philosophy. Not the least of the enigmas surrounding Freire's thinking is, therefore, how he succeeds in being both a Christian and a Marxist at the same time.

Perhaps the key philosophical and political moment in Freire's early life is his development of a new method of adult literacy education, which he first presented at Pernambuco in 1958 (Gadotti, 1994, p. 8). This new approach, which was built on a strong criticism of existing methods of literacy and more general education, forms the basis of his more evolved work, which we will analyse in this book. We can trace its first systematic exposition in book form in *Education as The Practice of Freedom* (2005a) and, of course, it will also serve as the theoretical and practical foundation for Freire's theses in *Pedagogy of the Oppressed* (1996a).

A new approach to literacy

Gadotti draws out the story of how this evolution of Freire's method began to engender political conflict in Brazil – this was 'the method which took Paulo Freire into exile' (Gadotti, 1994, p. 15). The emergence of this literacy method in Northeastern Brazil is not coincidental – in 1960 this area had an illiteracy rate of 75 per cent and a life expectancy of 28 years for men and 32 for women; in 1956, half of the land was owned by 3 per cent of the population; the income per capita was only 40 per cent of the national average (Elias, 1994). Of course, precisely at the heart of the threat this educational approach posed to the status quo was the fact that it went beyond the confines of ordinary methodologies – instead of being a 'method', we might describe Freire's approach as being rooted in an attempt to construct a new epistemology or theory of knowledge (Elias, 1994, p. 2, Gadotti, 1994, p. 16;). Or, as Linda Bimbi notes, the Freirean approach to literacy is linked to a 'total change in society' (quoted Gadotti, 1994, p. 17). While the first experiments began in 1962 with 300 rural farm workers who were taught to read and write in 45 days (Gadotti, 1994, p. 15), the following year Freire had been invited by the President of Brazil to rethink the literacy schemes for adults on a national basis. By 1964, 20,000 cultural circles were set up for two million illiterate people (Gadotti, 1994, p. 15). But, as Gadotti notes, 'the military coup, however, interrupted the work right at the beginning and cancelled all the work that had already been done' (Gadotti, 1994, p. 16). The military coup thus attacks the literacy and political programme at its very roots: Freire, along with many others, was jailed. This incarceration lasted for 75 days, with many instances of torture and murder of prisoners (most of whom were teachers and community workers). After release, Freire was encouraged to leave the country and he fled to exile in Chile.

Again and again throughout his texts, Freire will return to this time as constitutive for his understanding of the relation between politics and education, but, we might also say, for his sensitivity to the relation between personal existence and philosophy. This emphasis is evident in early works such as *Extension or Communication* (Freire, 2005b), which was written during his exile in Chile right up until later works such as *Pedagogy of Hope: Reliving Pedagogy of the Oppressed* (Freire, 1992), where Freire exactly 'relives' the initial attempts at political and educational transformation in Brazil. We will also explore how Freire's life and work can seen as coming full circle in his later return to Brazil. In 1980, 16 years after his initial exile, Freire is allowed to come back to Brazil where he becomes a Minister for Education in São Paulo. During this last period of his life, Freire teaches influentially at the University of São Paulo, while also being instrumental in the formation of the Brazilian Workers' Party (*Partido dos Trabalhadores*), led by later Brazilian President Lulu. His texts from this period constantly foreground the tensions of individual and collective freedom and responsibility. Freire died in 1997 but his legacy continues to be powerfully influential in Brazil and South and Latin America, as well as on a more worldwide level. Understanding Freire as philosopher, for us, will thus also be a process of coming to understand Freire as person, in an existential and political sense.

Overview: Freire and the discipline of the philosophy of education

Before looking at the detail of Freire's own texts, I will first situate Freire's work in the context of the discipline of the philosophy of education. The increased receptivity to Freire's texts in more mainstream philosophy of education in recent years has been due to what may be described as a *paradigm shift* in the latter discipline's self-understanding. While education has always been a significant theme in the work of philosophers from early Greek thinking onwards in 500 BC, with, for example, both Plato and Aristotle seeing education as an area of key philosophical contestation, the discipline of the philosophy of education is a relatively recent phenomenon, traceable from the work of Hirst and Peters in the UK in the early 1970s (Hirst and Peters, 1970). While John Dewey (Dewey, 1973) is now viewed as an earlier philosopher of education, Dewey's own significant contribution to philosophy per se (in terms of the movement of pragmatism) may be seen as somewhat overshadowing his work specifically as a philosopher of education (or as being indissociable from the latter). Hirst and Peters, in contrast, contributed significantly to the specific self-understanding of a distinct discipline of the philosophy of education, and in their eyes this discipline was grounded primarily in a Kantian and 'analytical' approach to education and philosophy, which focused most especially on conceptual issues (Blake *et al.*, 2003b). In simple terms, we can say that Freire's approach to the philosophy of education is significantly at odds with such conceptualism. However, in more recent years, the discipline of the philosophy of education (so long the bastion of the Anglo-American analytic tradition) has come face to face with the cutting edge of French and German continentalist postmodern theory. The signal importance of the groundbreaking work of such philosophers as Jacques Derrida (Derrida, 1978) and Michel Foucault (Foucault, 1998) for schooling and the relationship between education and culture has at long last become apparent. In the UK, this evolution of the discipline is being led by thinkers such as Paul Standish and Nigel Blake, who apply the insights of the theoretical work to the particular (changing) context of British education. The previously dominant analyticity and neo-Kantianism no longer seems so relevant in the context of an increasingly powerful politicization of education.

This insight, under the guise of the 'Critical Pedagogy' movement, is also being taken up in the USA. This movement, led by figures such as Peter McLaren, bell hooks and Henry Giroux, seeks to answer the needs of the increasing complexification of youth and urban culture, as they impact on education. *The key influence and acknowledged original source for this strand of pedagogical thinking is the work of Paulo Freire.* Under the tutelage of Freire, these philosophers recognize the need to pay homage to a romantic tradition of creativity and imagination in education, while reformulating some of the implicit utopianism of this romantic tradition through the addition of a healthy dose of urban and inter-cultural pedagogical experience. However, I want to claim that an analysis of Freire's work may also be seen as immensely significant not simply in the American context of education but also more globally. With regard to what Freire refers to as the 'Third World' (itself a constantly shifting concept in terms of its identification), we shall see how Freire's work is very explicit in its influence. But, as Freire's work constantly demonstrates and reiterates, the so-called First and Third worlds are in constant mutual interaction and reaction, and we shall also see how Freire's philosophy of education may be seen as increasingly relevant with regard to changes in the education systems of the UK and Ireland, among other countries. Within the UK, for example, alongside the practical connections, we can also see Freire's philosophy as connected to the evolution of the Birmingham Centre for Contemporary Cultural Studies (hereafter CCCS), in its initial forays into adult education and then with regard to the study of youth subculture. This nexus of influence and evolution, which has looked back to Marx (Marx, 1992a), Nietzsche (Nietzsche, 1998) and Gramsci (Gramsci, 1988) among others, may be seen as developing, with significant degrees of tension, through the 1980s and 1990s work in the philosophy of education, both in the USA and the UK. These respective developments of Freire's work share significant affinities but also manifest tensions with regard to their interpretations of Freire.

I will explore how the British example of the CCCS may be viewed as pushing beyond the limits of Freire's work while maintaining important connections to the latter; such extension should not of course be seen as simply negative. In recent critical anthologies devoted to his work, Freire has acknowledged the need for such challenging of his own approach. However, criticism of both Freire and the developments of his work have come from other sources. One accusation posits that critical pedagogy has taken an unnecessarily 'moralistic' stance on popular culture and contemporary subcultures, especially those associated with youth. This would seem to be at odds with the spirit of Freire's own work, which eschews formulaic or moralistic responses, in its emphasis on historicity. Some commentators have argued that such 'moralism' or rigid essentialism is already present in Freire's original work and is merely being mirrored in the critical pedagogy approaches. Another key aspect of such challenges to Freire and Freirean approaches concerns *the relation between modernity and postmodernity*. Freire's work has conventionally been seen as a kind of modernist 'emancipatory' approach. However, with regard to the interpretations of both critical pedagogy and the CCCS, and especially the latter and the development of a recent British continentalist philosophy of education, Freire's work has arguably been pushed in a direction which is too accepting of the dictates of postmodernism. As we will see below, in his later work, Freire argues for what he terms a 'progressive postmodernity' (Freire, 1992). However, the more or less whole-hearted embracing of Foucauldian and Lyotardian (Lyotard, 1986) discourse and politics by thinkers such as Standish (Dhillon and Standish, 2000) and Hall (Hall, 1996a) might be seen as betraying the more balanced perspective of Freire, who has always sought a *rapprochement* between the demands of an emancipatory modernism and a more ironical or deconstructive postmodernism.

Freire and Dewey

While Freire is often cited as a paradigmatic figure in the development of twentieth-century educational thought, his importance is often underestimated in favour of a foregrounding of the work of John Dewey (Dewey, 1973). Progressive educationalists have tended to look back to John Dewey as the great critic of traditionalism in schooling and the great visionary of a child-centred and active learning curriculum and school system. Moreover, Dewey and the wider movement of American pragmatism, including Charles Pierce and particularly William James, may also be seen as formative for the Vygotskian development of 'constructivist' learning theory in educational psychology (which has been such an unquestioned influence in recent Irish and global education). All of these thinkers share a modernist (and romantic) faith in individual human reason and democratic community. However, as Giroux and Stanley Aronowitz have pointed out in their text *Postmodern Education* (Giroux and Aronowitz, 1992), much of what passes for enlightened education and democracy in these times under the names of Dewey and Vygotsky seems hardly worthy of the title. This pragmatist and constructivist legacy has (arguably) failed to deal with the subtleties of contemporary culture and education. For Giroux and Aronowitz, these philosophies, whether through distortion or through contradictions internal to their own rationale, have become congealed into pedagogic instrumentalisms.

This issue of instrumentalism in education will be a recurring theme of this book. Oftentimes, this new epoch of technicism and instrumentalism is associated with the development of the 'postmodern' era in society and culture (for example, Jean-François Lyotard's text *The Postmodern Condition: A Report on Knowledge* becomes exemplary). Thus, such a pedagogical ethos (mostly associated with 'managerialism' and with 'rigorous assessment') seems to have taken on a kind of paradigmatic significance for those who wish to mark a clear demarcation between high modernity and the supposedly new epoch of postmodernity. Moreover, this rupture in epistemological reference is also seen as having revolutionary ethical and political implications for the way in which we understand knowledge and its connection to people's lives. Here, education is one of the crucial processes at stake. It is easy to jump (or it seems easy to jump) from Lyotardian performativity to the more recent paradigm shift in educational thinking and management, towards a new technicism and hegemony of positivistic assessment. There are undoubted connections in this context. For example, as we know, 'performativity' is one of the key terms, one of the key values, of the new management in education, what Fiachra Long has referred to in a recent essay (although not specifically in relation to Lyotard) as the 'rubricist' paradigm (Long, 2008). This ideological approach has also been aligned with a kind of New Right technocratic thinking as in Daniel Bell's *The Coming of the Post-Industrial Society* (Bell, 1973), and comes to stand for a postmodern exemplary hybrid of technicism, individualism and amoralism. However, for Giroux and Aronowitz, it is more appropriate to lay the blame for this reductionistic approach to pedagogy at the feet of modernism than postmodernism. In addition, their understanding of the latter involves a *redirection* of the former's potential, away from what they see as this more instrumentalist legacy.

Taking Dewey as an exemplary modernist, they state: 'postmodernism cannot be a simple rejection of modernity; rather, it involves a different modulation of its themes and categories' (Giroux and Aronowitz, 1992, p. 59). This different modulation is itself a response to the new vista which faces educationalists today. Taking the Irish educational context as an example, we may say that while the 1999 Primary School Curriculum (NCCA, 1999) instituted Deweyean principles of democratic education in Irish schools, much remains to be done at the level of the proper implementation of this curriculum in practice. While the talk may be Deweyean, the constraints on practice due to increased content and the multiplied roles of the individual teacher may often revert back to a more traditionalist ideology (Burke, 2007). We may also say, however, that even the proper implementation of Deweyean principles in practice may not be enough. Perhaps more fundamentally, we need to recognize the dawning of a 'different modulation'.

It is just such a 'different modulation' which this book seeks to foreground and explore through a detailed and rigorous analysis of the work of Paulo

Freire. I will argue that it is Freire's vision of education, perhaps more than that of Dewey, that has become increasingly relevant in a pedagogical context of increased diversity and tension, and a global political context of increasing stress on 'social movements', especially within the context of the Third World. Always alert to the specific contexts of the Third World, what makes Freire astute is his ability to see such contexts not in isolation but as significantly connected to the political and pedagogical sites of the First World. More and more, this seems to be an increasingly prescient insight. For example, in the more practical contexts of education and schooling, the contemporary (Irish) realities of disenfranchised youth, multicultural classrooms, linguistic diversity and conflicting ethoi, it appears that Dewey's own romantic vision of education may need to be re-evaluated. Garrison and Neiman refer to the 'poetic' pedagogy of Dewey and William James (Garrison and Nieman, 2003). It is no doubt time to look to how a rather different pedagogical poetics (for example, that of Freire) might inspire our conception of education.

Freire's own evolution and auto-critique

In this book, I want to look at the nature of Freire's highly significant influence and at Freire's relevance to the contemporary analysis of education and culture, most especially as these relate to the politicization of education and culture. I will argue that Freire's own intellectual development demonstrates significant self-critique, early to late, but that there still remain tensions in his work which are unresolved. As Freire notes, 'If you were to ask me, "are you attempting to put into practice the concepts you described in your book [*Pedagogy of the Oppressed*]?", of course I am, but in a manner in keeping with the times' (Freire and Torres, 1994, p. 106). Freire has thus always sought to evolve his own work and challenge his own presuppositions in the name of a radically historicized understanding of the nature of philosophical dialogue and dialectic (close, as we shall see, to the Platonic wellsprings of *elenchus* or 'refutation', constantly putting one's own position under interrogation). I will look at the origins and development of Freire's extraordinarily influential and profound philosophy of education, which sought to do justice to traditional ethical and spiritual concerns while also coming to terms with the most radical and revolutionary of contemporary events and ideas. Developing out of a complicated symbiosis between Christian and Marxist thought, Freire also sought to take on board the insights of existentialism and psychoanalysis. Freire's work is also notable for its constant emphasis on the need for *praxis,* for a practical exploration of the relation between philosophy and the world, so as to bring about real and progressive change in people's lives. In this measure, his influence has extended well beyond the academy, and has been the inspiration for significant political and revolutionary movements throughout the world.

Development of sections and chapters

Part One of the book – entitled 'Paulo Freire: origins and development' – will consist of four chapters which look at the genealogy of Freire's thinking, early to late. In Chapter 1, entitled 'From sectarianism to radicalization and *conscientização*: the politics of *Pedagogy of the Oppressed*', I look in detail at Freire's most famous and influential text. In this chapter, I focus on the political dimension to this work. For Freire, education and politics are always inextricably connected; education is always a political process through and through. Here, I look at what sense we can make of the political background to *Pedagogy of the Oppressed*, with Chapter 1 of that text being perhaps Freire's most explicitly political writing of this period. Employing the themes of 'sectarianism and radicalization' and *conscientização* (conscientization), I will explore how these concepts originate in his work, how they develop from an eclectic series of influences, but also how Freire operationalizes them in his own specifically powerful way. Moreover, these are concepts and themes which recur throughout Freire's work (as we shall see), often with slightly different inflections and 'modulations', depending on the context of the work, but always in some way returning to the original discussion in *Pedagogy of the Oppressed*. In Chapter 2, entitled 'From banking education to problem-posing education in *Pedagogy of the Oppressed*', I explore how Freire begins to make the links between education and politics. This is a book which is primarily focused on Freire's educational vision and, while in Chapter 1 we saw how, for Freire, education and politics are ultimately inextricable, we can also delineate the contours of Freire's own view of the specific challenges and dimensions of pedagogy. In this chapter, I explore this issue through Freire's famous and hugely influential distinction between what he calls 'banking' and 'problem-posing' education. In looking at banking education, I pay particular attention to what Freire calls the 'Teacher–Student contradiction' and the 'A–J of Banking Education', while with regard to his problem-posing alternative, I explore the nature of *freedom* in education for Freire, both for teacher and student. As we will see, this is never understood as a freedom in isolation, but rather as a valuation of freedom which takes account of the dialectical relationship between freedom and authority.

One of the problems in the secondary literature on Freire is that *Pedagogy of the Oppressed* gets such an extraordinary deal of attention while Freire's many other texts may often seem neglected. This is often based on the perception that Freire's work is consistent in its philosophical principles and ideas. While there is truth to the latter view, and while *Pedagogy of the Oppressed* is indeed an extraordinary text, too much attention to it and too little attention to Freire's other (highly voluminous) work can underestimate the degree of differentiation to be found within Freire's *oeuvre*. This refers not simply to Freire's texts written after *Pedagogy of the Oppressed* but also to those texts written before and, in Chapter 3, I explore in detail Freire's 'first text', or at least his first truly significant, independent text, *Education as the Practice of Freedom*. This chapter is thus entitled 'Before *Pedagogy*: *Education as the Practice of Freedom*' and the analysis here both allows us to get a sense of Freire's thinking before writing *Pedagogy of the Oppressed*, but also allows us to get a better sense of the genealogy of Freire's early thinking, right up to and including *Pedagogy of the Oppressed*. One of the distinctive aspects of the latter text is that it is very condensed, very theoretical and, uncharacteristically for Freire, lacking in the tendency to narrative and personal or existential anecdote which are common throughout his other work. *Pedagogy of the Oppressed* is, in many respects, more of an 'impersonal' text than Freire's others, and its process of coming-to-be is less visible than in Freire's other work (where the process is nearly always explicitly rendered). Therefore, we can only look to Freire's other texts of the period for clues, suggestions and evidence of the process which brought *Pedagogy of the Oppressed* to fruition. This process was obviously highly theoretical (and this is signposted to some extent in *Pedagogy* itself) but it was also deeply experiential and personal, when one considers that it developed out of Freire's own experience of a military *coup d'état*, imprisonment and exile. *Education as the Practice of Freedom* allows us to glimpse some aspects of this process of coming to be, especially in its analysis of the 'Brazilian situation'.

In Chapter 4, we develop this logic of the 'before and after *Pedagogy*', with an analysis of two further texts from this period of Freire's work, the first, *Extension or Communication* (Freire, 2005b), which was written in and around the same time or slightly before it and *Cultural Action for Freedom* (Freire, 1977), which was written at Harvard, where Freire had gone as a Visiting Professor in 1970, after the success of *Pedagogy* worldwide, as a text of educational concern. Both of these texts provide fascinating details which are relevant to our understanding of *Pedagogy of the Oppressed*, although, taken in themselves, they are significantly different texts. *Extension or Communication* was written by Freire specifically in relation to his experience in Chile, working with agricultural projects which had a highly 'developmental' emphasis. This text allows Freire to critique what he sees as a rather reifying tendency in agricultural projects of redevelopment in Chile, and this is also an interesting text because it pre-dates the military coup which was to take place in Chile in the early 1970s with General Pinochet (and which Freire will refer back to in his later text, *Pedagogy of Hope: Reliving Pedagogy of the Oppressed* (Freire, 1992)). The second text discussed in this chapter is equally significant as it is the first text which Freire writes explicitly to the audience in the 'First World', and here we see Freire defiantly extending the relevance of his work beyond Third World contexts. These thematics of oppression and domination cannot be seen as simply Third Worldist concerns, not least because (as Freire clearly outlines) the latter are constantly being shaped by the 'director societies' in the First World. In this context, we see the clear connections between Freire and Frantz Fanon, for example, which have already surfaced in *Pedagogy*. This text also has strong affinities with *Extension or Communication* in its unequivocal rejection of an ideology of the oppressor which remains residually present in developmentalist ideology. More generally, this thematic in Freire recurs throughout his *oeuvre* in relation to the complexities of the power relations between educator and educatee, whether we are talking about development in 'dependent' societies or about schooling in any society. This is also a theme which connects Freire's philosophy of education to the events of May 1968, and more widely to the movement of postmodern thought. As Freire outlines in *Pedagogy of Hope: Reliving Pedagogy of the Oppressed*, his is a work which self-describes as 'progressively postmodern'.

Part Two, entitled 'Impacts and legacies – from Freire's return to Brazil to critical pedagogy', will look at the eclectic influence and complex (and sometimes contradictory) legacy of Freire's work, both in relation to educational and political practice (in Brazil and beyond), but also in relation to his impact on a radically diverse series of philosophical and political movements, which range from Christian liberation theology to neo-Marxist groups to critical pedagogy, the latter which seeks to combine a political and educational project in the name of Freire. In seeking to assess Freire's work, one of the great benefits of looking to his own work is that it is acutely self-reflexive and self-referential. This tendency demonstrates not so much a narcissism as a powerful willingness to self-critique and evolve his work, depending on the insights and challenges of the circumstances. Freire's work consistently takes its cue from the situation in which it finds itself. To employ a concept of Freire's early work, which he often evokes, his philosophy looks to the '*generative themes*' of the contexts and the specific issues being addressed. Moreover, in each of these instances, the proffered solutions must come from the protagonists themselves rather than from Freire or whomever the supposedly 'expert educator' might be. In his text, published in 1994 *Pedagogy of Hope: Reliving Pedagogy of the Oppressed*, Freire exemplifies precisely this methodology in both looking back at and affirming elements of his original project and vision in *Pedagogy of the Oppressed*, while at the same time extending, challenging and rethinking elements which are anachronistic in the then present climate of the 1990s. Significantly, Freire had originally started to write this text as an 'introduction' to *Pedagogy*, but it evolved and developed into a full text in its own right. What this seems to signify in the context of this work is that, to a great extent, a renewed vision was now urgently required to engage the contemporary challenges of education and society. At the same time this text is also a 'reliving' of the original *Pedagogy* in a simpler sense. It articulates, through narrative and detailed description of personal experience, the process by which *Pedagogy* had come to be. In this sense, it also stands alongside the earlier Freirean texts as rich repositories of the more personalized Freire, a figure not so evident in *Pedagogy* itself.

Chapter 6 explores a significant episode in the development and history of Freire's work, namely his return to Brazil in the 1990s as Secretary for Education in *São Paulo*. One dimension to this story is the personal aspect, the sense of a man who had worked so hard to make his country a better and more equal place to live, exiled and brutalized by a regime which had interest only in its own power. However, Freire's return signals a revolutionary change in Brazil, accompanied by the increasingly significant role which the Workers' Party (*Partido dos Trabalhadores*) has in Brazilian politics (a party which Freire was involved in co-forming). My focus in this chapter will be on Freire's work in the educational sector in São Paulo, which as always with Freire, cannot be separated out from his political understanding and philosophy. What is most striking about Freire's work in São Paulo is its extraordinary fidelity to the Freirean principle of *praxis* – practice and theory working in symbiosis and reciprocal challenge. We are also lucky to have a very experientially and philosophically rich analysis of Freire's work in Brazil available to us in the shape of the work which Carlos Torres and others put together on this period (O'Cadiz *et al.*, 1998). I will have significant recourse to O'Cadiz *et al.* in this chapter, but I will also contextualize the São Paulo period in relation to Freire's work as a whole. Throughout Freire's life, whether in Brazil and Chile initially, or later in Tanzania and Guinea-Bissau, among other countries, Freire has practised what he preached, has walked the talk, but in São Paulo we have perhaps the most extraordinary and evocative of these examples.

Freire's influence on both theory and practice in education has been monumental and, alongside John Dewey, he is perhaps the most significant educational thinker and practitioner of the twentieth century. A sustained analysis of this influence would require many volumes but, in Chapter 7, I conclude the book with an exploration of two particularly significant strands of this influence, in the work of critical pedagogy and the Birmingham CCCS. Chapter 7 is entitled 'Postmodernist tension and creativity in Paulo Freire's educational legacy: from critical pedagogy to the Birmingham Centre for Contemporary Cultural Studies'. Here, I look first at how Freire's legacy has been developed in the USA, through the work of Peter McLaren (McLaren, 1994), Henry Giroux (Giroux, 2000) and bell hooks (hooks, 1994) among others. As with all of Freire's work, this influence is not without contestation or differentiation, but ultimately I argue for the vibrancy of this strand of thought. Second, I explore a more neglected connection to Freire's work (also influential on critical pedagogy itself) – the work of the Birmingham CCCS. Here, I pay particular attention to the work of Stuart Hall (one of the original founders of the CCCS) and that of Paul Willis, famous for his *Learning to Labour* (Willis, 1981) text. In both cases, there are affinities and disaffinities with the work of Freire, but again the work of the CCCS exemplifies the relevance of Freire's philosophy of education not simply for current debates in the USA but also in the UK and indeed more globally, cutting across as I have argued (and

Freire constantly argued) divisions between Third and First worlds. As the 'revolutions of democracy' continue to spread across the Arab world, from Tunisia to Egypt and to Libya, and as Western societies continue to struggle with issues of accountability and justice, Freire's insight and wisdom seem stronger and more of a needed resource for us than ever.

PART ONE

Paulo Freire – origins and development

CHAPTER ONE

From sectarianism to radicalization and *conscientização*

The politics of Pedagogy of the Oppressed

The influence of Marx on Freire

This first chapter focuses on Freire's most famous text, *Pedagogy of the Oppressed* (Freire, 1996a), originally published in the seminal year of 1968, which is also one of his earliest books. This text has received the most attention and discussion among scholars and also has arguably been the text which has influenced the most practical application of Freire's work, whether in terms of his own work, in places such as Guinea-Bissau (Freire, 1978) or as Secretary of Education in São Paulo (O'Cadiz *et al.*, 1998), but also in terms of the take-up of his work by political and educational groups, especially in Latin America. As we will see, this hermeneutic foregrounding of *Pedagogy of the Oppressed* is mostly justified, as it is a text of extraordinary philosophical richness and is especially effective in combining a philosophical and pedagogical emphasis. Moreover, it places education firmly within the ambit of politics and a revolutionary politics which seeks to redirect the vision of the West *vis-à-vis* the Third World. In this, it has strong similarities, for example, to Frantz Fanon's iconoclastic *The Wretched of the Earth* (Fanon, 1986b) and we will look at these similarities in more detail below. However, it may be argued that Freire's text has been the more influential insofar as it speaks not simply to a political or philosophical audience but also directly to the connections between the latter and practical educational systems and policies throughout the world.

We mentioned, in the Introduction, the influence of Marx on Freire, and this Marxian dimension is foundational to a reading of *Pedagogy*, in several respects. It is helpful to examine several of these strands before we undertake a more micro-level interpretation of Freire, as they may be said to structure the *meta-level* of Freire's work. In the first case, there is the sense that Marxism is not a philosophy in any ordinary sense. If Freire is influenced by Marx, it is first of all in terms of a *revolutionary* understanding of philosophy itself, as a discipline which, to invoke Frederic Jameson (Jameson, 2001), is 'unlike any other contemporary mode of thought, what I will call a unity-of-theory-and-practice' (Jameson, 2001, p. ix). This may be spoken of as Marx's complete revision of philosophy which Etienne Balibar has so powerfully described (Balibar, 2007, p.1ff.). For Balibar, while the early Marx starts out in a very philosophical mode, his mid to late work signifies a critique of philosophy's self-understanding as a kind of master discipline. Instead, Marx reinscribes philosophy in a process of life much greater than human thought, which determines or at least conditions what philosophy and philosophers are capable of. The most obvious instance of this is in Marx's text *Theses on Feuerbach* (Marx, 1992a), where he outlines that whereas previous philosophy had primarily sought to interpret the world, the point is 'rather to change it' (Marx, 1992a, p. 423). This is also clearly the Freirean position.

Second, there is the complex issue of the notion of *ideology* as it was originally introduced by Marx and developed in the Marxist tradition in various ways. The original notion is itself complex and ambiguous in Marx (Balibar, 2007, p. 42ff.) but came to be understood by succeeding Marxism as based on the 'false consciousness' of the people under capitalism. This was then complicated by thinkers influential on Freire such as Georgs Lukács, *who transferred the notion of falsity from consciousness to the situation*: 'the notion of ideology as thought true to a false situation' (Eagleton, 1994, p. 191). That is, this conception of ideology sees the problem as lying within the practical context of contemporary capitalist society rather than in some mode of cognitive misapprehension. This insight was then, in the case of Antonio Gramsci, deepened through his conception of *hegemony* (Eagleton, 1994, p. 197), which allowed for its sense to become more subtly connected to 'lived, habitual social practice' (Eagleton, 1994, p. 197). Here, the situation itself under capitalism was no longer simply false but *subject to contestation*. It is the latter view which is most influential on Freire, although aspects of the tensions outlined here are present in Freire's work as it relates to the concept of 'ideology' at alternate moments, insofar as he invokes, for example, Lukács, Althusser and Gramsci respectively, sometimes in the same text (Freire, 1996a).

One related, and crucially important, Marxist issue with regard to ideology concerns the problem of transformation or how much potential there is for change under the existing structures (of oppression). If ideology is all-encompassing, then there can be no possibility of authentic resistance and several Marxists seem to move towards this rather pessimistic conclusion. Pierre Bourdieu, for example, argues that 'the capacity for resistance, as a capacity of consciousness, was overestimated. It is clear that people are prepared to accept much more than we would have believed' (Bourdieu and Eagleton, 1994, p. 268). Althusser, through a different approach, seems to come to similar conclusions (Althusser, 1994), while simultaneously invoking a distinction between 'ideology' and 'science', which seems to reinforce the chasm between the 'masses' and the 'intellectuals'. For Althusser, the philosopher has access to a non-ideological knowledge which is not accessible to the common people. Again, Freire's work may be seen as strongly opposed to the latter claims, in all Freire's emphasis on, and affirmation of, 'popular' or ordinary consciousness, while still not accepting the exact terms of reference of the popular understanding. We can see this as strongly influenced by Gramsci's more positive understanding (Gramsci, 1988) of popular ideology:

> Popular consciousness is not to be dismissed as purely negative but its more progressive and more reactionary features must instead be carefully distinguished. The function of the organic intellectuals is to forge the links between theory and ideology, creating a two-way passage between political analysis and popular experience.
>
> (Eagleton, 1994, p. 198)

Third, and finally for our purposes in this context, we can foreground the Marxist understanding of the *concept of the subject*. As Balibar makes clear (Balibar, 2007, p. 29ff.), the question 'What is man?' may be seen as a relatively recent philosophical development, associated with the 'theoretical humanism' of the late eighteenth century. Balibar sees Kant, von Humboldt and Feuerbach as especially paradigmatic in this context, and also sees Marx as instituting a break with this humanist tradition (Balibar, 2007, p. 29) in his 'Theses on Feuerbach' (Marx, 1992a): 'But the human essence is no abstraction inherent in each individual. In its reality, it is the ensemble of social relations' (Marx, 1992a, p. 423). This text has often been seen as an example of the anti-subjective thrust of Marxism, such that Marx would have sought to, in effect, annihilate the individual or subjectivity. However, Balibar reads this text differently and it is this reading which we need to keep in mind when we come to explore Freire's understanding of subjectivity below. Whereas Althusser sees this as an example of Marx's privileging of the 'totality of the system over the individual historical subjects' (Kearney, 1986, p. 302), for Balibar it rather shows that Marx, while accepting the reality of subjectivity, none the less sees such subjectivity as ultimately constituted in the 'multiple and active *relations* which individuals establish with each other (whether of language, labour, love, reproduction, domination, conflict, etc)' (Balibar, 2007, p. 30; emphasis in original). In many respects, this exactly describes Freire's understanding of subjectivity and *intersubjectivity* (Balibar prefers the term 'transindividual'), as we shall see below.

Let us return to the problem of reading *Pedagogy of the Oppressed* itself. A key issue, in this context, is how representative *Pedagogy of the Oppressed* is of Freire's work as a whole. To the extent that this text is seen as paradigmatic of his work, there is a real danger that the complexity of Freire's work is simplified or reduced. This is particularly the case for two reasons. First, the fact that *Pedagogy of the Oppressed* is such an early text means that there is a danger that the texts which Freire produces both before and after *Pedagogy*, the latter which may be seen to extend over almost a 30-year period, will be neglected. As we shall see in this book, many of these varied Freirean texts are very significant in their own right. Second, there is the fact that perhaps more than most, Freire is a historical thinker, a thinker for whom development and revision of thought is a key tenet. As Freire notes in the 1990s, looking back at the publication of *Pedagogy*, 'If you were to ask me, "are you attempting to put into practice the concepts you described in your book?" [*Pedagogy of the Oppressed*], of course I am, but in a manner in keeping with the times' (Freire and Torres, 1994, p. 106). This emphasis on temporality and context is persistent in Freire's work. Therefore, to simply isolate one text from one specific period of his work distorts the nature and evolution of his thought. We will see this especially when we come to look at Freire's own meditation on his relation to *Pedagogy of the Oppressed*, in *Pedagogy of Hope: Reliving Pedagogy of the Oppressed* (Freire, 1992). Significantly, this latter text was initially intended to be written as an introduction to a new anniversary edition of *Pedagogy of the Oppressed*. However, once Freire began to write about *Pedagogy of the Oppressed*, he wished not simply to 'introduce it' but to 'rethink it'. *Pedagogy of Hope: Reliving Pedagogy of the Oppressed* demonstrates this rethinking in a powerful way and has become one of Freire's most important texts. But we will also see that many of Freire's other texts similarly rethink the original *Pedagogy* in different ways. Given Freire's varied career and life, where much of his work develops from specific contexts of education and political practice, his work is significantly diverse and eclectic.

However, in seeking to present Freire as a thinker whose thought is eclectic and diverse, we do not wish to suggest that *Pedagogy of the Oppressed* should not be studied in its own right. In a philosophical career of great complexity, it is undoubtedly Freire's most sustained and perfectly pitched work. In this chapter, I will look at the detail of this complex text and seek to trace the reasons for its importance, both pedagogically and philosophically. In the Foreword to *Pedagogy of the Oppressed*, Richard Shaull makes a key claim. He says that Freire 'incarnates a rediscovery of the humanising vocation of the intellectual, and demonstrates the power of thought to negate accepted limits and open the way to a new future' (Schaull, 1996, p. iv). For Schaull, Freire is able to do this because he operates on one basic assumption – 'that man's ontological vocation (as he calls it) is to be a subject who acts upon and transforms his world, and in so doing moves towards ever new possibilities of fuller and richer life individually and collectively' (Schaull, 1996, p. v). This point regarding subjectivity reiterates the aforementioned claim from Balibar that Marx's understanding of the subject (deriving from 'The Theses on Feuerbach' (Marx, 1992a)) is both positive and interrelational: here we see Freire's faithful development of this legacy. It is this dynamic or dialectic of transformation and hope which we see evidenced on every page of *Pedagogy* and it is to the detail of this text that I now turn.

Sectarianism and radicalization

In his own Preface to *Pedagogy of the Oppressed* (Freire, 1996a), we see Freire already struggling with some of the tensions in his work and that of his followers, particularly as he makes the distinction between 'sectarianism' and 'radicalization': 'sectarianism, fed by fanaticism, is always castrating; radicalization, nourished by a critical spirit, is always creative' (Freire, 1996a, p. 19). In particular, Freire's critique of what he terms 'leftist sectarianism' is significant for our purposes. The 'rightist sectarian' attempts to domesticate the present and hopes that the future will simply reproduce this domesticated present. The 'leftist sectarian', in contrast, considers the future pre-established. Both are caught within a fatalistic position or a 'circle of certainty' and both 'negate freedom' (Freire, 1996a, p. 19). Of his own radical perspective, he says that radicals are 'never simply subjectivists; rather the subjective, for the radical, exists only in relation to the objective; there is a dialectical unity between subjective and objective' (Freire, 1996a, p. 20). The sectarian, however, cannot perceive what Freire terms the 'dynamic' of reality. This creates 'alienation' ('sectarianism mythicises and thereby alienates' (Freire, 1996a, p.19)), which allows Freire to introduce this key concept, once more deriving from the early Marx, in this case from the latter's 'Economic and Philosophical Manuscripts' (Marx, 1992b).

Two things are worth noting here. First, Freire's own self-distancing from sectarianism, from the Right (which one would expect) but perhaps more surprisingly from the Left; subjectivity and freedom must be taken account of, fatalism is misguided and history (or what he terms 'historicity') is irreducible. Second, however, there is also a more problematic aspect to Freire's discussion. In outlining this key distinction between radical and sectarian, and placing his own thought firmly in the radical camp, there is a real danger here of intellectual and moral presumption. That is, one might argue that Freire's own discussion of the difference between sectarian and radical is itself based on a framework which is sectarian. Another way of asking this question is to query whether Freire's own thinking will really be as open to history, change and subjectivity as he likes to claim.

If we look at some of the detail of *Pedagogy of the Oppressed,* we can see moves in both directions; that is, intellectual and political moves which appear to be close to sectarianism and moves which appear closer to radicalization. For example, the very notion of an 'oppressed' people, the conceptions of sadism and masochism, the emphasis on liberation from oppression and the recurrent concept of emancipation, might be seen as more 'essentialist' ideas, thus bringing his thinking close to sectarianism. However, read in a different key, these aspects of Freire's work may be seen as radical. For example, they might be viewed as historical rather than *a priori* structures. The emphasis on reality as not fixed, the emphasis on transformation and change and the reversibility of the oppressor/ oppressed roles, as well as the nuanced discussion of subjectivity through psychoanalysis (at least in name), suggest a more radical and less sectarian perspective.

Freire has acknowledged that his earlier work runs the risk of becoming the very sectarianism it sets out to critique. We can trace this auto-critique of his own thought in Freire's later work which explicitly engages his earlier, more famous work, most paradigmatically, for example, in his *Pedagogy of Hope,* subtitled *Reliving Pedagogy of the Oppressed* (Freire, 1992). 'The radical does not consider himself the proprietor of history or of men, or the liberator of the oppressed; but he does commit himself, within history, to fight at their side' (Freire, 1996a, p. 21). Freire is delineating here the crucial dynamics of power within the relationship between oppressed and so-called liberators or emancipatory educators, a dynamics often occluded in other so-called emancipatory thinkers such as Louis Althusser (Althusser, 1994), as we suggested above. For Freire, as later for a thinker such as Jacques Rancière (Rancière, 1991), this dividing line is fatal for the educator, or at least the one who wishes to be radical rather than sectarian:

> The radical, committed to human liberation, does not become the prisoner of a 'circle of certainty' within which he also imprisons reality. On the contrary, the more radical he is, the more fully he enters into reality so that, knowing it better, he can better transform it. He is not afraid to confront, to listen, to see the world unveiled. He is not afraid to meet the people or to enter into dialogue with them.
>
> (Freire, 1996a, p. 21)

Freire adds here a reference to Rosa Luxembourg: 'as long as theoretic knowledge remains the privilege of a handful of academicians in the party, the latter will face the danger of going astray' (quoted Freire, 1996a, p. 21).

Crucial to this notion of radical education, then, is the notion of authentic communication and a critique of the paternalism which destroys all authentic communication. This was a paradigmatic theme of Freire's work even before *Pedagogy of the Oppressed*. In his early text *Extension or Communication* (Freire, 2005b), he demystifies all aid or helping relationships. He sees an implicit ideology of paternalism, social control and nonreciprocity between experts and 'helpees', and refers to the oppressive character of all nonreciprocal relationships (Freire, 2005b). We will look in detail at this earlier context of Freire's thinking in chapter 3. Here, I want to look at *Pedagogy of the Oppressed* specifically. In the following section, I will explore Freire's seminal 'Preface' in more detail, as well as his crucial conceptions of 'conscientization' and 'banking'.

Conscientização (conscientization) and Freire's progressivism

Already in the Preface to *Pedagogy of the Oppressed*, Freire has introduced some of the key foundational concepts which provide a backdrop to his famous distinction between 'banking' and 'problem-posing' education. With regard to the distinction between 'sectarian' and 'radical' that I have just discussed, Freire makes clear that his text is addressed to one of these groups only: 'the *Pedagogy of the Oppressed*, the introductory outlines of which are presented in the following pages, is a task for radicals; it cannot be carried out by sectarians' (Freire, 1996a, p. 19). But what Freire is advocating here is not some kind of dogmatism of its own. The open-ended aspect of his work, which we will be seeing developed in more detail in later chapters, as well as the evolution of a loyal but none the less critical tradition of neo-Freireanism, is exemplified already here in the opening Preface: 'I will be satisfied if among the readers of this work, there are those sufficiently critical to correct mistakes and misunderstandings, to deepen affirmations and to point out aspects I have not perceived' (Freire, 1996a, p. 21). This aspect looks forward to the work of Peter McLaren, Henry Giroux and bell hooks, amongst others (McLaren and Leonard, 1993a; hooks, 1994; Giroux, 2000). In addition, despite all the analysis of concrete situations and contexts, a tendency which, if anything, is exacerbated in Freire's later work (for example, the tendency towards personal testimony in *Letters to Cristina: Reflections on My Life and Work* (Freire, 1996b) or in *Pedagogy of Hope: Revisiting Pedagogy of the Oppressed* (Freire, 1992)), there is also a kind of romanticism or utopianism which remains. As Freire observes: 'from these pages, I hope at least the following will endure; my trust in the people and my faith in men and in the creation of a world in which it will be easier to love' (Freire, 1996a, p. 19).

A third phase of progressivism

Freire starts by making clear that the historical context for his work is his 'last six years of exile', the years thus from 1962 to 1968. In the analysis of Darling and Nordenbo of the phenomenon of educational progressivism (Darling and Nordenbo, 2003), this is the exemplary period of their 'third phase' of progressivism. We must not forget that Freire's *Pedagogy of the Oppressed* is published right on the cusp of this key moment and we will return to this below in terms of a discussion of Freire's relation to progressivism and later to a wider discussion of his relation to the movement of postmodernism. Here, however, it is worth noting that Freire's six years of exile have provided insight which builds on Freire's previous educational activities in Brazil and, again, the national context is crucial for an understanding of Freire. What this work has allowed Freire to achieve is a foregrounding of the concept of 'conscientization' and the ability to develop actual experimentation with a genuinely liberating education (Freire, 1996a, p. 15).

The translator (Myra Bergman Ramos) gives a useful definition of this complicated term in Freire's work; 'the term *conscientização* [conscientization] refers to learning to perceive social, political and economic contradictions, and to take action against the oppressive elements of reality' (translator's note, Freire, 1996a, p. 15). The obverse of this process of critical emancipation is what Freire already here refers to as 'the fear of freedom', which he discusses in detail in the first chapter of this book, and which links his work explicitly to Erich Fromm (Fromm, 2001). One of the elements which is linked to the fear of freedom in this context is a kind of scaremongering regarding the 'possible effects of *conscientização* ... [which] implies a premise which the doubter does not always make explicit; it is better for the victims of injustice not to recognize themselves as such' (Freire, 1996a, p. 15). This, it is often said, is because of the destructive consequences of such a consciousness-raising, but Freire makes clear that he does not agree with the logic of such an argument:

> In fact, *conscientização* (conscientization) does not lead men to 'destructive fanaticism'. On the contrary, by making it possible for men to enter into the historical process as responsible subjects, *conscientização* (conscientization) enrols them in the search for self-affirmation, and thus avoids fanaticism.
>
> (Freire, 1996a, p. 18)

Again, the translator's note is helpful: 'the term *Subjects* denotes those who know and act, in contrast to those who are *objects*, who are known and acted upon' (translator's note: Freire, 1996a, p. 15). However, for Freire, subjects must never be understood in a narcissistic or self-enclosed meaning.

Freire labels the latter version of subjectivity 'subjectivism' (Freire, 1996a, p. 20), where the self becomes hubristic. Indeed, this is going to be one of the key difficulties in Freire's later problematic relationship to postmodernism, which he accuses of a tendency towards subjectivism. This discussion also connects very clearly to our earlier elaboration of the problematic of subjectivity in the early Marx texts (Marx, 1992a). Like Marx, Freire is seeking to balance the individual and collective poles, without overemphasizing either one. 'The radical is never a subjectivist. For him, the subjective aspect exists only in relation to the objective aspect (the concrete reality, which is the object of his analysis). Subjectivity and objectivity thus join in a dialectical unity producing knowledge in solidarity with action, and vice versa' (Freire, 1996a, p. 20).

One of the problems which Freire faces, an age-old problem for philosophy but especially for the Marxist tradition and the latter's concept of 'false consciousness' or 'ideology' (Eagleton, 1994), *is why subjects or individuals allow themselves to remain objects or to be objectified?* Freire, in *Pedagogy of the Oppressed* (Freire, 1996a), seeks to develop a more refined answer to this traditional question and, in the Preface, he already gives a schematic outline of it. 'Fear of freedom, of which its possessor is not necessarily aware, makes him see ghosts' (Freire, 1996a, p. 18). In invoking the Hegelian dialectic (Hegel, 1979) in this context as an explanatory framework, Freire foregrounds the whole problematic of modern freedom. Quoting Hegel in relation to the individual paralysed by fear of freedom, Freire observes:

> Such an individual is actually taking refuge in an attempt to achieve security, which he prefers to the risks of liberty. As Hegel testifies, it is solely by risking life that freedom is obtained; the individual who has not staked his life may, no doubt, be recognized as a Person; but he or she has not attained the truth of this recognition as an independent self-consciousness.
>
> (Freire, 1996a, p. 18)

The Hegelian (Hegel, 1979) element in Freire's thought is paradigmatic of a specific kind of modern 'idealism' which *Pedagogy of the Oppressed* develops and which, for example, Balibar reads as being continued and radicalized from Hegel in Marx's approach to philosophy (Balibar, 2007, p. 23ff.). It is this radicalized element which is more important than borrowing from an idealist tradition in itself. If there is a Hegelian element in Freire's thinking, it is now an element significantly transformed from the original and somewhat 'out-of-joint'. Freire is clear from the beginning that the methodology of his work will not be conventional philosophy, especially of the idealist type. 'Thought and study alone did not produce *Pedagogy of the Oppressed*. It is rooted in concrete situations and describes the reactions of labourers [peasant or urban] and of middle class persons whom I have observed directly or indirectly through the course of my educative work' (Freire, 1996a, p. 19). We can say that this emphasis on 'concrete situations' once more clearly demonstrates Marx's influence on Freire, not so much in a philosophical contents sense (although we will see that there is that also) but more in the sense of Marx's complete revision of philosophy which Etienne Balibar has so powerfully described (Balibar, 2007). This revolutionary approach to philosophy is also clearly enacted by Freire and, in the Preface, this Marxian moment is marked with the reference to 'concrete situations' and his educational 'observations'. However, as Balibar also notes, whether intentionally or not, Marx's critique of philosophy had the paradoxical effect of *renewing* philosophy (Balibar, 2007, p. 2).

Another aspect of Freire's work which is clear from the Preface to *Pedagogy of the Oppressed* is his refusal to hide from negativity and conflict (perhaps also an inheritance from Hegel's dialectic): 'this volume will probably arouse negative reactions in a number of readers' (Freire, 1996a, p. 19). Here, he confronts head-on those different schools of thought which might counter the assumptions or detail of his work in *Pedagogy of the Oppressed*. 'Some will regard my position *vis-à-vis* the problem of human liberation as purely idealistic, or may even consider discussion of ontological vocation, love, dialogue, hope, humility and sympathy as so much reactionary "blah"' (Freire, 1996a, p. 19). However, as with all of Freire's work, as well as delineating opposition, he is also keen to identify connections and affinities:

> This admittedly tentative work is for radicals. I am certain that Christians and Marxists, though they may disagree with me in part or in whole, will continue reading to the end. But the reader who dogmatically assumes closed 'irrational' positions will reject the dialogue I hope this book will open.
>
> (Freire, 1996a, p. 19)

Here, we see Freire's key distinction between radicalization and sectarianism, as well as a pronounced emphasis on dialogue and openness of philosophical and political position. But the reference to two specific groupings is hugely important: 'I am certain that Christians and Marxists, though they may disagree with me in part or in whole, will continue reading to the end' (Freire, 1996a, p.19). Christians and Marxists are here singled out, groups of course who have hardly seen eye-to-eye, although there have been attempted reconciliations. It is important to remember Freire's Latin American background in this context – in Latin America, the conjunction of Christian and Marxist (Freire, 1985) is perhaps less surprising than it would be elsewhere, due most especially to the importance of so-called liberation theology, both philosophically and politically, not least in Brazil (Torres, 1993; Gutierrez, 2001). None the less, Freire also intimates here that he is neither an orthodox Marxist nor an orthodox Christian: 'though

they may disagree with me in part or whole.' Freire seems to be designating
here a fundamentally progressive or 'progressivist' element of his thinking.
As some commentators have argued, progressivism is never an absolutist
or fixed philosophical position but is best understood in the sense of a
specific reaction to the crisis of the times (Darling and Nordenbo, 2003),
and Freire's work can helpfully be seen in this light. It can only be properly
understood, on this reading, through taking account of its time, place and
contextual positioning, although that is far from saying that it is simply
reducible to those coordinates. In the following section I want to look
at how Freire develops this progressivist mode of thinking in a vehement
critique in *Pedagogy of the Oppressed* of what he terms 'banking education'
and a militant espousal of what he terms 'problem-posing education'.

Freire and 1968

Freire's prose has a way of alternately confronting problems directly and
elliptically. Each sentence carries a heavy weight. Freire often comments on
his love of language and his concern with the 'form' of his texts, and with
the process of writing itself. In this, we see a Freirean connection to the work
of postmodernist philosophy, most especially with the work of Jacques
Derrida (Derrida, 1982). We have looked at how the Preface to *Pedagogy of
the Oppressed* is important in a number of respects, but especially insofar
as it delineates a key distinction between the concepts of 'sectarianism' and
'radicalization'. As his thinking develops in Chapter 1, we see Freire dealing
with issues at both a macro- and micro-level. He begins by foregrounding
the problematic of 'humanization' which will be so central to the book as
a whole. He states the following: 'while the problem of humanization has
always been, from an axiological point of view, man's central problem, it now
takes on the character of an inescapable concern' (Freire, 1996a, p. 25). The
translator's note is again helpful in clarifying the meaning of Freire's notion
of 'axiological': 'An axiological viewpoint is one which involves the ethical,
the aesthetic and the religious' (translator's note; Freire, 1996a, p. 25). This
notion of the 'axiological' is significant in Freire's work and we will return
to it at several points. This seems important in at least two respects. In the
first case, Freire is foregrounding the interconnections between the 'ethical,
aesthetic and the religious'. Although not cited here, it would seem that he
is looking back at Kierkegaard's schema of existential life, or life's three
stages of the aesthetic, the ethical and the religious (Kierkegaard, 1992;
Gardiner, 2002). However, unlike in Kierkegaard, where we get a sense of
hierarchy between these three levels, here we just get a sense that each phase
or stage is indispensable to the whole. This makes sense of Freire's continual
return to the aesthetic and to art as key components of his thinking, and
also the foregrounding of the religious looks to his involvement and affinity

with liberation theology (Freire, 1985; Torres, 1993; Gutierrez, 2001). The ethical perhaps requires little explanation, although in Freire there is always a sense that ethics is located within the broader purview of the political, which itself ties Freire's work to contemporary political thinkers such as Chantal Mouffe (Mouffe, 2005), who argues against what she sees as a 'moralization' of politics in her recent work.

A preoccupation with human being

Freire also clarifies a specific distinctiveness in today's moment: while humanization has always been a concern, it now takes on an especial or 'inescapable' importance. Why? A footnote, which is easy enough to miss, provides the historical (and political-cultural) context for this sense of inescapability. The book is written in 1968 and Freire takes his chance to refer to 'the current movements of rebellion, especially those of youth' (Freire, 1996a, p. 25). We thus have a direct connection between Freire's work and the movements centred around May 1968, most particularly in France but also worldwide. In this context, I want to foreground several important points which Freire makes in the footnote concerning 1968. First, Freire is honest that each of the manifestations of the diverse 1968 movements are peculiar to their time and context: 'they necessarily reflect the peculiarities of their respective settings' (Freire, 1996a, p. 25). However, this is not all we can say about them. Rather, Freire wants to move beyond their specific contexts to something more generalizable, more universal: 'these movements manifest in their essence this preoccupation with people as beings in the world and with the world, a preoccupation with what and how they are "being"' (Freire, 1996a, p. 20). There is then, according to Freire, some essence to be spoken of here and it is a preoccupation with 'human being' or, to invoke his earlier phrase, it is a preoccupation with the problem of 'humanization' which has now become 'inescapable'.

Second, there is in this context a focus on the notion of 'being'; this is most reminiscent of an existentialist emphasis in Freire, one which connects him to thinkers such as Jean-Paul Sartre (Sartre, 2007) and Erich Fromm (Fromm, 2001). Freire seems to be suggesting that the student movements want to foreground our problem of how to 'be', when in contemporary culture all the emphasis is on 'having'; we have thus forgotten how to be. In this context, he singles out certain aspects of the students' critique as especially relevant for his purposes:

> As they place consumer civilisation in judgement, denounce all types of bureaucracy, demand the transformation of the universities [changing the rigid structure of the teacher-student relationship and placing that relationship within the context of reality], propose the transformation of reality itself so that universities can be renewed.
>
> (Freire, 1996a, 25)

'Consumer civilization' is a key target and Freire is in line with a whole tradition of Neo-Marxism leading back to Marx himself: the critique of capitalism and consumerism, a thread which we will foreground throughout our own reading of Freire. Crucially, however, Freire refers to the universities. There is a 'demand' from the students that the universities be 'transformed'. He refers to the 'rigid nature of the teacher–student relationship' and placing 'that relationship within the context of reality' (Freire, 1996a, p. 25). And, finally, he refers to the need for a 'transformation of reality itself' so that universities might be 'renewed' (Freire, 1996a, p. 20). This analysis seems crucial from a number of points of view. In the first case, by focusing on universities, Freire is once again affirming the connection between many of the social movements in 1968 and student contexts. Second, much of the analysis of Freire's work has been seen as relevant for adult education or primary education, but we should not lose sight of the importance of Freire's work for the university and what universities are for, especially in the context of 1968 when *Pedagogy of the Oppressed* was originally written (perhaps not enough has been made of the original dating of the text).

Two more points can be made in this context, just in terms of the claims implicit in this footnote. In the final part of it, Freire refers, first, to the need for 'men' to become 'subjects' of decision. But Freire is also clear that this emphasis on 'humanization' is not traditionalist. It will 'attack old orders and established institutions'. That is, on our terms, it is undeniably progressive. And finally, it is more 'anthropological' than 'anthropocentric'. This latter Freirean claim seems to try to resist criticism of his work as excessively humanist, since we must remember that many of the 1968 movements were premised on an 'anti-humanism' (although this has also become something of a caricature in the representation of the 1968 movements from critics on the New Right and the new philosophers or *nouveau philosophes*). Rather, what Freire's work allows is a reimagination of the 1968 movements as a process of 'humanization', which is progressivist and radical rather than traditionalist or sectarian. This is undoubtedly a new way of thinking about the human.

Humanization

Freire now goes on to explicate in more detail his meaning for the concept of *humanization* which is so central to his work. He contrasts humanization with dehumanization: 'while humanization and dehumanization are real alternatives, only the first is man's vocation; this vocation is constantly negated, yet it is affirmed by that very negation' (Freire, 1996a, p. 20). This is significant insofar as it demonstrates Freire's commitment to a human 'vocation' by which he seems to mean a human teleology. This will cause certain difficulties for Freire, as we shall see. Is Freire entitled to be definitive philosophically, in elaborating a humanist vocation, and if Freire is a humanist in just this way, what distinguishes his humanism from other types? Second, this passage also shows that Freire is not simply talking in an intra-theoretical way. Rather, we are talking about the human being's vocation in history which also is not an easy task. Rather, Freire points to the very real hindrances to humanization. However, rather than showing the futility of the latter, this very negation of humanization seems to point towards this vocation or need which never goes away. An important point to bear in mind here is that Freire seems to see humanization and dehuman-ization as existing in some sort of *dialectical* relationship. We must be careful in not going too far beyond the letter of the text but certainly we can see an element of the Hegelian influence on Freire in this context (Hegel, 1979). Could it be that dehumanization is an example of the negativity which, for instance, Hegel sees as inevitable and essential in history?

If we are looking for an understanding of what dehumanization means, we can cite what Freire says here about how humanization is thwarted; 'it is thwarted by injustice, exploitation, oppression and the violence of the oppressors' (Freire, 1996a, p. 20). These are concepts which we will return to below: *injustice, exploitation, oppression, violence and the very concept of the oppressors themselves.* We will see the connections, for example, with a thinker like Frantz Fanon (Fanon, 1986b) and I would argue that we should not decontextualize this analysis from the Third World context, although of course there is the issue of the students' movements in the West and the wider political movements of 1968 (which were primarily located in the First World). To complicate this matter further, as Kristin Ross has shown (Ross, 2004), the 1968 movements were in many ways influenced by a Third Worldism (Ross, 2004). But if we know what dehumanization is, what about humanization? What sense can we make of a substantive basis to what humanization might mean, as a concept or a reality? Freire gives us a positive statement of how we might envisage it here: 'it is affirmed by the yearning of the oppressed for freedom and justice; and by their struggle to recover their lost humanity.' Freedom and justice are key concepts. Freire's work is at the very heart of the debate over the proper attribution of these concepts. Do they belong, in terms of political ideologies, to socialism, communism, anarchism, liberalism or even libertarianism? Certainly, 'freedom' is a key contested concept and, most especially in recent times, the term has become a battleground for opposed ideological forces (Moseley, 2008). Moseley, for example, makes a key distinction between a 'classical liberal' position and a more 'modern liberal' position which asserts freedom only in the context of a human equality. That is, whereas the classical liberal position is unequivocally individualist, the modern liberal position is more socialistically inclined, or inflected with egalitarianism.

If people are being dehumanized, as Freire tells us, then someone or something must be doing this dehumanizing. One of the most original aspects of Freire's work is the way in which he sees this as being a dialectical relationship. This dialectic works both ways, making the oppressor and oppressed co-dependents rather than opposed. On the one side, the process is not simply positive for the oppressor. Rather, there is an ultimately negative aspect for those doing the oppressing, a dependency which gives the lie to the supposed autonomous power which oppressing is meant to give them. On the other side, the oppressed are not simply innocent victims, but are also complicit with the oppressor in the oppression. Thus the process of oppression, the *pedagogy of the oppressed* per se, is not a one-way process. Rather, it is enigmatic and, in some key respects, mutual. While Freire brings an original analysis to bear on this issue, none the less this dialectic of oppressor–oppressed does look back to Hegel's master–slave dialectic (Hegel, 1979). 'Dehumanization. Which marks not only those whose humanity has been stolen, but also [though in a different way] those who have stolen it' (Freire, 1996a, p. 20). This leaves us with some interesting questions regarding the motivation of the oppressors, but it will also connect with Freire's discussion later in *Pedagogy of the Oppressed* of the concepts and processes of 'sadism' and 'masochism'. Freire develops this problematic with an appeal to the concept of 'distortion' and the sense of a distortion of something that is a 'vocation'. Freire is also adamant that this is not just a question of which perspective you take, as in some form of historical and interpretative relativism. Although 'dehumanization' occurs in history, it cannot be the historical vocation of humanity: 'but it is not an historical vocation. Indeed, to accept dehumanization as a historical vocation would lead to either cynicism or total despair' (Freire, 1996a, p. 26). The second point is also significant. Not only is it not a historical vocation but to accept this would lead to 'either cynicism or despair'. Freire's work is thus set up very clearly against both cynicism and despair.

Freire gives us again a sense of what his key struggles are in *Pedagogy of the Oppressed*: 'The struggle for humanization, for the emancipation of labour, for the overcoming of alienation, for the affirmation of human beings as persons' (Freire, 1996a, p. 26). Thus we have here a four-pronged assault to create a more positive ambition for humanity: humanization (which we have already spoken about), emancipation of labour (which refers to Marx's theory of labour value (Marx, 1992b)), the overcoming of alienation (a key concept which owes something to Marx and Hegel, and indeed to Plato and the Allegory of the Cave (Plato, 1961)) and the 'affirmation of human beings as persons'. For Freire, this is all the result of an 'unjust order' (Freire, 1996a, p. 26) which 'engenders violence in the oppressors' (Freire, 1996a, p. 26). The *violence of the oppressors* is also foregrounded as another key concept for Freire.

The struggle between the oppressed and the oppressors

Another aspect of the teleology we see being stressed by Freire is the sense that the struggle will take place, as he puts it, 'sooner or later'. Once again, there is an inevitability or relative inevitability about this. This is a matter of the oppressed being driven to seek out the very humanity which has been denied to them. However, Freire is keen once more to stress the dangers of this struggle, the pitfalls which this struggle for freedom and justice entails for the oppressed. The key danger is *complicity with the oppressors* or even, in overturning them, turning into a new form of oppressor. The oppressed must not, in seeking to retain their humanity (which, in existentialist mode, Freire describes as a way to 'create' their humanity) become, in turn, oppressors of the oppressors but rather 'restorers of the humanity of both' (Freire, 1996a, p. 26). There are two key points here being adumbrated by Freire.

The first is a point one would almost not even notice. Freire here seems to acknowledge the tensions between a recognition and the creation of identity. This, among others, is a Sartrean problematic which Sartre outlines paradigmatically in his text *Existentialism and Humanism* (Sartre, 2007). Are we existentialists or essentialists? Sartre foregrounds the problematic in these diametrical terms and it is a little like Freire's similarly dichotomous choice of either being for or against in terms of education, as there is never a neutral position to take up. Freire, if we are going to follow Sartre's ultimatum to choose, is definitely on the existentialist over the essentialist side. Thus, he seems to suggest that the creativity and inventiveness of identity is something that must not be compromised. However, there are also essentialist elements in his dialectic of recognition, and it is this tension between existentialism and essentialism in Freire which remains unresolved. The second point regarding the danger of the oppressed in seeking recognition and liberation, becoming in turn a form of oppressor themselves, is a problematic that we know goes back to Hegel's dialectic. But this is also the very meaning of 'humanization'. Liberation alone is not enough or rather Freire is calling into question the philosophies which would seek to define freedom, liberation and emancipation as decontextualized from any dialectic of humanization or compassion for the oppressor. The oppressor him or herself is also a victim, Freire is telling us: 'this then is the great humanistic and historical task of the oppressed: to liberate themselves and their oppressors as well' (Freire, 1996a, p. 26).

At the root of this analysis is a conception of power, a very specific and counter-cultural conception of power: 'Only power that springs from the weakness of the oppressed will be sufficiently strong to free both [i.e. oppressed and oppressor]' (Freire, 1996a, p. 26). Thus power stems from weakness rather than strength for Freire. This again has, among other antecedents, Christian roots in the *Beatitudes* and the notion of 'blessed are the poor in spirit', but it does not necessarily require a supernatural explanation or justification. Freire is also keen, in this context, to stress that this renewal must be genuinely revolutionary. He seems to critique any notion of reformism or minor changes in power relations (and this is relevant for the debate which looks at the tensions in Freire's work between reformism and a more revolutionary spirit (Quinn, 2010)). This is a debate which goes all the way back, for example, to the discussion regarding Freire's original project in Brazil, where many in the Brazilian context have spoken of Freire as originally a reformer rather than a revolutionary thinker and pedagogue (Torres, 1993). It is present in the more contemporary debate in critical pedagogy as to whether Freire's understanding of education requires a parliamentary democracy in order to succeed and flourish (Da Silva and McLaren, 1993). We will also see it raised as an issue in terms of the Workers' Party in Brazil and Freire's involvement in the education and political administration in São Paulo (O'Cadiz *et al.*, 1998) in the late 1980s and early 1990s. There, in the context of a capitalist democracy (or 'liberal' democracy), the Workers' Party claims to be a 'democratic socialist' party.

The dialectic between the oppressor and the oppressed is thus complicated and often subject to reversal. Freire is also sensitive to moves within this process which seem to involve the oppressed receiving more power or concessions, but which, in his view, simply reinforce the problem of power. He observes: 'any attempt to "soften" the power of the oppressor in deference to the weakness of the oppressed almost always manifests itself in the form of false generosity; indeed the attempt never goes beyond this' (Freire, 1996a, p. 26). Reformism, Freire is saying, runs the risk of 'false generosity'. This is important with regard to Freire's understanding of parliamentary democracy. Although in principle this view leans towards a more revolutionary politics, in practice Freire's work has taken place very much within the terms of reference of democracy. None the less, for example in Brazil, as we have seen, the Workers' Party maintains a 'democratic socialist' line, at least ideologically. Second, there is a clear critique of the kind of paternalism which is often associated with development approaches in the West and indeed especially associated with Christian or religious mission in the Third World. Freire's analysis bears the marks of Nietzsche, for example, and his critique of *ressentiment* (simultaneously 'resentment' and 'reactiveness') in *On the Genealogy of Morals* (Nietzsche, 1998). While we must be wary of the oppressors' false charity, we must also be wary of the oppressed becoming riven by *ressentiment*. Rather, the whole discourse is guided by a notion of love, which connects with Nietzsche and, in this emphasis, also connects with later thinkers such as Alain Badiou (Badiou, 2001). There are, in addition, elements of Sartre's critique of 'bad faith' here, which he elaborates in *Existentialism and Humanism* (Sartre, 2007). 'True generosity consists precisely in fighting to destroy the causes which nourish false charity' (Freire, 1996a, p. 27). Again, what is significant is that

Freire is not content to simply critique but also seeks to provide a genuine alternative.

Freire illustrates the process of this becoming liberated in detail. Describing the situation from his own experience, Freire is implicitly drawing on elements from his earlier work in Brazil and Chile, and also in his earlier texts, *Education as The Practice of Freedom* (Freire, 2005a) and *Extension or Communication* (Freire, 2005b), which were not published in English until 30 years later. 'Almost always in the initial stages of the struggle, the oppressed tend to become sub-oppressors. The very structure of their thought has been conditioned by the contradictions of the concrete, existential situation by which they were shaped' (Freire, 1996a, p. 27). What is noteworthy is the reference to a concrete existential situation, the notion of a structure of thought that is 'conditioned', which connects Freire with all the emphasis on false consciousness, or what Lukács called 'a true thought of a false reality' (Eagleton, 1994) in earlier Marxism, and the reference to contradiction. We will return to this notion below in the emphasis on a *teacher–student contradiction* in Chapter 2, but here the notion is more generalized and specifically looks back to Marx's conception of contradiction in the capitalist system (Marx, 1992b). As the translator notes, 'the term "contradiction" denotes the dialectical conflict between opposing social forces' (translator's note: Freire, 1996a, p. 28). However, the struggle as yet has not truly materialized, in the measure to which the oppressed continue to see themselves as 'opposite': 'their [the oppressed] perception of themselves as opposites of the oppressor' (Freire, 1996a, p. 27). What is thus required is a more authentic consciousness-raising, which links back to the discussion of conscientization. Freire also makes clear that at no stage can one say that the oppressed are without any consciousness of their situation: 'this does not necessarily mean that the oppressed are not aware that they are downtrodden; but their perception of themselves is impaired by their submersion in the reality of oppression' (Freire, 1996a, p. 27).

At no point, consequently, are the oppressed completely ignorant of what is going on but, even at the second stage of gaining in greater consciousness, there are still clear limitations on the emancipatory project or dialectic. 'In this situation, the oppressed cannot see the "new man" as the person to be born from the resolution of this contradiction' (Freire, 1996a, p. 28). For Freire, then, they are more keen, it seems, to become like their oppressors, to take over the power the oppressors once had, or to perhaps oppress the oppressor. What they don't see, Freire says, is the need for the 'new man'. At this point, Freire is telling us that the oppressed are still caught in a vicious circle, and even their vision of emancipation remains caught within the prejudices or biases of the previous 'oppressor' framework: 'their vision of the new man is individualistic; because of their identification with the oppressor, they have no consciousness of themselves as persons or as members of an oppressed class' (Freire, 1996a, p. 28). This is not just a question of reform vs. revolution, where reform would come off badly by always containing a residue of the old oppressiveness. For Freire, even revolution itself runs this risk, in theory and in practice. Freire refers to revolution as being about a 'process of liberation'. Perhaps this is the key – what we have here is a *process* rather than a destination.

The fear of freedom

But what is standing in the way to some kind of proper or authentic human-ization, if even revolution has taken place? Freire introduces a concept which seems to derive from a fellow thinker, Erich Fromm, what he terms the 'fear of freedom' (it is here introduced in quotation marks, indicating the citation of Fromm) (Fromm, 2001). This notion of a 'fear of freedom' (Freire, 1996a, p. 28) is developed by Freire specifically in relation to the oppressed and their fear of overcoming the position of being oppressed. Thus, in the first instance, this fear constitutes a reason or a motivation to stay oppressed, to maintain the status quo and to be complicit in this maintenance. However, it may also relate to a tendency to 'desire the role of the oppressor' (Freire, 1996a, p. 28). What Freire seems to be suggesting, then, is that the oppressed have only negative reasons for wishing to become the oppressors. There is nothing affirmative or positive in this desire. Freire relates this to a psychological internalization of the oppressors' ideology. 'The oppressed, having internalised the image of the oppressor and adopted his guidelines, are fearful of freedom' (Freire, 1996a, p. 29). While the analysis points towards the value of freedom for the oppressed, we should remember that while regarded as a positive notion, freedom remains a contested ideal. Freire tries to explicate what exactly he means by freedom when he says, 'freedom would require them to eject this image and replace it with autonomy and responsibility. Freedom is acquired by conquest and not by gift. It must be pursued constantly and responsibly' (Freire, 1996a, p. 29). But he is again unequivocal in his dual tendency to see freedom as linked to human essence and also to seeing the possibility of freedom as indispensable to human flourishing, as the very condition to make human flourishing a reality: 'freedom is not an ideal located outside of man; nor is it an idea which becomes myth. It is rather the indispensable condition for the quest for human completion' (Freire, 1996a, p. 29).

The notion of a pedagogy of the oppressed

It is at this point that, for the first time, Freire introduces the specific concept of the *Pedagogy of the Oppressed*, a notion that will have such significance in his own name. At the root of this pedagogy must be an acknowledgement and critique of what Freire calls the 'duality' at the heart of the self-identity of the oppressed peoples, and this notion connects with Fanon's work *The Wretched of the Earth* (Fanon, 1986b) but perhaps even more especially with *Black Skin, White Masks* (Fanon, 1986a): 'the oppressed suffer from the duality which has established itself in their innermost being. This book will present some aspects of what the writer has termed the pedagogy of the oppressed' (Freire, 1996a, p. 30). Key for Freire is not just an identification of the pedagogy but the very process by which this pedagogy will be instantiated and brought to fruition: 'a pedagogy which must be forged *with*, not *for* the oppressed' (Freire, 1996a, p. 30; italics in original). The conflict lies in the choice between being wholly themselves or being divided. In moving beyond this psychological and sociological duality, we must be wary of the power relationship which exists in political groups and also in the relationship between oppressor and oppressed. What is at stake, according to Freire, is an *ejection* of the oppressor. More sociologically, it involves a choice between 'alienation' and human or communal 'solidarity' (Freire, 1996a, p. 31).

Freire seems intent on respecting the autonomy and freedom of the oppressed themselves. What is the point in affirming the freedom of the oppressed if the very political and educational means by which we bring this about, or seek to bring this about, exemplify paternalism, thus taking away the freedom we seek? What kind of freedom would we envisage which would be brought about through coercion? This is the question with which Freire's work is especially concerned and he is highly conscious of the tendency for Marxism and leftist movements to be tempted by power plays which further reinforce the problem of oppression rather than in any way undermine or subvert it. That is, a pedagogy of the oppressed which is 'for' the oppressed is not an authentic pedagogy, in Freire's eyes, although many such emancipatory pedagogies manifest themselves in reality in these ways. Freire is critical, for example, of the neo-Marxist thinker Georg Lukács in Chapter 1 of *Pedagogy of the Oppressed* on exactly this point: 'Lukács refers to "explaining to the masses their own action". For us, however, the requirement is seen not in terms of explaining to, but rather entering into a dialogue with the people about their action' (Freire, 1996a, p. 35).

So freedom has been affirmed and, now, dialogue, but issues remain. While one critique of the tendency towards paternalism in Marxism and leftism sees both of the latter as power-hungry, another view sees the problem as with the very condition of the oppressed themselves. If the oppressed are truly manipulated by their oppressors, are they in any fit state to bring about revolution or even to see some aspect of their oppression? Freire categorically rejects a blanket or determinist reading which would see the oppressed as wholly conditioned by false consciousness. Again, we see the importance of the discussion of the concept of ideology, as outlined in the Introduction to this chapter. Freire clearly rejects the view of ideology as all-encompassing, which we might associate, for example, with certain aspects of Althusser (Althusser, 1994) or Bourdieu's (Bourdieu and Eagleton, 1994) thought. None the less, while positing an awareness of oppression, *Pedagogy of the Oppressed* also clearly outlines the complex machinations of the oppressive regime, which make it very difficult for people to resist and which foster what Freire calls a 'fear of freedom'. So his central problem, as he calls it, becomes the following: 'the central problem is this. How can the oppressed, as divided, unauthentic beings, participate in developing the pedagogy of their liberation?' (Freire, 1996a, p. 30). How can they achieve such a critical discovery when they, as well as the oppressors, have become dehumanized? Freire cautions against utopianism: 'this solution cannot be achieved in idealistic terms ... they [the oppressed] must perceive the reality of oppression' (Freire, 1996a, p. 31).

The whole issue of *idealism* is a complex one in Freire, in both the senses of idealism. In the first case we have idealism in the more 'ordinary' parlance of utopianism. This, although it seems simple enough in Freire, is itself complex and problematic. While he constantly affirms the need for realism, he is also in many ways tied into a more aspirational or even utopian construct for the vocation of man, and 'man's historical destiny'. In the *Institute* texts (Freire, 1995b), for example, Freire is unequivocal in his affirmation of the need for a specific form of utopianism, which he links to hope. Second, there is the issue of 'idealism' as we know it in a more specifically philosophical context, where it is contrasted with materialism. Here, the key to this distinction (although the opposition goes back further) is that between German idealism and materialism, and most especially the debate between Hegel and Marx. Marx sees his own work as a refutation of the false premises of idealism but, as several commentators have shown, most notably Etienne Balibar (Balibar, 2007), Marx's materialism is far from eschewing idealism completely. In many respects, materialism is a continuation of idealism (Balibar, 2007). We will see how, like Marx, Freire's affirmation of materialism is not exclusive of a certain idealism. Indeed, to adopt Balibar's understanding, we can say that materialism and idealism are co-dependent (Balibar, 2007). This view makes Freire's perspective less contradictory and more compatible with a *both/and* perspective rather than an *either/or* viewpoint. Freire also refers to his idealism as speaking of the possibility of transformation, that is, 'not as a closed world from which there is no exit but as a limiting situation which they can transform' (Freire, 1996a, p. 31).

Throughout this chapter, Hegel's philosophy has been in the background and Freire now explicitly cites Hegel's *Phenomenology of Mind*:

Nor does the discovery by the oppressed that they exist in dialectical relationship to the oppressor, as his antithesis – that without them the oppressor could not exist – in itself constitute liberation. The oppressed can overcome the contradiction in which they are caught only when this perception enlists them in the struggle to free themselves.

(Freire, 1996a, p. 31)

It is not simply the question of dialectic and contradiction/opposition which here binds Freire's analysis to that of Hegel, but also the conception of perception which liberates and the very valuation of freedom itself.

As always with Freire, however, this notion of freedom which underlies his pedagogy is not a freedom to do whatever, or a freedom which inculcates and reinforces the individualism of the contemporary age. We have already seen how Freire expresses an affinity at the very beginning of the book with social movements and especially the student movements of May 1968, which he explicitly links to his own liberatory pedagogy. Central to his conception of pedagogy and politics then is a conception of 'solidarity' which must be understood as providing the context, the wider societal or community context, within which the value of freedom is affirmed. This takes his conception of freedom out of a standard classical liberal understanding towards a more socialist or Marxist view, although we have already spoken of the evolution within the self-understanding of modern liberalism towards a more egalitarian perspective (Moseley, 2008). He describes such 'solidarity' as a 'radical posture': ' if what characterises the oppressed is their subordination to the consciousness of the master, as Hegel affirms, true solidarity with the oppressed means fighting at their side to transform the objective reality which has made them these "beings for another"' (Freire, 1996a, p. 31). The reference to Hegel is significant in terms of his master–slave dialectic and the emphasis on transformation and consciousness-raising. Again, we must avoid becoming or being determined as 'beings for another'.

Solidarity

But how can such solidarity come about in reality, in history? For Freire, solidarity is not something just felt among the oppressed class. Rather, for the dialectic of progress, or progressivism, to be successful, it must also include the oppressors. Such solidarity must exist between the oppressed themselves but also from the oppressor to the oppressed and finally from the oppressed to those who oppressed them. Again, most especially in terms of the relation between the oppressor and the oppressed, what Freire seems to be especially cautioning against is the idea of 'false generosity' or 'false charity'. Thus we must be careful not to mistake these false charitable gestures for real solidarity between oppressor and oppressed. Freire refers to these gestures condescendingly as 'pious, sentimental and individualistic gestures' (Freire, 1996a, p. 32), contrasting them with what he calls 'an act of love' (Freire, 1996a, p. 32) which must be risked. 'When he stops making pious, sentimental and individualistic gestures and risks an act of love. True solidarity is only found in the plenitude of this act of love, in its existentiality, in its praxis' (Freire, 1996a, p. 32).

All the emphases are here – existentiality, love, praxis. These will return, for example, even in Freire's latest work, where they are often seen as symptoms of a postmodern turn in his work. But whereas there are definite changes of emphasis and context in Freire's work, early to middle to late, none the less perhaps what is most striking is the continuity in terms of purpose and conceptuality. We have already seen Freire distinguish his thought very clearly from both materialism and idealism, or at least seek to position his thought in a more complicated relationship to both. Here, now, he also wishes to evolve his discussion of subjectivity, and its role in the political and pedagogical struggle. Certainly, Freire is clear that we need to avoid individualism or simply individualistic gestures, whether charitable or otherwise, but here he is also concerned that we do not derive from this some kind of complete disavowal of subjectivity. Freire is keen to stress the irreducibility of a certain kind of subjectivity here:

> to present this radical demand for the objective transformation of reality is not to dismiss the role of subjectivity in the struggle to change structures ... Neither objectivism nor subjectivism nor yet psychologism is propounded here, but rather subjectivity and objectivity in constant dialectical relationship.
>
> (Freire, 1996a, p. 32)

Marx and subjectivity

What is also significant about this section of *Pedagogy of the Oppressed* is that Freire is not simply intent on distinguishing his own work here as relying on a notion of subjectivity but also with offering revisionist accounts of Marx's own thought, with which he obviously feels most affinity at this point, connecting explicitly with our earlier analysis of this relation. 'Marx does not espouse such a dichotomy, nor does any other critical, realistic thinker' (Freire, 1996a, p. 33). What Marx criticized and scientifically destroyed was not subjectivity but subjectivism and psychologism. Without subjectivity, it seems that there is no real chance of transformation, political-educational or otherwise. But this is not subjectivity in some kind of vacuum or tending towards the dangers of narcissism. What is at stake in this context is oppression, and the possibility of a liberation from this oppression, which can only come about through critical awareness of such oppression. This, it would seem, requires subjectivity and subjects, because, without subjects, who exactly is going to be able to have awareness of oppression and critical insight? Central to this and indeed to Freire's wider project is the operationalization of this subjective critical insight in action, and this action must take place between subjects, who exist in solidarity, a notion we can connect with Marx's conception of the subject as constituted by its 'relations', which he elaborates in 'The Theses on Feuerbach' (Marx, 1992a). Such relationality between subjects becomes fully evident only in action, in practice, which again develops Marx's key claim from 'The Theses on Feuerbach' (Marx, 1992a) concerning the intervention of philosophy in the world. *Praxis* for Freire means something very important but also something very simple: 'praxis – reflection and action upon the world in order to transform it' (Freire, 1996a, p. 33). Freire also quotes here from José Luís Fiori in order to demonstrate the difficulty of this task: 'Liberating action necessarily involves a moment of perception and volition. ... the action of domination, however, does not necessarily imply this dimension, for the structure of domination is maintained by its own mechanical and unconscious functionality' (Freire, 1996a, p. 33). That is, domination works by the unconscious and by repetition. Praxis must fight hard to resist and overcome this predicament of oppression.

So many distinct aspects seem to stand in the way of this liberation. We mentioned earlier 'fear of freedom'. Freire refers also to the 'rationalization' (Freire, 1996a, p. 33) of oppressions by those who realize it, even the oppressed themselves. At all times, however, we must avoid fatalism and live in hope for the future. This is because the human being is a "project" (Freire, 1996a, p. 35). 'There would be no human action if man were not a 'project', if he were not able to transcend himself, to perceive his reality and understand it in order to transform it' (Freire, 1996a, p. 35).

Freire derives, in this context, very positive conclusions from his use of Marx, Hegel and dialectic. This, in effect, is the thrust and direction of his very specific form of progressivism. At the root of it is a simultaneous critique of idealism and materialism understood in a simple sense as too much emphasis on either reflection or action: 'action is human only when it is not merely an occupation but also a preoccupation, that is, when it is not dichotomised from reflection' (Freire, 1996a, p. 35). Freire is advocating that reflection is essential to and constitutive of action. *Action must become a reflective preoccupation if it is be fully human.* Against those who caution against philosophy for its mere 'interpretation' of the world (a misreading of Marx in 'The Theses on Feuerbach' (Balibar, 2007, p. 13)), Freire is calling for a realization of the dialectical relationship between thought and action, individual and world. But what is also clear throughout Freire's work is that he won't settle for mixed motives or half-measures in pedagogy. He is highly critical of humanitarian rather than humanist generosity, which he sees as reinforcing the problem of oppression, or an 'egoism cloaked in the false generosity of paternalism' (Freire, 1996a, p. 36). This maintains and embodies oppression; he even goes so far here as to call it 'an instrument of dehumanization' (Freire, 1996a, p. 36). Quoting from Marx's 'Theses on Feuerbach' (Marx, 1992a, p. 422) once more, Freire tells us something he will reiterate in different language throughout his work: *the educator him or herself needs educating.*

One of the recurring Freirean issues is how to move from a condition of oppression to a condition of freedom, especially when the agents of change, the oppressed themselves, seem to have such a tentative hold on the awareness of their oppression and, when all around them, society seems to scheme to keep them in shackles. A key issue is thus *power*. Freire acknowledges that if education is going to be the vehicle for change then this cannot happen in terms of what he calls 'systematic education' (Freire, 1996a, p. 36), in the shorter term, by which he means school and curriculum development. This more centralized education system is more under the control of the oppressor class and, as such, can only 'be changed by political power' (Freire, 1996a, p. 36). However, Freire wants to clarify a key distinction for him between this form of systematic education and what we might call non-formal 'educational projects' (Freire, 1996a, p. 36), which should be carried out with the oppressed in the process of organizing them. Here, we are talking about more micro-level projects of education at a grass-roots level. Significantly, it is arguable that, even when in Brazil, Freire was always more involved in systematic education or the critique of it, so it is interesting to question whether this distinction really holds for his work. In addition, the changes which his work developed in Brazil, it might be argued, especially the later changes at a Brazilian Department of Education level, ran the risk of being too complicit with the power of systematic education. This is a question to which I will return, especially in terms of Chapter 6, with special reference to Brazilian education and, more generally, the practical component of Freire's work in politics and education.

The politicization of the oppressed

For Freire, education must never be understood in isolation from politics. One of his key texts is emblematically entitled *The Politics of Education* (Freire, 1985). In Chapter 1 of *Pedagogy of the Oppressed*, Freire refers several times to key theorists who also connect the educational to the political, for example, Frantz Fanon, Albert Memmi and Erich Fromm. All the while, Freire is reiterating his key insights that man's ontological and historical vocation is 'to be more fully human' (Freire, 1996a, p. 26). Freire is very insightful but also controversial in his understanding of global politics and the relation between the First and Third worlds. These are issues which also connect very clearly to Freire's work earlier than *Pedagogy of the Oppressed*, collected in *Education for Critical Consciousness* (Freire, 2005c), as well as the work directly following which was developed out of his work in Harvard; that is, his *Cultural Action for Freedom* (Freire, 1977).

What concerns Freire in Chapter 1 is the often problematical critique directed at oppressed peoples when they use violence against their oppressor. The violence of the oppressed against the oppressor leads to them being called '"barbaric", "wicked" or "ferocious"' (Freire, 1996a, p. 38). Thus there is a kind of inevitable movement here: the oppressor forces the oppressed into submission and labels them savage. When the oppressed become critical and try to react against this violence, they have no other means than violence itself as this is what the system is founded upon. In responding with violence, they confirm the image of the colonized as savage and they thus justify ever more increasing put-downs or domestications to keep these savages in their place. Freire, unsurprisingly, sees a different meaning and also a very different potential in these moments of crisis and violence, often connected to revolutionary moments and the revolutionary assertion of a native people. Of course, this was a time of such tumult in Africa most especially, which we should not take in isolation from both the May 1968 movement, very much grounded in disgust over the Algerian war and the Vietnam war (both of which may be seen as First World vs. Third World conflicts) and also Freire's own involvement with African and Latin and South American liberation movements (Freire, 1985; Torres, 1993). This also explains the significance of Fanon (Fanon,1986b) and Memmi's (Memmi, 1975) respective work for Freire. In contrast to those who would see such revolutionary violence as reactive or simply as a sign of the natives' savagery, Freire argues that 'paradoxically it is in this response that a gesture of love may be found .... It is only the oppressed who, by freeing themselves, can free their oppressors' (Freire, 1996a, p. 38). We can see Freire's logic here – the violence of the oppressor is oppressive and dehumanizing because it destroys the humanity of the oppressed. On the other hand, the violence of the oppressed is an attempt to liberate themselves from oppression and thus to become fully human. Thus, this violence is not oppressive. Moreover, if understood correctly, or if directed properly, the violence of the oppressed must also be seeking to liberate the oppressors from their own predicament. All the less then is it oppressive violence for 'an act is oppressive only when it prevents human beings from being more fully human' (Freire, 1996a, p. 39).

This is potentially dangerous talk, it may be argued, and it is certainly one of the most controversial passages in Freire, at least in *Pedagogy of the Oppressed*. Is it giving licence to any revolutionary group to take up arms? We might think, for example, of Freire's analysis of the social movements and especially the students' movements which develop out of 1968. We now know that 1968 was to lead, in this line of enquiry, to groups such as *Baader Meinhof*. Is Freire implicitly agreeing with this line of development? Certainly, in Fanon, there is at the very least an implicit affirmation of such revolutionary violence and it would seem to be also the case here, although Freire is more equivocal on this point than Fanon. Some commentators, for example, Paddy Quinn, foreground a change of Freirean tone regarding violence and politics from the early to the later work, contrasting the affirmation of violence in these early works to a less revolutionary later work in the texts on universities, etc., where Quinn sees Freire's language and politics as more reformist (Quinn, 2010). But alongside the thematic of revolutionary violence which is left ambiguous and unresolved, we also have a return to the thematic of how society operates to keep the oppressed seduced and/or dominated. Freire invokes Erich Fromm's (Fromm, 2001) analysis in some detail in terms of his key distinction between 'being and having' and the concomitant understanding of a sadistic consciousness which seeks to possess everything and which is thus necrophiliac. In a short space, Freire has thus invoked three key concepts of his analysis: *sadism*, *masochism* and *necrophilia*. Freire also links this (in almost Heideggerian mode) to the advent or at least the intensification of science and technology. He also cites in the footnotes Herbert Marcuse's key work on 'dominant forms of social control', relating to Marcuse's text *One-Dimensional Man* (Marcuse, 2002) (Freire, 1996a, p. 42). Once more, there is a sense that these manipulative societal controls won't be easy to overcome with a re-emphasis on the duality of oppressed consciousness and the admiration of the colonized for the colonizer (Freire often speaks of this as the way in which the oppressed 'introject' the oppressor consciousness). Here, Freire additionally cites Fanon in his *The Wretched of the Earth* and Memmi's *The Colonizer and the Colonized* (Freire, 1996a, pp. 44–45).

The subjectivity of the oppressed

So is this oppression insurmountable? Should we see the manifestation of the violence of the oppressed as somehow a last cry in the wilderness, a useless and pointless exercise in nihilism? No, Freire emphatically answers, and the ultimate response and answer seems to lie in *dialogue*. There can be no question of vanguard leaderships or rule by an intellectual or political elite. 'The conviction of the oppressed that they must fight for their liberation is not a gift bestowed by their revolutionary leadership; but the result of their own *conscientização* (conscientization): the oppressed must reach this conviction as Subjects and not as objects' (Freire, 1996a, p. 49). This consciousness-raising will hope to take people out of their situation as objects among objects, as things. This of course is a thematic of objectification or reification which extends right through the neo-Marxist heritage, but it also raises a potential problem for Freire here. That is, Freire needs to be careful of this ambivalence or ambiguity between two ways of interpreting the political and educational situation which runs through his work: (1) That all people are reduced to things in some blanket kind of objectification and that alienation is full and complete; and (2) that this domination is only partial. It would seem that Freire needs to avoid the talk of total domination, but he is also right to point to the revolutionary method as itself problematic in this respect. If Freire is orthodox in the ambiguity regarding the dominant/non-dominating tendencies, he is less orthodox and more progressive in recognizing that the revolutionary pedagogy itself is often complicit with reactionary forces and simply serves to consolidate class and oppressive interest. As he says in a phrase which will become very influential for bell hooks, for example: 'they cannot enter the struggle as objects in order *later* to become human beings' (Freire, 1996a, p. 50; emphasis in original). Of course, the irony here, as hooks is the first to point out, is that Freire's own original declaration of this humanization was couched in sexist or gendered terms: Freire originally referred to 'men' becoming human (hooks, 1994), although this was revised in later editions. This caused many feminists to turn against Freire's work, simply on these terms. We will see in a later chapter how hooks (while critical of this dimension of Freire's original work) none the less sees Freirean pedagogy and politics as potentially compatible with many aspects of the feminist struggle.

The pedagogical character of the revolution – politics and education

Amidst all this talk of revolution and politics, Freire wants to reiterate the importance, the indispensability of the pedagogical dimension: 'the object in presenting these considerations is to defend the eminently pedagogical character of the revolution' (Freire, 1996a, p. 49). In Chapter 2, we will see how Freire starts to more explicitly engage the pedagogical and educational implications of the political situation he has described. Thus, in terms of the teacher–student relation, 'a humanising pedagogy … expresses the consciousness of the students themselves' (Freire, 1996a, p. 51). Quoting Vierira Pinto, Freire notes that 'the essence of consciousness is being with the world' (Freire, 1996a, p. 51). For Freire, teachers and students, as irreducible subjectivities, are 'co-intent on reality' (Freire, 1996a, p. 51). That this should come at the very end of Chapter 1 of *Pedagogy of the Oppressed* raises a number of important issues. Does politics come first for Freire? Is education really only a secondary or derivative element in his philosophy? Certainly, in trying to write a book about his 'philosophy of education', I am conscious of the significance of this issue. Second, in writing about not just a political but also an educational experience which is first and foremost Third World and Brazil-based, we have to ask about the applicability of Freire's analysis to the wider world, and especially the First World which he himself engaged so directly with, both in his theoretical work and his life and practical projects (especially or perhaps unavoidably because of his exile from Brazil). Freire himself has spoken about precisely this connection or sometimes disconnection between Third and First worlds, regularly and in detail. His major point, as we will see, is that there can be no simple conversion from Third World to First World, or vice versa. The latter was in effect the basis of his critique of American literacy programmes applied to Brazil in the first instance (as we see in his first book, *Education as the Practice of Freedom* (Freire, 2005a)). For Freire, then, no culture can simply transfer its method to another, full stop. Indeed, this is partly due to the specificity of the culture but also because

Freire's philosophy, of education and of literacy, was never intended as a method. The fact that it has been so taken is part of the very system of education and politics (in effect, a positivism) which he criticizes. However, this is not how Freire's work should be deployed and he is unequivocal on this. Finally, we might say that if we are looking to the relationship between politics and education, that no one should look further for an example of their interconnectedness than to the 1968 moment. Immortalized in Freire's own 1968 work *Pedagogy of the Oppressed*, on the first page of his first chapter in an extended footnote, which cuts typographically across the page of the English translation, these very student and workers' movements exemplify the fierce intersection of education and politics, under conditions of societal crisis, witnessed in 1968 but also, to a great extent, being witnessed again in our own time.

CHAPTER TWO

Developing the analysis of *Pedagogy of the Oppressed*

From politics to the concept of banking education

Contextualizing Freire's philosophy of education

If Chapter 1 of *Pedagogy of the Oppressed* (Freire, 1996a) gives us a provocative political analysis of what Freire designates unequivocally as 'oppression', then Chapter 2 gives us an equally provocative analysis of the alienation endemic to the educational context, as Freire sees it. Implicit in this analysis, and made explicit in some instances, is the complex relation between politics and education. Freire sees both as distinct but as indissociable. This, as we have seen and will return to below, has been a major criticism of Freire, coming from within and outside Brazil, that Freire all too easily conflates education and politics (Torres, 1993). In this chapter I will argue that this accusation underestimates the complex and specific analysis which Freire gives of education and the pedagogical process. Certainly, in *Pedagogy of the Oppressed* (Freire, 1996a), the perspective on education is powerfully influenced by some of the political conflicts Freire has been involved in, before and during the period of the text's writing. For example, we can say that the analysis of education in *Pedagogy* (Freire, 1996a) is more revolutionary in intent than his exploration of education and pedagogy in the earlier *Education as the Practice of Freedom* (Freire, 2005a) (which we will look at in Chapter 3), and that this renewed emphasis on a revolutionary pedagogy owes a great deal to Freire's experience of political alienation and exile from Brazil. Freire says exactly this in his later retrospective analysis of this situation in *Pedagogy of Hope: Reliving Pedagogy of the Oppressed* (Freire, 1992). In the very revolutionary flavour of the pedagogical process as described, however, we should not lose sight of Freire's recognition that education is a process which must be understood in its own right, as well as in its connections to politics.

As the Introduction explored, Freire is a key figure in the transformation of philosophy of education (as a discipline) from being neo-Kantian and rationalist (as well as individualist) to being grounded in a more socio-political understanding of pedagogy (Blake *et al.*, 2003b, p. 5). One way to understand this move is to speak of a transition from an *analytic* to a more *continentalist* philosophical framework, while another (more politicized reading) is to view it as a transition from a more liberal to a more social-democratic understanding of education, or a move from a modernist to a postmodernist view. Freire aligns his own work in Brazil with the Workers' Party, which describes its ideology as 'democratic socialist'. Another important issue in this context concerns what Blake *et al.* refer to as 'the ambiguity of liberalism between political and economic forms' (Blake *et al.*, 2003b, p. 5) in the measure to which economic liberalism tended to be grounded in a 'social and educational authoritarianism' (Blake *et al.*, 2003b, p. 5). This latter becomes synonymous with what Freire will describe as the machinations of 'banking education'.

Blake and colleagues (Blake *et al.*, 2003b, p. 14) point to three key elements which might inform any renewed understanding of the discipline. First, a concern for language and for conceptual clarity, with more connections made to postmodern developments in theory. Second, an interdisciplinary dialogue between the disciplines of education (philosophy, psychology, sociology, history) where the philosophy of education can play a dialogical and distinctive role, but where it can no longer be regarded as the master discipline as it has been in the past. Third and more ambitiously, philosophy of education can engage in 'the exploration of what education might be or might become, a task which grows more compelling as the politics of the obvious becomes more oppressive' (Blake *et al.*, 2003b, p. 14). As we will see, in each of these three ways, but especially in the last case, Freire's work will take up this challenge, both originally and creatively.

With regard to their renewed vision for the philosophy of education as a discipline, Blake and colleagues have referred rather negatively to what they see as a failure to interrogate the very concept of educational practice itself in more recent American critical pedagogy approaches, which claim to take their cue from Freire's work (Blake *et al.*, 2003b, p. 50). They describe the critical pedagogy approaches as simultaneously 'utopian' and 'instrumental', insofar as they seem to eschew philosophical interrogation and self-critique in favour of the positing of a more ideological, politicized project. We will examine in Chapter 7 whether this interpretation of critical pedagogy is wholly accurate. In Freire's case, however, the analysis of education as a process in *Pedagogy of the Oppressed* (Freire, 1996a), and throughout his work, exemplifies that such an accusation cannot really hold. Freire's pedagogical work (for example, Chapter 2 of *Pedagogy of the Oppressed* (Freire, 1996a)) is nothing but a relentless questioning of the concept of educational practice, as well as an exploration of the very nature and experience of the practice itself. This symbiotic approach to pedagogy (conceptual and practical) is what Freire exactly means by '*praxis*'.

Critiquing education

On first inspection, Chapter 2 develops its thematic in the line of progressive education from Dewey (Dewey, 1973) to Buber (Buber, 2002), with a foregrounding of the 'teacher–student relationship': 'A careful analysis of the teacher–student relationship at any level, inside or outside the school, reveals its fundamentally narrative character' (Freire, 1996a, p. 52). Narrative in this context is intended as a pejorative concept and designation – it signifies that there is only one narrator of the educational story, a teacher-centred education. Moreover, it is not only a matter of the teacher being the exclusive agent of education. The problem also relates to what the teacher signifies or teaches about reality: 'the teacher talks about reality as if it were motionless, static, compartmentalised and predictable; or else he expounds on a topic completely alien to the existential experience of the students' (Freire, 1996a, p. 52). There are two related, but distinct, elements here which recur throughout *Pedagogy of the Oppressed* and indeed Freire's work as a whole. First, the thematic of reality and its distortion in most conventional forms of education. Second, the gap between what is taught, the content of the curriculum or the educational programme, and what Freire refers to as the 'existential experience' of the students. This latter phrase already gives a sign of the key importance of the philosophical movement of existentialism for Freire's work (for example, Jean-Paul-Sartre and Simone de Beauvoir are cited favourably in this very chapter). Indeed, in many respects, one may refer to Freire's work as *existentialist*, as an existentialist philosophy of education.

Freire invents a name for the negative kind of education which has become infamous – he refers to it as 'banking education'. In Chapter 2 of *Pedagogy of the Oppressed*, we get the most detailed examination of what exactly he means by this notion of pedagogy and education. While recognizing the distinctiveness of the critique of education, we must also not lose sight of the dialectical relationship between politics and education. Indeed, this is also a dialectical relation between Chapters 1 and 2 in Freire's most famous text (Freire, 1996a). In other words, banking is not simply an educational programme or approach. It is also, perhaps more significantly, a political programme, and one of our questions will be the relationship between the political and educational dimensions of this predicament. Which came first – banking education or banking politics?

In order to answer this question, we must first be clear on what we mean specifically by banking education and Chapter 2 provides a detailed and thorough analysis of this approach. Freire (1996a, p. 53) gives a useful summation:

> Education thus becomes an act of depositing, in which the students are the depositories and the teacher is the depositor ... this is the 'banking' concept of education, in which the scope of action allowed to the students extends only as far as receiving, filing and storing the deposits.

As always with Freire, however, it is not simply the question of educational content that bothers him but the effect of this kind of pedagogy on the person, not simply as a learner, but in terms of his or her very own personhood. If education aspires to be a humanizing process where individuals can come to self-realization, then the problem with this kind of pedagogy is that, in the name of education, it does exactly the opposite: 'but in the last analysis, it is the people themselves who are filed away through lack of creativity, transformation and knowledge in this [at best] misguided system. For apart from inquiry, apart from the praxis, individuals cannot be truly human' (Freire, 1996a, p. 53). Freire refers to this banking system of education as 'at best misguided'. As we shall see, his critique of this kind of pedagogy extends far beyond simply any notion of it being simply misguided. Banking education is an invidious kind of pedagogy with pernicious effects on human individuals and on the possibility of community or inter-subjective solidarity.

The teacher–student contradiction

All the while in this chapter, Freire is keen to provide more than simply a critique of existing pedagogy and knowledge. Rather, his aim is to contrast some of the existing problems with a more aspirational model of pedagogy, which he labels 'problem-posing education'. So what sense are we to make of this pedagogical alternative? How does it work? 'Knowledge emerges only through invention and re-invention, through the restless, impatient, continuing, hopeful enquiry human beings pursue in the world, with the world, and with each other' (Freire, 1996a, p.53). The sense of creativity which is associated with this kind of problem-posing knowledge and education is contrasted rather drastically with the process (or *lack of process*) by which banking education works: 'In the banking concept of education, knowledge is a gift bestowed by those who consider themselves knowledgeable upon those whom they consider to know nothing' (Freire,

1996a, p. 53). This knowing nothing or at least the designation of students as such is something Freire sees as central to the banking mindset and system of control. This constitutes for Freire an 'ideology of oppression' (Freire, 1996a, p. 53), which is not simply faulty as an educational approach but actually 'negates education and knowledge as processes of enquiry' (Freire, 1996a, p. 53). Central to this system of oppression is the way in which the teacher–student relationship is defined and corralled: 'the teacher presents himself to his students as their necessary opposite; by considering their ignorance absolute, he justifies his own existence' (Freire, 1996a, p. 53). This in effect is what Freire means by the *teacher–student contradiction*, which he here compares to Hegel's master–slave dialectic in *Phenomenology of Spirit* (Hegel, 1979), with one crucial difference. 'The students, alienated like the slave in the Hegelian dialectic, accept their ignorance as justifying the teacher's existence – but, unlike the slave, they never discover that they educate the teacher' (Freire, 1996a, p. 53).

In the master–slave dialectic, while contradiction exists, it is resolved or at least in principle is resolvable through the realization that although the relationship appears to be one of complete independence and complete dependency, in reality the relationship is one which is much more accurately described as *co-dependent*. The problem with the teacher–student contradiction in the banking system is that this co-dependency is never properly acknowledged. The student remains in an apparent position of subordination but, for Freire, this is to misunderstand the dialectics of oppression. To think that the oppressor remains independent of the oppressed in both education and politics is, for Freire, to miss the fact that the oppressor is also oppressed by the banking system. The mastery which seems to result for the teacher/oppressor is really only apparent. In effect and in reality, the teacher remains just as dependent upon the student and vice versa. The teacher–student contradiction is thus, for both teachers and students, a vicious circle on Freire's terms. In more practical terms, we can refer this abstract discussion back to Freire's approach to literacy education: *the educator him or herself needs educating* (Marx, 1992a, p. 422). An educator or teacher who seeks to maintain an absolute distance between him or herself (as expert) and the student (as passive learner) is involved in self-deception. Education, to be authentic, must be a mutual process of dialogue, and anything less involves an objectification and reduction of the possibilities for both student *and* teacher.

For Freire, banking education so called is not education in any real sense and so education has not yet begun in the banking system. For authentic or real education to begin properly requires, for Freire, 'the solution of the teacher–student contradiction, by reconciling the poles of the contradiction; so that both are simultaneously teachers *and* students' (Freire, 1996a, p. 53: emphasis in original). That is, one cannot posit a solution to the crisis of banking education for humanity from within banking education: 'the solution is not (nor can it be) found in the banking concept. On the contrary, banking education maintains and even stimulates the contradiction through the following attitudes and practices, which mirror oppressive society as a whole' (Freire, 1996a, p. 54). We will see below how important this is in terms of delineating very clearly that any attempt to liberate human beings from the banking system or society must divorce itself completely from any banking ideology or psychology. The threat is twofold; the first, and a threat which has plagued Marxism in its most politically institutional form, is that, in the idea of a certain transitional period, similar structures of power can be maintained in the revolutionary period from what went before (although obviously with a change in who holds power). The emphasis here is on a transitional phase. The problem historically, if not also in principle, has related to the transitional phase becoming a more permanent state of affairs. This has been the main basis of the historical and ideological feud between Marxism and anarchism, for example, that between Marx himself and Mikhail Bakunin (Irwin, 2010c). At the root of this issue is the question of authority and its connection to government and power. Even if only defended temporarily, the transitional 'dictatorship' highlights a residual elitism in Marxism (or at least this was Bakunin's claim).

The second issue relates to a more invidious residue of the 'oppressor mentality' even after such a transitional phase. Again, we are back to Hegel and the relationship of dependency which exists between master and oppressed. Freire is not just talking in the abstract but also in terms of several examples of revolutions which have already taken place or are in the process of erupting. In each case (and he cites in this context Fanon (Fanon, 1986b) and Memmi (Memmi, 1975) most especially), there is the acknowledgement that the oppressed maintain an ambivalent relationship to the power of the oppressor, which they resist but also admire and, paradoxically (in some cases at least), seek to emulate. Thus, for an authentic revolution to take place, what is required is a genuine move beyond the oppressor consciousness as mimicked by the oppressed in any attempt to revolutionize a society.

Freire's primary concern in Chapter 2 is none the less education rather than politics (although they are, on his terms, ultimately indissociable). Freire refers to the *mirroring* of the educational problems in the society as a whole (Freire, 1996a, p. 54). This concept of 'mirroring' is often used by Freire but it may, and has been, criticized, for an excessive literalism or simplification in the understanding of the relation between education and society/politics (McLaren, 1994). We should also note that some commentators at least regard Freire's positions on this relation between education and society as changing from his early to his late work (for example, Paddy Quinn's analysis of Freire's supposed turn to a later non-revolutionary 'reformism' (Quinn, 2010)). It should also be added that this relation bears somewhat on an even more significant relation between (economic) base and (socio-cultural) superstructure, where Freire inherits a complex Marxist heritage (Althusser, 1994). At this point in the text, Freire delineates the key differences between the teacher and the student under the banking system, although they are less differences as such and more oppositions which, drawn together, create the dynamic which keeps the banking system afloat and, in some cases, vibrant.

The A–J of banking education

Freire gives an A–J of the banking system and seems to present us with a simple dialectic of contradiction between the respective attributes of the teacher and student under the banking system. One may wonder at Freire's motivations here. The very description of such simplified opposition seems itself to partake of a banking mentality and method. Certainly, while one way of looking at the banking system is to see it in such stratified terms, it is none the less clear from Freire's more sustained analysis in *Pedagogy of the Oppressed* that the banking system is far more complex and nuanced than this 'A–J' would suggest. Thus, we should not read this list so literally. However, in its very simplification, the 'A–J' provides a useful grid on which to plot the more complex relation of teachers and students to the banking method and psychology and, as such, provides a useful starting point. Of particular note, for example, are the following 'contradictions' between teacher and student:

(b) the teacher knows everything and the students know nothing

(d) the teacher talks and the students listen – meekly

(e) the teacher disciplines and the students are disciplined.

(Freire, 1996a, p. 54)

In this brief resumé, Freire gives us much to think about and foregrounds the key concepts of his analysis: students in a position of complete ignorance, as empty vessels, a consequent student passivity, a disciplining of the students (which, of course, may imply some student resistance, at least initially). Freire complexifies this relationship between teacher and student with '(g) the teacher acts and the students have the illusion of acting through the action of the teacher' (Freire, 1996a, p. 53). This notion of *illusion* being endemic to the education process, and especially the illusion of action hiding an underlying passivity, connects readily to the discussion in the Marxist tradition of 'false consciousness' and the wider notion of 'ideology' itself (Žižek, 1994a). Indeed, this notion has deeper philosophical antecedents in Plato's original distinction between appearance and reality, for example, in his paradigmatic Allegory of the Cave (Plato, 1961).

The last two elements of the 'A–J' of banking education are particularly revealing. First, item 'I': '(i) the teacher confuses the authority of knowledge with his or her professional authority, which she and he sets in opposition to the freedom of the students' (Freire, 1996a, p. 54). We will see that the question of authority (and its relation to freedom) is key to Freire's analysis of education. The issue of authority and freedom became the defining conception within the movement of progressive education, which we will discuss in more detail in Chapter 5 (Darling and Nordnebo, 2003). For Darling and Nordenbo, for example, the third wave of progressivism was associated with an emphasis especially on the freedom of the child versus the authority of the teacher. In many respects, and this is acknowledged by the authors, this is a vulgarization of the authentic meaning of the progressivist emphasis on childhood and freedom, as the latter should be understood as a corrective emphasis to counter the traditionalist emphasis on an unaccountable authority of the teacher (in effect, a traditionalist authoritarianism). That is, the progressivist movement never wanted to jettison the authority of the teacher per se, but to create a dynamic between authority and freedom. This is precisely John Dewey's insistent point in *Experience and Education* (Dewey, 1973), against those who sought to reduce his own philosophy of education to the vulgarized version of progressivism.

But what is Freire trying to do here with this progressivist legacy in the restricted environment of his 'A–J' of banking education? '(i) the teacher confuses the authority of knowledge with his or her professional authority, which she and he sets in opposition to the freedom of the students' (Freire, 1996a, p. 54). We may best understand Freire, in this context, as precisely seeking to engage the very problematic of authority and freedom which I have just described, in a suggestive rather than a finalized way. Freire is indicating that authority in teaching and education is a complex and enigmatic phenomenon, which, as a value, may be at odds with itself, or which can have contrary claims made for it. In this case, Freire seems to be distinguishing between the teacher's 'professional authority' and the 'authority of knowledge'. Freire accuses the banking educator or teacher of 'confusing' or conflating the two. What Freire seems to be suggesting is that education (or teaching) cannot survive without authority as a value, particularly in the context of the authoritative value which must attach to authentic knowledge. However, *this is confused too often with the mere professional authority of the teacher*, that is, the authority which is designated as the teacher's in the context of institutionalized schooling. These two kinds of authority are not the same, and Freire also makes the assertion of the teacher's professional authority synonymous with an 'opposition to the freedom of the students'. Thus, in banking education, the teacher's professional authority is used to suppress the student's freedom. It is this kind of repressive (and arbitrary) authority that must be unequivocally rejected by the student. However, in re-asserting the freedom of the student, there should be a simultaneous respect for *the continuing value of authority*, albeit an authority which goes beyond the teacher and student, and resides in the value of knowledge itself. For Freire, authority and freedom must both be respected as authentic values in education, although often what is claimed as authority and freedom is inauthentic. Moreover (and we will return to the important issue of progressivism in Chapter 5), progressivism is misunderstood when it is cited as sanctioning the jettisoning of authority in favour of freedom in education and schooling. Finally, in this context, there is the sense of a kind of teacher authority which is opposed to freedom absolutely, an authoritarianism of the teacher. This latter view understands subjectivity (so dear to Freire's heart) as exclusively an attribute of the teacher identity while students or children are divested of the capacity for subjectivity or automony per se. With regard to the students, we can rather speak of a thorough objectification: 'pupils are mere objects' (Freire, 1996a, p. 54).

Developing critical consciousness in *Pedagogy*

There is thus a constant interplay between what happens in education and how this process is played out in terms of social and political roles. The more the student becomes immersed in banking education, the less chance there is of 'critical consciousness'. We can see the key connections between *Pedagogy* (Freire, 1996a) and the more differentiated work collected in *Education for Critical Consciousness* (Freire, 2005c): 'the more the students work at storing deposits, the less they develop the critical consciousness which would result from their intervention in the world as transformers of that world ... the more they tend simply to adapt to the world' (Freire, 1996a, p. 54). This concept of *adaptation* was central to the early part of *Education as the Practice of Freedom* (Freire, 2005a) and indeed we can read *Pedagogy of the Oppressed* as a distilled, and more politically refined, translation of some of the key concepts of the earlier text. What does Freire mean by 'adaptation'? In a manner similar to that announced by other Marxist thinkers such as Marcuse (Marcuse, 2002), adaptation refers to the assimilation of individuality within a 'massified society'. Freire also takes this idea of 'massification' from Gabriel Marcel, a Christian existentialist, again demonstrating the eclecticism of his work. The references to existentialist thought are particularly pronounced in this chapter, with key references to Sartre, Beauvoir and Erich Fromm. In each instance, the key theme is one of 'domination' (Freire, 1996a, p. 55), which Freire first relates here to Simone de Beauvoir: 'the interests of the oppressors lie in changing the consciousness of the oppressed; not the situation which oppresses them, for the more the oppressed can be led to adapt to that situation, the more easily they can be dominated' (Freire, 1996a, p. 55).

There is a paradigmatic connection between education and society; 'the oppressors use the banking concept of education in conjunction with a paternalistic social action apparatus' (Freire, 1996a, p. 55). Freire, as we have seen, has already referred to this process as a 'mirroring', although this would seem to be somewhat simplistic. It is also a theme he complexifies in his later work, especially in his confrontation with postmodernism, through the work of Peter McLaren among others (Freire, 1993; McLaren and Lankshear, 1994b).

Freire invokes in this context the existentialist distinction between 'beings for others' and 'beings for themselves' which he relates to 'student *conscientização*' or conscientization. 'The oppressed have been made "beings for others" … the solution is not to "integrate" them into the structure of oppression but to transform that structure so that they can become "beings for themselves"' (Freire, 1996a, p. 55). He also makes the distinction between his thinking and a specific form of 'humanism' (Freire, 1996a, p. 54) of the banking approach; the latter masks the effort to turn women and men into automatons. This constitutes the very negation of their ontological vocation to be more fully human.

But how can such a liberation or a searching for emancipation begin or be generated in the first instance, especially if the process by which people are maintained in oppression is so powerful (those processes such as 'objectification', for example)? The key concept, for Freire, seems to be (as it was for Marx) 'contradiction': 'if men and women are searchers, and their ontological vocation is humanization, sooner or later they may perceive the contradiction in which banking education seeks to maintain them, and then engage themselves in the struggle for their liberation' (Freire, 1996a, p. 55). In the banking concept of education, there is a whole philosophy of *man and world* or *person and world* which is inherently contradictory. In this context, we might refer, as an example, to the complicated debate about Freire's use of language and the re-translation of *Pedagogy* to make it more feminist in its employment of language and predication (hooks, 1994).

The travesty of education under the banking system is that it *miseducates*. Instead of educating us into self-realization, it reinforces the problem of what Freire calls 'adaptation' and 'domination': 'education should make them more passive still, and adapt them to the world; the educated person is the adapted person, because he or she is a better "fit" for the world … how little they question it' (Freire, 1996a, p. 55). There is a reference to Sartre's existentialism in a footnote. This reference invokes what Sartre calls the 'digestive' or 'nutritive' concept of education, in which knowledge is fed by the teacher to the students to fill them out (Freire, 1996a, p. 57). However, for Freire, this system seems to be in some inevitable process of breakdown or crisis.

Solidarity

In a language which in effect anticipates much of the more recent development of leftist and Marxist theory through figures especially associated with May 1968 (Rancière, Badiou, Balibar, etc.), Freire speaks of a 'solidarity': 'one must seek to live with others in solidarity' (Freire, 1996a, p. 57). Although the banking system is premised on 'security', for Freire this is a sham. There is no authentic security here. 'The bank clerk educator does not realize that there is no true security in his hypertrophied role, that one must seek to live with others in solidarity; solidarity requires true communication' (Freire, 1996a, p. 57). This is how meaning is generated and communicated for Freire, a meaning concerned with 'reality'. For Freire, one cannot extract or abstract from existential reality which must be the basis of all meaning and thus of all pedagogy and politics. Otherwise, one has what he terms here a kind of 'hypertrophy'. This is also connected to Freire's distinction which he borrows from Erich Fromm, of 'biophily' and 'necrophily'; 'because banking education begins with a false understanding of men and women as objects, it cannot promote the development of what Fromm calls "biophily", but instead produces its opposite, "necrophily"; this clearly is a love of life versus a love of death' (Freire, 1996a, p. 57).

Freire delineates in more detail what this key concept of 'necrophilia' means on his terms: 'For the necrophiliac, having rather than being is what counts; he loves control; oppression, overwhelming control, is necrophilia; it is nourished by love of death not life; the banking concept of education, which serves the interests of oppression, is also necrophiliac' (Freire, 1996a, p. 57). We see the way Freire constantly juxtaposes and connects paradigmatic concepts in his work, here 'banking' and 'necrophilia'. As with his earlier discussion in the Preface to *Pedagogy of the Oppressed*, of sectarianism and radicalization, Freire's targets are more generalized than one might at first expect. If necrophilia can be associated for Freire with rightist sectarianism, it is no less associable with leftist sectarianism, where a similar or at least related process of 'indoctrination' goes on. This is what Freire calls 'education and the practice of domination'. 'Education as the exercise of domination, the ideological intent (often not perceived by educators) of indoctrinating them to adapt to the world of oppression' (Freire, 1996a, p. 57).

What Freire is seeking to extract from this discussion is the possibility of what he calls a 'true humanism' ((Freire, 1996a, p. 57), and that he wishes to distinguish from those philosophies and politics which seek to lay claim to the title of humanism, while contradicting the very basis of such a philosophy. Key to this move beyond a false humanism is Freire's warning or 'accusation' that any attempt to use banking or 'domination' methods at the service of revolution (or especially in some transitional revolutionary phase, such as the phase of 'dictatorship of the proletariat') is misguided and fatal, as Freire observes: 'this accusation; its objective is to call attention of true humanists to the fact that they cannot use banking educational methods in pursuit of liberation' (Freire, 1996a, p. 59). Freire dwells on this point as it connects with so many of his other themes in *Pedagogy* and beyond, most notably the danger in colonial societies of the oppressed simply inverting the age-old political structures when they gain power. This is far from simply an abstract argument – for example, it is precisely the problematic transition to independence in much of Africa in the 1970s which was used as an explanation by many leftists for moving to the political middle ground, or further to the Right, as Kristin Ross has suggested (Ross, 2004). Freire, as always, sees this as more than simply a political issue. It is also a pedagogical issue: 'authentic liberation – the process of humanization; is not another deposit to be made in men. Liberation is a praxis, the action and reflection of men and women upon their world in order to transform it' (Freire, 1996a, p. 57). As with Marx, praxis comes to designate for Freire a key symbiosis between reflection and action, and develops the paradigmatic theme of Marx's 'Theses on Feuerbach' (Marx, 1992a).

Problem-posing education

As an alternative to banking, Freire now starts to delineate the detail of his alternative conception of what he calls 'problem-posing education' (Freire, 1996a, p. 60). Here, the concept of consciousness will be fundamental and again we see the interrelatedness to the early texts such as *Education for Critical Consciousness* (Freire, 2005c). We must 'reject the banking concept and adopt instead a concept of men and women as conscious beings; and consciousness as consciousness intent upon the world' (Freire, 1996a, p. 60). We have already spoken of Freire's link to the existentialist philosophers. Here again, when he invokes the paradigm of consciousness, we might be initially fearful that he is falling back into the rubric of some kind of vulgar idealism. But Freire is too subtle for this and indeed one of his great strengths is his constant dialogue with contemporary and 'progressive' philosophy, not simply in a political sense but also, perhaps more importantly, in an epistemological sense. Several commentators have drawn attention to the importance of epistemology (Elias, 1994) in Freire, and here he draws on the phenomenological tradition, as it also evolves into the existential phenomenological tradition (Kearney, 1986). As it concerns consciousness, this phenomenological tradition dovetails with problem-posing education, as Freire calls it: 'problem-posing education ... epitomises the special characteristic of consciousness; being conscious of, not only as intent on objects, but as turned in upon itself in a Jasperian split; consciousness as consciousness of consciousness' (Freire, 1996a, p. 60).

All the while, Freire moves the problematic back and forth from a more intra-philosophical terrain to a pedagogical and political domain. He returns to the topic of problem-posing education and the resolution of the 'teacher–student contradiction'. Fundamental to this contradiction, as Freire sees it, is the complex relation of authority and freedom: 'problem-posing education can fulfill its vocation as a practice of freedom only if it can overcome the above contradictions ... the teacher is also taught in dialogue; authority must be on the side of freedom and not against it; people teach each other' (Freire, 1996a, p. 60). This is an age-old problem in educational studies of the complex relation of authority and freedom, which, for example, thinkers as diverse as Martin Buber (Buber, 2002) and John Dewey (Dewey, 1973) have sought to solve. Freire assumes much of this tradition in his analysis here but it is clear that he does not see this as an either/or choice, although he is often represented as believing this. Rather, there is a properly dialectical relationship between authority and freedom and an affirmation of a both/and rather than either/or structure. He makes a clear distinction between what he sees as this dialectical element of problem-posing in two stages of education (Freire, 1996a, p. 61) and the more stultified and reifying approach of banking education. It is problem-posing which affirms students and teachers as 'critical co-investigators' (Freire, 1996a, p. 61) and this is (to invoke Plato's old distinction, Plato being another key influence here) *doxa* (opinion) superseded by *logos* (knowledge): 'problem-posing education strives for the emergence of consciousness and critical intervention in reality' (Freire, 1996a, p. 62).

On a meta-level, Freire makes clear that this is not exclusively or simply a 'theoretical question' (Freire, 1996a, p. 62), but a problematic to be developed in what he terms a 'total context': 'they apprehend the challenge in terms of total context rather than just as a theoretical question' (Freire, 1996a, p. 62), and he cites as influences here with regard to *Education as the Practice of Freedom* (Freire, 2005a) both Sartre, in terms of the connection between consciousness and world, and Husserl, with regard to background awareness (Kearney, 1986). At issue is not simply an epistemology but a whole ontology of the world: 'they come to see the world not as a static reality but as a reality in process; in transformation; the dialectical relations of men and women. Reflection must not be dichotomised from action' (Freire, 1996a, p. 64).

At this point of the text, Freire sets up problem-posing very clearly and somewhat polemically in opposition to banking education in a number of key paradigmatic areas: 'the two educational concepts and practices come into conflict' (Freire, 1996a, p. 64). There are several key quarrels which problem-posing and banking education run into here. First, banking involves itself in a 'mythicizing' (Freire, 1996a, p. 64) of reality where problem-posing, in contrast, 'demythologizes' (Freire, 1996a, p. 64). Banking education resists dialogue whereas problem-posing regards dialogue as indispensable and problem-posing thus creates the space for critical thinkers. Again, banking education 'inhibits creativity and domesticates the intentionality of consciousness, by isolating consciousness from the world' (Freire, 1996a, p. 64). In contrast, problem-posing education 'bases itself on creativity and stimulates true reflection and action upon reality' (Freire, 1996a, p. 64). A significant element in this contrast is rooted in the contested understanding of history: 'banking education fails to acknowledge men and women as historical beings; problem posing theory and practice take the peoples' historicity as their starting point' (Freire, 1996a, p. 64). Again, we can see that the phenomenological and existential strands of thought have had an influence on Freire's thinking which he assimilates in his usual eclectic way, with the latter eclecticism having its advantages and disadvantages. The advantages are clear: a sense of contemporaneity and an absorption of some of the most important philosophical ideas of the time. This very eclecticism also reflects positively on Freire's own genuine affirmation of and fidelity to some kind of 'historicity'. Freire's own openness to different strands of 'new thought' is genuine and causes some difficulties for his own thinking insofar as it challenges the basis of the latter. It also shows Freire's willingness to evolve his own thought in terms of what he calls in *Pedagogy of Hope: Revisiting Pedagogy of the Oppressed* (Freire, 1992) 'new thought's new ways of thinking'. However, there is also a more potentially negative side to this eclecticism. In taking and borrowing many different theories from many different thinkers and reabsorbing them back into the very specific history of his own thought, Freire runs the risk of distorting the true meaning of these ideas and simply using them for his own purposes (Elias, 1994). There is a danger of reductionism here as well as a superficial appearance of openness, which masks a greater grand mastery (it is reminiscent of Thomas Aquinas' claim to have developed a *perennial philosophy* which can assimilate all that went before).

Moving back to Freire's conception of problem-posing education, we may say that there is also a crucial conception in this context of 'human being' as unfinished:

> problem- posing affirms men and women as beings in the process of becoming; as unfinished, uncompleted beings in an unfinished reality. In this incompletion and this awareness lie the very roots of education as an exclusively human manifestation, the unfinished character of human beings and the transformational character of reality necessitate that education be an ongoing activity.
>
> (Freire, 1996a, p. 64)

Again, the resonances to Sartre and Husserl are powerful, and what does this tell us about the process of education itself? 'Education is thus constantly remade in the praxis; in order to be, it must become' (Freire, 1996a, p. 65).

Freire clarifies that underlying this notion of problem-posing and connected to his previous emphasis on historicity and consciousness, this must not be understood as in any way an idealism of consciousness. Rather, in an existentialist vein, we can never see people in this kind of abstraction: 'since people do not exist apart from the world, apart from reality, the movement must begin with the human–world relationship. Accordingly, the point of departure must always be with men and women in the here and now; which constitutes the situation in which they are submerged' (Freire, 1996a, p. 65). This 'submergence' is rather similar to Sartre's notion of 'facticity' (Sartre, 2003) but it is also aligned with a radical anti-determinism (as also in Sartre): 'to do this authentically, they must preserve their state not as fated and unalterable, but merely as limiting ... and therefore challenging' (Freire, 1996a, p. 65). This connects additionally with Freire's conception in Chapter 1, that the truth must be both discovered and created, and thus *recreated*.

Problematization

The very term used in the new kind of education is significant in this context, 'problem-posing': 'Whereas the banking method directly or indirectly reinforces the human's fatalistic perception of their situation, the problem-posing method presents this very situation to them as a problem' (Freire, 1996a, p. 66). Why is this problematization important? Precisely because it avoids fatalism and determinism, aspects of behaviour which Freire sees as plaguing the oppressed and their conditions as well as their possibilities for overcoming oppression, most especially in the Third World. This allows the overcoming of 'the magical or naive perception which produced their fatalism' (Freire, 1996a, p. 66). This is important for the sense of Freire's critical relation to superstition, magic and even a certain religion, and we can relate this to *The Politics of Education* (Freire 1985), which thematizes Freire's relation to liberation theology. He has already referred to problem-posing education as 'prophetic' (Freire, 1996a, p. 66), which has religious overtones. But Freire also maintains a harsh critique of a certain vulgar religion or, as he says here, 'the magical or naïve perception' which realistically is often connected with the 'massification' of religion in orthodox approaches to the Church (Freire, 1985). All is not lost however – there is a way out of this impasse and Freire is a constantly affirmative and optimistic thinker. Here we have an affirmation of the possibility of 'consciousness raising': 'a deepened consciousness of their situation leads people to apprehend their situation as an historical reality susceptible of transformation' (Freire, 1996a, p. 66). 'Resignation' gives way to the 'drive for transformation and inquiry, over which human beings feel themselves to be in control' (Freire, 1996a, p. 66). What this moves very radically against is the tendency to 'objectification' (Freire, 1996a, p. 66), which is the drive to alienate human beings from their own decision-making and 'to change them into objects' (Freire, 1996a, p. 66).

Erich Fromm and 'being' and 'having'

To conclude the chapter, Freire returns to his earlier interlocution with Erich Fromm (Fromm, 2001), a thinker to whom he has constantly referred as a key influence. He is especially concerned with Fromm's understanding of the relation between 'being and having'. What we need to affirm is a process of 'humanization' based on what he has earlier called a 'true humanism' but we must be wary of distortions of this vocation, which can look similar. 'This movement of inquiry must be directed towards humanization; the peoples' historical vocation; the pursuit of full humanity, however, cannot be carried out in isolation or individualism, but only in fellowship and solidarity' (Freire, 1996a, p. 66). Freire is cautioning here against an over-hasty identification of humanism and individualism, and cutting to the core of one of the main problems of defining liberalism in the contemporary age. It is arguable (Moseley, 2008) that liberalism has sought to become more 'social' and has sought to define itself in contrast to a more classical liberalism which emphasized the individual, above all else. For Freire, this earlier kind of liberalism is misguided and we also know that it has powerful contemporary resonance in terms of what has become known as 'neoliberalism', and in terms of a more intellectual debate, in terms of the discussion around 'libertarianism'. 'Attempting to be more human, individualistically, leads to having more, egotistically, a form of dehumanization' (Freire, 1996a, p. 66). Freire also cautions against a naïve romanticism which would eschew all 'having' in favour of 'being': 'not that it is not fundamental to have in order to be human. Precisely because it is necessary, some men's having must not be allowed to constitute an obstacle to others having, must not consolidate the power of the former to crush the latter' (Freire, 1996a, p. 66). This leaves the thorny issue of the status of the 'individual' as opposed to individualism in Freire. We know from an earlier discussion that the status of the individual was always very problematic in Marx and yet the individual was seen as thriving in the communist society (Marx, 1992a; Balibar, 2007).

Freire prefers the word or concept of 'subject' or 'subjectivity' to that of 'individual': 'problem-posing education, as a humanist and liberating praxis, posits as fundamental that the people subjected to domination must fight for their emancipation, enables teachers and students to become *subjects* of the educational process, by overcoming authoritarianism' (Freire, 1996a, p. 67). By the same token, Freire cautions against what he terms as 'an alienating intellectualism' (Freire, 1996a, p. 67). The best way out of this is to avoid didacticism: 'the revolutionary leaders must be revolutionary – that is to say, dialogical – from the outset' (Freire, 1996a, p. 67). Another aspect of this which Freire has previously clarified is that there must be a dynamic relation between reflection and action, a reciprocal relation where both are affirmed simultaneously, in what Freire (following Marx) calls 'praxis'.

From hollow 'activism' to rhetorical 'verbalism' – concluding *Pedagogy of the Oppressed*

Chapter 3 of *Pedagogy of the Oppressed* begins with a key point regarding the relationship between reflection and action. We have seen that this is a paradigmatic relation for Friere, what he terms *praxis*. However, this is often misunderstood to be synonymous with an emphasis on action rather than reflection. Freire makes clear in this chapter that praxis is a balance or a symbiosis between action and reflection. Thus, activism per se is not something which Freire lauds or even affirms. Rather, activism per se consti- tutes a 'sacrifice of reflection' (Freire, 1996a, p. 68). By the same token, on the other side, 'sacrifice of action' (Freire, 1996a, p. 68) constitutes 'verbalism' (Freire, 1996a, p. 68), that is, an excess of words, and, at various points, Friere returns to these twin mistakes in pedagogy and politics. He has interesting things to say in the Brazilian context about the mistaking of verbalism for dialogue, which he discusses in *Education as the Practice of Freedom* (Freire, 2005a), again showing the key intersections between these early texts. As far as Freire is concerned, it is a fundamental error to consider that verbalism is dialogue. Rather, verbalism destroys dialogue, and cultures that are synonymous with 'verbalism', as Freire says Brazil was, are not good at dialogue. But how does such dialogue take place?

Dialogue and love

In his explanation of the genealogy of dialogue, and how it can best take place, Freire introduces a theme which links him with later thinkers such as Alain Badiou (Badiou, 2001) and Jacques Rancière (Rancière, 1991), and this is also a key theme of the existentialist movement: 'dialogue cannot exist however in the absence of a profound love for the world and for people; the naming of the world, which is an act of creation and recreation, is not possible if it is not infused with love' (Freire, 1996a, p. 70). Here, Freire invokes Che Guevara's words: 'I am more and more convinced that true revolutionaries must perceive the revolution, because of its creative and liberating nature, as an act of love. [In the words of] Che Guevara, "the true revolutionary is guided by strong feelings of love"' (Freire, 1996a, p. 70).

Freire goes on to explicate this complex and enigmatic relation between dialogue and love: 'love is at the same time the foundation of dialogue and dialogue itself; it is thus necessarily the task of responsible subjects and cannot exist in a relation of domination' (Freire, 1996a, p. 70). Here, we see love being linked with other key themes in Freire's work, the concepts of domination and that of responsible subjectivity, which will fight such domination and its attendant divesting of subjectivity into objectification. Freire also here draws on concepts which he has looked at in more detail in earlier chapters – sadism and masochism, concepts also linked to Sartre and Fromm. It is love which brings us beyond fear, beyond the fear of freedom, as an act of courage. The emphasis on pathology indicates the psychoanalytic dimension of Freire's analysis, which owes a lot to Fromm (there are also Hegelian resonances in this discussion). As Freire notes, 'domination reveals the pathology of love; sadism in the dominator and masochism in the dominated. Because love is an act of courage not of fear, love is commitment to others' (Freire, 1996a, p. 70). We can clearly contrast Freire's reading of love and his analysis of relationality with, for example, that of Sartre's in *Being and Nothingness* (Sartre, 2003), the latter interpretation being far more negative and objectifying. For Sartre, in complete contrast, love is pathological.

Freire makes clear that this emphasis on love is not to be misunderstood as a naïve sentimentalism or romanticism (certainly, however, there are undoubtedly romantic elements to it). Rather, this thematic of love is connected to the theme of liberation and of dialogue. 'As an act of bravery, love cannot be sentimental. As an act of freedom, it must not serve as a pretext for manipulation; it must generate other acts of freedom; otherwise, it is not love' (Freire, 1996a, p. 71). We see the connection between love and freedom, and whereas love might be accused of romanticism, the emphasis on freedom once again returns us to the problematic of liberalism (as discussed, for example, by Moseley, 2008). But for Freire, love is not possible in the current situation of oppression. In the context of dehumanization there is *a distinct lack of love*, an incapacity to love, which also connects with Freire's themes of sadism and masochism and brings us back to Fromm. 'Only by abolishing the situation of oppression is it possible to restore the love which that situation made impossible. If I do not love the world, if I do not love life, if I do not love people, I cannot enter into dialogue' (Freire, 1996a, p. 71). For Freire, this authentic dialogue which he is searching for will bring about what he terms the condition for 'encounter' (Freire, 1996a, p. 71): 'someone who cannot acknowledge himself to be as mortal as everyone else still has a long way to go before he can reach the point of encounter' (Freire, 1996a, p. 71). This is, for Freire, primarily a matter of 'naïve thinking' versus 'critical thinking' (Freire, 1996a, p. 71). On the side of naïve thinking, there is an attempted 'normalization', whereas what Freire terms critical thinking seeks rather the 'transformation of reality' (Freire, 1996a, p. 73). Freire quotes here from the philosophy of time: 'the goal will no longer be to eliminate the risk of temporality by clutching to guaranteed space but rather to temporalise space; a domain which takes shape as I act upon it' (Freire, 1996a, p. 73). This notion of the 'risk of temporality' is especially evocative and connects Freire to existentialism.

The human and the animal

I have mentioned existentialism, and one of the key elements which Freire inherits from the existentialist movement (and especially in its Christian guise) is the emphasis on the demarcation between the human and the animal: 'the people, unlike animals, not only live but exist; and their existence is historical' (Freire, 1996a, p. 80) In the English language, the terms 'live' and 'exist' have assumed implications opposite to their etymological origins. As used here, 'live' is the more basic term, implying only survival. 'Exist implies a deeper involvement in the process of becoming' (Freire, 1996a, p. 80). Again, we can stress the existentialist dimension of Freire's thinking. But if humans and animals are so distinct, what is it about the human that makes it especially human? 'Humans, however ... exist in a dialectical relationship between the determination of limits and their own freedom; people overcome the situations which limit them, the "limit situations"' (Freire, 1996a, p. 80). This idea of 'limit situation' is connected to Karl Jasper's existentialist work (Jaspers, 1971), but Freire makes an important distinction between Jasper's use of the term which is more pessimistic in meaning and the way that Vierira Pinto speaks of 'limit situation', which is the view he wishes to affirm: 'limit situations are the frontier which "separates being from being more"' (Freire, 1996a, p. 80). Against the pessimism of Jaspers, they are not the 'impassable boundaries where possibilities end but the real boundaries where all possibilities begin' (Freire, 1996a, p. 80). This is, in effect, what Freire terms 'utopianism', not an unrealistic idealism but an optimism which looks to possibility rather than to obstacles.

Of course, not all humans behave in this way and some may be said to live a life which is more akin to the animal, immersed in society and what Freire elsewhere calls 'massification', which is a kind of 'animalization' of man. In many ways it is even more serious than this, as the human can go lower than the animal for Freire. A human who is unfulfilled exists at a lower stratum than simple animal 'specialization' (a view which Freire borrows or develops from the Christian thinker Jacques Maritain) (Maritain, 1943). However, thankfully, many humans can overcome this submersion in objectified reality:

> humankind emerge from their submersion and acquire the ability to intervene in reality as it is unveiled; intervention in reality – historical awareness itself – thus represents a step forward from emergence and results from the *conscientização* of the situation; *conscientização* is the deepening of the attitude of awareness characteristic of all emergence.
>
> (Freire, 1996a, p. 90)

Freire concludes Chapter 3 with a cross-reference to *Education as the Practice of Freedom* (Freire, 2005a) which develops this issue in more detail ('regarding the generative word, see my *Education as The Practice of Freedom*' (Freire, 1996a, p. 91)) and clarifies that this process of conscientization is not simply subjective but dialectical: 'obviously *conscientização* does not stop at the level of mere subjective perception of a situation, but through action prepares men for the struggle against the obstacles to their humanization' (Freire, 1996a, p. 91).

This leads into the fourth and final chapter of *Pedagogy of the Oppressed* (Freire, 1996a). Freire starts by reaffirming his commitment to a humanism which sharply differentiates itself from animality. Here, he wants to connect this thematic of humanism to a proper definition of praxis which he wishes to disconnect from reductionist notions of praxis as activism: 'I shall start by reaffirming that humankind, as beings of the praxis, differ from animals, which are beings of pure captivity' (Freire, 1996a, p. 106). In a sense, then, we may say that, on Freire's terms, pure activism is a kind of animality. Human action, in contrast, or human praxis, is a symbiosis:

> human activity consists of action and reflection: it is praxis. It is transformation of the world, and, as praxis, it requires theory to illuminate it. Human activity is theory and practice, it is reflection and action. It cannot, as I stressed in chapter 2, be reduced to either verbalism or activism.
>
> (Freire, 1996a, p. 106)

This is very important because, in educational terms, it shows the importance of theory for education, which has often been undermined in the study of education.

Freire quotes Lenin favourably in this context: Lenin's famous statement in *What Is To Be Done?* that, 'without revolutionary theory, there can be no revolutionary movement' (Freire, 1996a, p. 106). On Freire's terms this means that the revolution is achieved with neither verbalism nor activism, but rather with praxis, that is, with reflection and action directed at the structures to be transformed. This raises the crucial question of power: who does the deciding or how democratic will the revolutionary movement be? 'The revolutionary effort to transform these structures radically cannot designate its leaders as its thinkers and the oppressed as mere doers' (Freire, 1996a, p. 106). This is an age-old problem in the Marxist movement, for example in Althusser's distinction between 'science' and 'ideology' (Althusser, 1994), and one that Freire is unequivocal on. There can be no vanguard revolution: it must involve the respect for and full participation of 'the people'. In this context we see the crucial importance of dialogue. Revolution and dialogue go hand in hand, for Freire, which also means that revolution must be democratic. This raises the issue of the tensions between reformism and revolution in Freire's work and several commentators have questioned the revolutionary credentials of his thinking insofar as, for example, the process of conscientization as he describes it would require a democratic society to achieve (Torres, 1993). This also connects with the tension between the subjective and the objective in Freire's work, a tension which goes back to Hegel and Marx, so influential on Freire:

> Dialogue with the people is radically necessary to every authentic revolution. This is what makes it a revolution, as distinguished from a military coup. One does not expect dialogue from a coup; only deceit (in order to achieve legitimacy) or force (in order to repress).
>
> (Freire, 1996a, p. 106)

While revolutionaries may use various justifications for putting off dialogue, for deferring it:

> sooner or later, a true revolution must initiate a courageous dialogue with the people; its very legitimacy lies in that dialogue. It cannot fear the people, their expression, their effective participation in power. It must be accountable to them, must speak frankly to them of its achievements, its mistakes, its miscalculations, and its difficulties.
>
> (Freire, 1996a, p. 106)

Freire goes on to quote Fidel Castro in this context, which shows that he is not simply speaking in the abstract but in terms of real struggles in Latin America at the time. '"While we might obtain some benefit from doubt", said Fidel Castro to the Cuban people as he confirmed the death of Guevara, "lies, fear of the truth, complicity with false illusions, and complicity with lies, have never been weapons of the revolution"' (Freire, 1996a, p. 109).

Once again clarifying the false identification of activism with praxis, Freire tells us that 'critical reflection is also action' (Freire, 1996a, p. 109). Freire continues his critique of activism by clarifying its false connections to a revolutionary spirit: 'on the other hand, it would be a false premise to believe that activism (which is not true action) is the road to revolution; revolutionary leaders cannot think without the people nor for the people but only *with* the people' (Freire, 1996a, p. 112). This is one of Freire's most famous principles. *We must think with and not for the people*: 'revolutionary leaders cannot think without the people, not for the people but only with the people' (Freire, 1996a, p. 112). It is through this encounter between the people and the revolutionary leaders, which Freire, following Buber (Buber, 2002), refers to as their 'communion' (Freire, 1996a, p. 164), that a true revolutionary praxis can be built and evolved.

Conclusion: is there a change of emphasis, a Freirean turn?

Paddy Quinn states in his essay 'Paulo Freire's Theory of Education as Political Transformation' (Quinn, 2010) that a change of emphasis takes place in Freire's later work. Quinn associates Freire's later philosophy with the next statement made at the discussion concerning university education in Mexico in 1984: 'Paulo Freire, one of the most important 20th century philosophers of education, at a conference on higher education in Mexico city in autumn 1984, insisted that he was never inclined to believe that education could be the lever for political revolution' (quoted Quinn, 2010, p. 83). Quinn goes on to elaborate why he considers this view to represent a paradigmatic change from Freire's earlier work:

> For those, who like myself have read his earlier works on education, especially *Pedagogy of the Oppressed* and *Cultural Action for Freedom*, both published in the early 1970s, this claim seems at odds with his earlier view where the impression is given that a liberating education constitutes the central lever for revolutionary, political transformation.
>
> (Quinn, 2010, p. 83)

We have already discussed Freire's *Pedagogy of the Oppressed* (Freire, 1996a) in great detail in the last two chapters. Often Freire's early work (if not indeed his corpus as a whole) is seen as defined by *Pedagogy of the Oppressed*, as a text.

However, Freire has significant pre-*Pedagogy* work, and his work written immediately after *Pedagogy of the Oppressed*, such as *Cultural Action for Freedom* (Freire, 1977), is also very significant in understanding some of the implicit assumptions of the educational and political philosophy contained in *Pedagogy of the Oppressed* and Freire's subsequent intellectual and political development. As we will see, it is an oversimplification to regard Freire's work as, first, defined by *Pedagogy of the Oppressed* and, second, as continuous in theme and perspective. While there are certainly consistencies in Freire's work, early to late, it is also the case that significant shifts of emphasis take place. Quinn's argument about just such a conflict in Freire's development is thus a useful way into the discussion of Freire's early work, other than *Pedagogy of the Oppressed*, and most especially his conception there of the relation between education and politics. It provides us with a useful hermeneutic framework to analyse Freire's early work and to contrast it with the evolution of his later work, which we will discuss in subsequent chapters. There, we will return to the claims of Quinn and other commentators concerning the supposed stark chasm between Freire's early and later work.

CHAPTER THREE

Before *Pedagogy of the Oppressed*

Education as The Practice of Freedom

A reading hermeneutic for Freire's texts

In this chapter, I seek to provide some background context for the overwhelming importance of Freire's text, *Pedagogy of the Oppressed* (Freire, 1996a). Certainly, the latter has been Freire's most influential text but an exclusive focus on the textual detail itself can blind us, as readers, to the importance and relevance of several of Freire's other early texts, both those which immediately precede *Pedagogy* and those which immediately follow. To this end, this chapter will explore the first of these avenues of investigation. Paul Taylor, in his seminal work on interpreting Freire's overall hermeneutic, refers to three main approaches to be taken, what he calls the 'triple redaction reading' (Taylor, 1994, p. 3). First, there is the 'auto or bio-text' (Taylor, 1994, p. 3); that is, the relationship between the work and Freire's biography and lived existential experience. Second, there is the 'grapho-text', the reading of Freire's texts themselves in significant detail (Taylor, 1994, p. 3). Third, there is the 'con-text', that is, the relation between Freire's work and the wider group of thinkers and the tradition which have influenced his thinking (Taylor, 1994, p. 3). There is obviously some overlap and intersection between these three categories of interpretation, while each is none the less distinct. One way to introduce the importance of *Education for Critical Consciousness* (Freire, 2005c) is to say that it provides us with more of the 'auto or bio-text' of Freire's early years and development than *Pedagogy of the Oppressed* did, which was more explicitly concerned with the 'grapho text' and the 'con-text' of

Freire's work. Similarly, in focusing too much on the specific 'grapho-text' of *Pedagogy of the Oppressed*, we also miss out on Freire's more complex and varied 'grapho-text', which encompasses over 20 independent books.

There are two key books which precede *Pedagogy*, and which have become known in translation (collected together) as *Education for Critical Consciousness*, and each will be examined separately. The early text from 1964, *Education as the Practice of Freedom* (Freire, 2005a) gives us a rare insight into Freire's work before his exile to Chile and then Geneva. The key themes are already in place but the differences in emphasis are noteworthy, especially perhaps as the earlier book is espoused in a less strident or revolutionary tone (Freire's original work in Brazil was more reformist than revolutionary) (Torres, 1993). This dialectic of reform/revolution is ever present in Freire's work as we shall see, although it takes different modes at different times. In Freire's later work, for example, there is a tension between a 'utopianism' (Freire, 1995b) which views education as the paradigmatic lever that can bring political revolution, and a more moderate view which views the best approach as a kind of antagonistic educational politics that can bring about minor reform, without changing the overarching terms of reference (Freire *et al.*, 1994). If *Pedagogy of the Oppressed* is associated with the more utopian and revolutionary perspective in Freire (Quinn, 2010), then *Education as the Practice of Freedom* is of a more moderate tenor.

Education as the Practice of Freedom: critical consciousness as the motor of cultural emancipation

Denis Goulet's 'Introduction' (Goulet, 2005) to *Education for Critical Consciousness* is a useful place to start a contextualization of Freire's early work, even that which comes before *Pedagogy of the Oppressed*. As Goulet (2005, p. vii) makes clear,

> the unifying thread in this work is critical consciousness as the motor of cultural emancipation. *Education as the Practice of Freedom* grows out of Paulo Freire's creative efforts in adult literacy throughout Brazil prior to the military coup of April 1, 1964, which eventually resulted in his exile.

This notion of 'critical consciousness' (which Freire also sometimes refers to as 'conscientization') is a paradigmatic notion throughout Freire's work and it is fascinating to see it used here so centrally in the early texts, albeit with perhaps less of a developed sense than it achieves in the later work.

Goulet also refers to the importance of 'cultural emancipation'. Freire's work is perhaps unusual in its constant referencing of 'culture' and the politicization of culture. For Freire, even at this early point, culture is a key concept in its opposition to nature. Whereas nature stands for what humans cannot change, the concept of culture represents rather *the malleability of existence* and the chance for people to transform their situation. As we shall see, it will also paradoxically return as a preoccupation for many of Freire's followers in the critical pedagogy movement, although there the terrain of conversation will be primarily media culture and youth culture (Giroux, 2000).

It is also noteworthy that perhaps Freire's most important early essay names the concept of 'freedom' in the title (Freire, 2005a). In Chapter 1 we foregrounded the problematic status of the concept of 'freedom' in Freire's work and the way in which it cuts across the whole tradition of liberalism, and the distinction between what has become known as classical liberalism on the one side, and modern liberalism on the other (Moseley, 2008). In this context we see this concept as central, right at the heart of Freire's early work. Goulet makes the point that Freire's concept of freedom is quite specific (Goulet, 2005, p. vii). Goulet states that 'Freire's notion of freedom has always been dynamic and rooted in the historical process by which the oppressed struggle unremittingly to "extroject" [the term is his] the slave consciousness which oppressors have introjected (into the deepest recesses of their being)' (Goulet, 2005, p. viii). Certainly, as Goulet suggests, we should be attentive to the specificity of the concept of freedom which Freire uses. We must be wary of occluding the differences between alternative conceptions of freedom used in different educational theory, whether between, for example, Freire and Buber (Buber, 2002) or between Freire and Dewey (Dewey, 1973), although these differences should also not hide the similarities or affinities. However, as Goulet notes (Goulet, 2005, p. vii), Freire himself uses this concept rather differently in different contexts and phases of his own work. For example, it is arguable (and implicit in Goulet's analysis) that his early use of the concept of freedom in *Education as the Practice of Freedom* is rather naively drawn; 'yet in recent years, Freire has grown ever more attentive to the special oppression masked by the forms of democratic "freedom" or civil "liberty"' (Goulet, 2005, p. viii). It is not so much a case of affirming freedom per se than of seeking to affirm a specific (and dialectical) concept of freedom.

Another aspect that is noteworthy relates to something which readers of Freire who begin with *Pedagogy* (Freire, 1996a) are bound to miss – the emphasis on literacy which defined Freire's early period work, and not simply a theoretical interest but a very strong practical-political interest and intervention, grounded in Freire's own background in Brazil. Indeed, it is this political and practical-educational background which leads to Freire being exiled. Any simple theoretical account of *Pedagogy of the Oppressed* must take account of this empirical context. As Goulet observes,

'American readers of *Pedagogy of the Oppressed* will find in *Education as The Practice of Freedom* the basic components of Freire's literacy method' (Goulet, 2005, p. viii). However, we must immediately make some qualifications. There is no Freirean method as such (in terms of a literacy method or any other method), as Freire tells us again and again. We might say that Freire's method is to disavow any kind of formulaic methodology. We will see this expressed in a most extraordinary way (exactly faithful to Freires' consistent philosophy) in his practical work at the Education Secretariat in Brazil in the 1990s (O'Cadiz *et al.*, 1998). Thus, when we look at his approach to literacy education, we are immediately struck by the multi-layered and explicitly interdisciplinary approach he takes to literacy education. Another key component is Freire's stress on the need for what he terms 'generative themes', and indeed a generative methodology, which must continuously be reinterrogated as we develop our understanding (and which constitutes a kind of *anti-methodology*). In addition, key to his approach is a *cooperative relationship* between teacher and student, where there is certainly a distinction between these roles, but here the teacher's role is more to problematize than to in any way provide an answer. It is arguable that, in such a practical–educational context, we can see the very same structure which Freire will later theorize more systematically in *Pedagogy of the Oppressed* and in his later texts. Elias, for example, sees the latter text as constituting an exploration of the 'post-literacy' phase of Freire's work, whereas *Education as the Practice of Freedom* is focused more specifically on the 'literacy' phase (Elias, 1994, p. 19).

Culture circle

Thus, as Elias (Elias, 1994, p.18) has shown, in Freire's early work we already see his radical pedagogical practice. We can cite the replacement of the concept of school or class with the notion of *culture circle* or the subversion of the teacher's role with the concept of a coordinator. We can cite this coordinator as becoming an 'educatee' and a concept of critical understanding which eschews abstraction and becomes embedded in real contexts of action. This is what Freire means by freedom, and this approach also stresses his conception of a *fundamental equality* between teacher and student. 'Education in the Freire model is the practice of liberty because it frees the educator no less than the educatees from the twin thrall-dom of silence and monologue' (Goulet, 2005, p. viii). We know that Freire's approach to literacy education was highly successful in Brazil in the early 1960s (this indeed was the main reason why Freire was exiled). This success was not, however, based on some kind of literalist education (Araújo Freire and Macedo, 1998, p. 19). Rather, literacy education for Freire is always intrinsically socio-political in orientation and it emphasizes the necessity of self-transformation. In addition, Freire's method is always linked to what he terms the '*post-literacy*' process, although notably in Brazil (in the early 1960s) the Freirean process never reached the post-literacy stage insofar as the military coup cut it off mid-stream (Elias, 1994, p. 19). As Elias observes, 'while he was still director of the national literacy training program in Brazil, Freire mapped out a postliteracy campaign for those who had already passed through the first stage of literacy training. He was never able to implement this program because of the military coup' (Elias, 1994, p.19).

However, all was not lost here. 'Freire did however put into effect this part of the method in Chile and *Pedagogy of the Oppressed* presents a further development of the postliteracy phase. Freire's literacy effort in Africa provided new practical contexts to work out this program' (Elias, 1994, p. 19). It is interesting to think of *Pedagogy of the Oppressed* as part of the post-literacy campaign. More importantly, Freire's understanding of the relationship between literacy and post-literacy is not one of simple succession, as if post-literacy represents a final stage (in some Hegelian dialectic of synthesis). Rather, as we see from the trajectory or chronology of his work, Freire's post-literacy work takes place in *Pedagogy of the Oppressed*, but much of his later work returns to the literacy problematic, both in African countries (for example, in Guinea-Bissau (Freire, 1978)) and also in his later work in São Paulo (O'Cadiz *et al.*, 1998).

We have already seen that the concept of critical consciousness (or *conscientização*) is key for Freire. In addition to this, we may also say that Freire has a specific understanding of what he terms 'problem-posing' or the employment of an approach of 'problematization'. As Goulet observes, 'Paulo Freire's central message is that one can know only to the extent that one "problematises" the natural, cultural and historical reality in which he/she is immersed; problematising is the antithesis of the technocrat's "problem-solving" stance' (Goulet, 2005, p. ix). Goulet goes on to explicate the specific meaning Freire ascribes to problematization: 'to problematise in his sense is to associate an entire populace with the task of codifying total reality into symbols which can generate critical consciousness and empower them to alter their relations with nature and social forces' (Goulet, 2005, p. ix). There is, of course, danger in this approach, particularly in terms of a tendency to indulge a more subjectivist element: 'this reflective group exercise is rescued from narcissism or psychologism only if it thrusts all participants into dialogue with others whose historical vocation is to become transforming agents of their social reality; only thus do people become subjects, instead of objects of their own history' (Goulet, 2005, p. ix). This is reminiscent of a phrase which Freire uses in *Pedagogy of the Oppressed* (and which many later authors (for example, bell hooks (hooks, 1994)) have cited as especially important for their own development; 'one cannot enter the process of history as objects in order later to become subjects'.

Theory and practice

Another important element of this early work in *Education as the Practice of Freedom* (Freire, 2005a) is that Freire has already a well-worked-out and coherent understanding of the relation between theory and practice. Again, we can cite Goulet; (2005, p. ix):

> Freire knows that action without critical reflection and even without gratuitous contemplation is disastrous activism. Conversely he insists that theory or introspection in the absence of collective social action is escapist idealism or wishful thinking. In his view, genuine theory can only be derived from some praxis rooted in historical struggles.

As we shall see, Freire's conception of *praxis* (with such strong references back to Marx and Hegel) is exactly the harmony between theory and practice, the virtuous and hermeneutic circle of thought and action.

Finally, there is a theme of 'cultural invasion' which pervades all the early texts being discussed in this and the following chapter (this is less of a theme in *Pedagogy of the Oppressed* and has led to the misunderstanding of the latter). In particular, we will see that *Cultural Action for Freedom* (Freire, 1977) constitutes an attempt to clarify in hindsight what *Pedagogy of the Oppressed* was trying to say on this score; that is, the relevance of Freire's work for First World contexts. As Goulet makes clear, one cannot simply transfer Freire's work from one context innocently to another. This is a point reinforced by Coutinho in his Preface to *Cultural Action for Freedom* (Coutinho, 1977) but here Goulet states the same case: 'this is why Freire cannot be the theorist of social revolution in the United States. Only those who are historically "immersed" in the complex forms of oppression taken by life in the United States can identify the special garb worn by "cultural silence" in this society' (Goulet, 2005, p. ix). Goulet then goes on to ask what might be understood as the particular coordinates of oppression particular to the United States? 'What is it then that blocks oppressed Americans from controlling their own social destiny? Is it because the psychic boundaries between oppressors and oppressed in the United States are so fuzzy?' (Goulet, 2005, p. ix). In Freire's later work (Freire, 1992), there is a constant call for a *psychoanalysis* of the specific culture concerned. Coupled with Freire's emphasis on *interdisciplinarity*, we can see how Freire has never tried to employ a reductive analysis in relation to the complexity of the problems which he faces. But, additionally here, we have another aspect to emphasize: each problematic culture is specific to itself, while it may have a share in generalizable characteristics of the wider situations of humankind. This is not to say that Freire's work cannot be relevant to this struggle – quite the contrary in fact – but a simple transposition or translation would be immensely counter-productive and reductive.

Helpfully, we can say that Freire's understanding of culture as a complex form of life can be very enlightening in our analyses. This also connects with what might be termed a 'cultural turn' in later critical pedagogy, especially in the work of Henry Giroux (Giroux, 2000) and Peter McLaren (McLaren, 1994), for whom cultural studies becomes a key area of contestation (we will return to a discussion of critical pedagogy and Freire's 'culturalist' legacy in Chapter 7).

Education as the Practice of Freedom: analysing the text

Here, I want to look in particular at Chapter 1 of *Education as the Practice of Freedom* (Freire, 2005a), entitled 'Society in Transition'. This is a complex chapter which can be very useful in our contemporary educational context to the extent that it attempts to map out a whole index of revolutionary struggles in education, pinpointing the points of stress in the effort to get beyond banking education, as a mindset and a reality, in both political and pedagogical situations. Although this text is often seen as one of Freire's less theoretical texts (in comparison, for example, to *Pedagogy of the Oppressed),* it is significant that he introduces the analysis in his first chapter with a heavy theoretical discussion of existentialism, which invokes Karl Jaspers, a paradigmatic existentialist thinker (Jaspers, 1971). Another point worth stressing is the way in which Freire continues to attack the edifice of Westernized politics, especially insofar as it cuts across Third World liberationism, and yet he simultaneously draws on an intellectual heritage that is strongly Western and canonical. None the less, there are exceptions to this rule, such as Freire's work in Guinea-Bissau (Freire, 1978) and his relation to Fanon (Fanon, 1986b), and he tends to emphasize Western dissidents such as Sartre (Sartre, 2003) and Fromm (Fromm, 2001). Moreover, his eclectic approach might be seen as subverting the canon from within. Karl Jaspers' (Jaspers, 1971) work is relevant to use, first, just simply in terms of his framework for describing our *being-human in the world.* This is a paradigmatic example of Freire's vision of a 'true humanism', a thematic to which he will return significantly throughout his work.

Human and animal

In Chapter 1, we saw Freire introduce the distinction between the animal and the human (Freire, 1996a). Here, in an earlier text, we can see a related but more enriched discussion of the same theme. So what is it to be human specifically, according to Jaspers and, by extension, for Freire? As Freire starts by observing, 'to be human is to engage in relationships with others and with the world. It is to experience that world as an objective reality, independent of oneself, capable of being known' (Freire, 2005a, p. 3). Freire contrasts the human situation with that of the animal: 'animals submerged within reality, cannot relate to it. They are creatures of mere contacts, but the human being's separateness from and openness to the world distinguishes him or her as a being of relationships' (Freire, 2005a, p. 3). This is an interesting way to look at the human and it coheres with much of the emphasis, for example, in a key existentialist text such as Sartre's *Existentialism and Humanism* (Sartre, 2007). The human is individual before anything else: our *existence* (or ex-*ist*ence) is precisely, etymologically and semantically, an ability to stand outside ourselves and our world, which animals are fundamentally incapable of, at least on this interpretation. For Freire, 'human beings, unlike animals, are not only in the world but *with* the world' (Freire, 2005a, p. 3; italics in original). Not the least of the problematic aspects in this context, for Freire, might be the tension which exists between his sense of the human as subject and his sense of the human as a 'being-in-the-world' or with the world, which is also *with others*. For Freire, these seem not to be mutually exclusive but complementary: we are subjects *and* fundamentally inter-subjective. One of our key questions to return to will be to what extent, if any, there is indeed a tension here or not.

Second, this also relates to the whole issue of 'critical consciousness' or conscientization as Freire calls it elsewhere: 'human beings relate to their world in a critical way; they apprehend the objective data of their reality (as well as the ties that link one datum to another)' (Freire, 2005a, p. 3). For Freire, this is not simply critical consciousness, *it is also, precisely, literacy*: political, social and philosophical literacy which allows people to both read the word and 'read the world'. This capacity is not something that always exists for human beings in whichever culture. Rather, it depends upon the literacy of the culture which allows critical consciousness to thrive. This then is 'humanization', a possibility that, it seems, is denied to non-human societies. However, it is also a possibility of literacy that is denied to humans if the culture has a tendency towards education as domination (Freire, 2005a, p. 3). In 'illiterate cultures, the "weight" of such illiteracy hinders people from having such a critical consciousness' (Freire, 2005a, p. 3). Crucial here is an understanding of time or temporality: 'the dimensionality of time is one of the fundamental discoveries in the history of human culture. In illiterate cultures, the weight of apparently limitless time hindered people from reaching that consciousness of temporality and thereby achieving a sense of their historical nature' (Freire, 2005a, p. 3). Temporality and a consciousness of temporality is thus something unique to the human being's sense of reality and this connects with Freire's ongoing thematic of 'historicity', which he inherits from phenomenology and existential phenomenology (Sartre, 2003). This possibility is absent in animals: 'a cat has no historicity; his inability to emerge from time submerges him in a totally one-dimensional "today" of which he has no consciousness: human beings exist in time, they are inside and they are outside' (Freire, 2005a, p. 3). This creativity is what allows the human being to achieve *agency*, and to break with the kind of mechanisms of adaptation and massification that Freire is so critical of in *Pedagogy of the Oppressed* and elsewhere. These processes, precisely because of the capacities that Freire here describes, are processes of *dehumanization*. We should note that this whole diagnosis and critique by Freire and the very identification of 'dehumanization' (as well as the attendant notion of humanization) could be and is radically questioned by an alternative philosophical understanding. This latter interpretation refuses to accept the presuppositions of humanism, whether of the more traditionalist version or even the presuppositions of the supposedly more authentic or revisionist humanism espoused by Freire and others.

If, however, these distinctions or this bar between the human and animal worlds is not so a priori or essentialist, if it is rather existentialist or materialist, then certainly there is a possibility of it being reversed or radically questioned under different social and political conditions. Where one sees a real potential problem in this context, for Freire, is in terms of his understanding of Christian theology and eschatology, which itself might be overturned by an existentialism, insofar as the latter tends towards a more human-centred and less theo-centric perspective.

For Freire, what is so positive about this element of the human situation which he describes is that it eschews any passivity and embraces action, although an action which is founded on authentic reflection: 'As human beings emerge from time, discover temporality and free themselves from today, their relations with the world become impregnated with consequence. The normal role of human beings in and with the world is not a passive one' (Freire, 2005a, p. 4). This allows for and indeed encourages intervention rather than adaptation or objectification: 'because they are not limited to the natural [biological] sphere but participate in the creative dimension as well, human beings can intervene in reality in order to change it. Human beings enter into the domain which is theirs exclusively – that of History and Culture' [Freire's capitals]' (Freire, 2005a, p. 4). Freire makes a subtle distinction between a more negative 'adaptation' and a more positive 'integration': 'Integration with one's context, as distinguished from adaptation, is a distinctively human activity; integration results from the capacity to adapt oneself to reality plus the critical capacity to make choices and to transform that reality' (Freire, 2005a, p. 4). This is then distinguished clearly from mere adaptation: 'to the extent that a human being loses their ability to make choices and is subjected to the choice of others ... he or she is no longer integrated; rather they have adapted; they have adjusted' (Freire, 2005a, p. 4). Fundamental here is a distinction which Freire has made earlier between subject and object: 'the integrated person as subject. In contrast, the adaptive person is person as object' (Freire, 2005a, p. 4). Again, Freire is keen to stress the element of fundamental distortion or what he terms 'dehumanization' which is at work (Freire, 2005a, p. 4).

Epochal shifts and paradigms

Freire now shifts his focus from the struggles of the individual in history to the wider problematic of epochal shifts and paradigms. As Freire observes, 'As human beings create, re-create and decide, historical epochs begin to take shape; and it is by creating, re-creating and deciding that human beings should participate in their epochs' (Freire, 2005a, p. 4). We have already seen how Freire emphasizes the value of historicity, deriving from his analyses of Husserl and existential phenomenology most especially (Sartre, 2003). I have also stressed how crucial an understanding of the historical context of Freire's own work is (Araújo Freire and Macedo, 1998, p. 19; Elias, 1994, p. 19ff.), deriving as it does from such a value-laden and paradigmatic moment as 1968, in terms of the key moment of the publication of his text *Pedagogy of the Oppressed* (Freire, 1996a). Freire balances the sense of the ideal and the empirical in terms of his analysis of epochs, at the same time stressing the ideal values and the concrete contexts.

As Freire notes with regard to the understanding of epochs as such: 'an historical epoch is characterised by a series of aspirations, concerns, and values in search of fulfillment; the concrete representations of many of these aspirations, concerns and values, as well as the obstacles to their fulfillment, constitute the themes of that epoch, which in turn indicate tasks to be carried out' (Freire, 2005a, pp. 4–5). This sense of 'tasks to be carried out' is a locus of attention for Freire as it also designates the historical responsibility which we all face as individuals and groupings in a 'society in transition'. This essay almost reads like a manifesto for *progressivism* (Darling and Nordenbo, 2003) in any epoch, although Freire is never far away from the specificity of his own problematic. 'The epochs are fulfilled to the degree that their themes are grasped and their tasks solved; and they are superseded when their themes and tasks no longer correspond to newly emerging concerns' (Freire, 2005a, p. 5).

Again, this is an interesting way to look at things. First, the sense that problems really can be solved or resolved. What Freire's work in Brazil suggests is that this may not be so easily achieved in reality (as opposed to in principle). Second, the sense that there will always be 'emerging concerns'. This seems to relate to Freire's emphasis on an irreducible historicity which cannot be overcome in any simple dialectical or finalized sense. Freire is keen that this emphasis on epochs should not give an overarching sense of some kind of historical fatalism. All the while in this emphasis on epochs, Freire wants to stress the key role human beings and indeed human subjectivities or individuals can play in 're-creating' the issues or solutions of their times:

> human beings play a crucial role in the fulfilment and in the super-
> seding of the epochs; whether or not human beings have perceived the

epochal themes and above all how they act upon the reality within which these themes are generated will largely determine their humanization or dehumanization, their affirmation as subjects or their reduction as subjects.

(Freire, 2005a, p. 5)

We can see an interesting juxtaposition, in this context, of the theme of perception with the age-old relation between 'discovery' and 'invention', a tension which Freire's work keeps in ambiguous relationship rather than seeking to resolve. The danger, it seems, is not perceiving the real themes of the moment, and, in such a case, one is destined to be a mere 'onlooker': 'for only as human beings grasp the themes can they intervene in reality instead of remaining mere onlookers' (Freire, 2005a, p. 5).

Adaptation and integration

For Freire, the key contrast is between adaptation and integration. Adaptation is when we are unable or unwilling to intervene in terms of the need for change: we become assimilated and dehumanized. In contrast, a critical attitude allows us to intervene in our epoch and have a more affirmative perspective, where we can achieve integration rather than mere adaption. This way lies humanization: 'And only by developing a permanently critical attitude can human beings overcome a posture of adjustment in order to become integrated with the spirit of the time' (Freire, 2005a, p. 5). There are some concerns one might express in this context, for example, a tendency on Freire's part to an excessive binarism, in this case between adaptation and integration. We might test out this tendency in terms of Freire's own achievements and problems in the practical Brazilian context of education and politics (O'Cadiz *et al.*, 1998), and we will return to this problematic in detail in Chapter 6.

We have spoken already of the tension in Freire's work which problema-tizes the status of the individual *vis-à-vis* the collective responsibility of the epoch and the society. But if there was any doubt that Freire keeps the subjective dimension alive, one should look to his critique of the way in which the individual can be annihilated by the adaptation process. This shows directly that Freire's work is, among other things, *a defence of the individual against the system*. His description of the destruction of the individual in his or her authenticity under the system is poignant:

But unfortunately what happens to a greater or lesser degree in the various "worlds" into which the world is divided is that the ordinary person is crushed, diminished, converted into a spectator, maneuvered by myths which powerful social forces have created. These myths turn against him or her, they destroy and annihilate him or her.

(Freire, 2005a, p. 5)

'These myths turn against him or her' – this is undoubtedly true.

But Freire is also insightful in terms of how individuals panic in these situations in an effort to survive this challenging context: 'On the other hand, fearing solitude, they gather in groups lacking in any critical and loving ties which might transform them into a cooperating unit, into a true community' (Freire, 2005a, p. 5). So there are many communities which appear as if they might be true or authentic and based on solidarity, but which fall victim to the same forces of destruction and complicity with adaptation. Freire's sensitivity to the psychological pitfalls of group psychology and indeed politics is interesting and shows a sensitivity to subjectivity and subjective authenticity. The important distinction which Freire makes here is between 'solidarity' and 'gregariousness'. '"Gregariousness is always the refuge of mediocrities, said … Dr Zhivago". It is also an imprisoning armour which prevents human beings from loving' (Freire, 2005a, p. 5).

Freire describes this as 'tragedy of modern humanity', that of our 'domination', a thematic which links Freire to specific thematics on the Left, such as Althusser's conception of ideology (Althusser, 1994) and Marcuse's understanding of domination in *One-Dimensional Man* (Marcuse, 2002). It also potentially puts him at odds with an alternative strand of Leftist thinking associated with, for example, Henri Lefebvre (Lefebvre, 2002) or Slavoj Žižek (Žižek, 1994a), who would see capitalist 'consumption' as a more positive possibility, and would view the notion of domination or 'false consciousness' (Žižek, 1994a) as too reductionistic. We have traced the status of this question of ideology in Chapter 1, in relation to the later text *Pedagogy of the Oppressed*. But here, at an earlier juncture, Freire seems to invoke a concept of 'false consciousness': 'by the force of these myths and their manipulation by organized advertising, ideological or otherwise, gradually, without even realizing the loss, the human being relinquishes their capacity for choice; they are expelled from the orbit of decisions; ordinary people do not perceive the tasks of the time' (Freire, 2005a, p. 5). This is in line with leftist thinking but runs the risk of setting up the very opposition between ordinary and extraordinary thought that Freire seems to want to undermine. However, Freire is not so much suggesting that ordinary people cannot perceive the tasks of the time as that they are not allowed to: 'the latter [tasks of the time] are interpreted by an "elite" and presented in the form of recipes or prescriptions; and when human beings try to save themselves by following the prescriptions, they drown in levelling anonymity, without hope and without faith; "domesticated and adjusted"' (Freire, 2005a, p. 5).

Freire quotes and cites Erich Fromm (Fromm, 2001) here, a constant companion in these endeavours. He is keen to stress Fromm's sense of the powerlessness of contemporary humanity:

> As Fromm said in *Escape From Freedom*, … modern human beings are overcome by a profound feeling of powerlessness which makes

them gaze towards approaching catastrophe as though they were paralysed.

(Freire, 2005a, p. 5)

The sense of paralysis is significant and the human alienation from what we really need and want, a being rather than simply a having, which of course is one of Fromm's central themes (Fromm, 2001). What is also significant is that this repressive adaptation of humanity to the surrounding capitalist context gives the mirage of a kind of cornucopia of delight, when in fact humanity seems to be reduced to such a primitive state of passivity and dehumanization, or turned into the disintegrated animal state which Freire describes at the beginning of this section.

Freire is especially conscious of the 'crisis' which comes with the move from one epochal period to another and, undoubtedly, he is thinking here of his own Brazilian society, although the 'Society in Transition' chapter may also be seen as prescient in terms of the events of 1968.

An especially flexible critical spirit is required if society moves from one epoch to another. Lacking such a spirit, human beings cannot perceive the marked contradictions ... the time of epochal transition constitutes the historical-cultural 'tidal-wave'; as the contradictions deepen, the tidal wave becomes stronger and its climate increasingly emotional.

(Freire, 2005a, p. 5)

Freire is conscious of the real difficulties of such a period of transitional crisis. In speaking of the 'emotional' climate, a climate 'increasingly emotional', we can say that this is a euphemistic description of what Fanon unequivocally labels 'violence' and Freire will experience this himself in 1964 in his exile from Brazil (Elias, 1994: p. 19). *Education as the Practice of Freedom* (Freire, 2005a) was first published in 1965 and so captures the respective moments when Freire is working in Brazil before exile *and* the fall-out of the explusion from his home country (this is not mentioned explicitly in the book but implicitly one can read about its effects). This book thematizes the complex question of a 'time of decision' which however is illusorily presented as a time of 'choice': 'choice is illusory to the extent that it represents the expectations of others' (Freire, 2005a, p. 6). So, it is a time of decision but there is no individuality to make a decision. The decisions are already made, Freire seems to be suggesting. Again, the Brazilian context would seem to bear out this reading in terms of a *society in transition*.

Brazil in transition

Freire moves to the specificity of the Brazilian context in the next section of the essay. 'Brazil, in the 1950s and early 1960s, was precisely in this position of moving from one epoch to another' (Freire, 2005a, p. 7). If the old themes of the closed society were no longer relevant, Freire wishes rather to foreground the themes of the new Brazilian society. Freire delineates the key theme as 'cultural alienation. Elite and masses alike lacked integration with Brazilian reality' (Freire, 2005a, p. 7). We may also note that a transition can take place across a wide expanse of time, with various stages and phases, and later in the chapter on Brazil we will return to this thematic of a society in transition, to see how Freire's analysis is borne out in later periods (O'Cadiz *et al.*, 1998). Freire's description of such a society in transition posits a kind of brinkmanship between positive and negative capabilities or possibilities. 'If Brazil was to move surely towards becoming a homogenously open society, the correct perception of new aspirations and a new perception of old themes was essential' (Freire, 2005a, p. 7). This is a significant statement: 'a correct perception of new aspirations and a new perception of old themes'; this is almost a definition of progressivism on Darling and Nordenbo's (Darling and Nordenbo, 2003) terms, which we have referred to in the Introduction. Without this correct perception of old and new however, the risk of the transition was very strong, with very destructive possibilities for the society. What makes this analysis all the more powerful is that we know the outcome of this society's development, which Freire could not foresee when he wrote the text. The risk of a massified and distorted society was strong: 'should a distortion of this perception occur however, a corresponding distortion in the transition would lead not to an open society but towards a "massified" society of adjusted and domesticated human beings' (Freire, 2005a, p. 7). 'A society of adjusted and domesticated human beings': here we can see where the language of *Pedagogy of the Oppressed* comes from. For Freire, beneath the veneer of contemporary society's freedoms lies the reality of massification and adjustment; or normalization and domination. The translator here gives us a useful definition of massification, the term having originally been coined by the Christian humanist Gabriel Marcel:

> A massified society is one in which the people, after entering into the historical process, have been manipulated by the elite into an unthinking, manageable agglomeration; this process is called massification. It stands in contrast to *conscientizacao*, which is the process of achieving a critical consciousness [translators note].
>
> (Freire, 2005a, pp. 16–17)

This, then, is not simply a political issue but a pedagogical one, an issue of education. 'Thus, in that transitional phase, education became a very important task' (Freire, 2005a, p. 7). Freire outlines the specifics of the Brazilian context from which he is working. 'The starting point for the Brazilian transition was that closed society to which I have referred ... backward, illiterate, anti-dialogical. Elitist' (Freire, 2005a, p. 8). In contrast and in opposition to this, Freire calls for a process of radicalization, which is not sectarianism, whether rightist or leftist. 'Radicalization involves increased commitment to the positions one has chosen; it is predominantly critical, loving, humble, and communicative and therefore a positive stance. He tries not to convince and convert, not to crush his opponent' (Freire, 2005a, p. 8). Dialogue is thus crucial in this context.

In this battle for radicalization, the designation or labelling of action takes on a political significance. In a footnote, Freire clarifies a point which will take on added importance in *Pedagogy of the Oppressed,* in relation to a discussion of Fanon, Memmi and the situation of colonial and anti-colonial violence. 'Among the innumerable rights claimed by the dominating consciousness is the right to define violence; and to locate it. Oppressors never see themselves as violent' (Freire, 2005a, p. 17). Freire is treading a thin line, on the one side criticizing those who label the anti-colonial violence as pathological, while at the same time warning against the sectarianism which Freire is especially conscious of on the Left. This is already a balancing act. Moreover, what it also demonstrates is that Freire's work, which is often seen as very conciliatory, is, in fact, quite aggressive with regard to competing political philosophies, on the Left most especially.

Freire's work emphasizes *problematization,* and especially problemati-zation of dogmatism. He always seems wary of the 'fascism of everyday life', as Foucault puts it ('the fascism in our heads') (Foucault, 2004). What is crucial in this context is the emphasis on dialogue as constitutive, but we might also say that this is philosophical through and through in the original sense of philosophy as a process of *elenchus* or 'refutation': philosophy is against sectarianism of all kinds. Freire here runs the risk of being accused of a certain romanticism, naïve in the extreme, because of his emphasis on love. This is indeed the basis of Freire's critique of sectarianism in this context:

> The sectarian creates nothing because he cannot love. Disrespecting the choices of others, he tries to impose his own choice on everyone else. Herein lies the inclination of the sectarian to activism; action without the vigilance of reflection. The radical in contrast rejects activism and submits his action to reflection.
>
> (Freire, 2005a, p. 9)

This is very important: the *'radical rejects activism'*. If there is one sectarianism which is often associated with Freire but which completely fails to read him, it is the sectarianism which is bred around the opposition between theory and practice, affirming practice without reflection, what Freire here calls activism.

Freire cannot be unaware of the polemical import of what he is saying in this situation. Political activism per se is to be rejected as unreflective and naïve. This naivete at best (or knowing dogmatism at worst) is complicit with the forces of adaptation and massification. It leaves the interlocutors of this kind of discourse locked into a pre-established knowledge: 'sectarians can never carry out a truly liberating revolution because they are themselves unfree' (Freire, 2005a, p. 9). This links with Freire's emphasis on freedom and the problematic aspect of this to the extent in which it partakes of some of the issues which I have already outlined with regard to liberalism and the contestation of freedom as value and concept (Moseley, 2008). Freire has already discussed the intensification of the emotional climate around these issues, and here he now mentions the term 'fanaticism' which, he says, flourishes in such a context. For Freire, the matter is unequivocal: 'Fanaticism flourished. This fanaticism, which separated and brutalized human beings, created hatred' (Freire, 2005a, p. 10). This hatred, rather than sustaining, can be seen to drain, for Freire at least, all the positive resources from radicalization and the possibility of real change in the society and the educational sector.

Seeing the alignments and disalignments across the political spectrum can be one of the most interesting challenges when reading Freire. Here, matters are especially complicated, as Freire himself notes. First of all, he tells us that 'in the Brazilian transition, it was the sectarians especially those of the right, who predominated rather than the radicals' (Freire, 2005a, p.10). But the footnote which develops from this point complexifies the situation still further, once more highlighting perennial themes in Freire of progressivism and the relation between progressivism and religion, especially Christianity and liberation theology movements. Freire is foregrounding here the issue of how different movements and ideologies can be split between progressive and reactionary elements, for example, both Christianity and leftism, as Freire understands them. Freire approvingly cites Emmanuel Mounier, the Christian personalist or existentialist thinker (Freire, 2005a, p. 17), and makes an important distinction between progressivist Christians and more reactionary or sectarian Christians, although neither the progressives nor the sectarians in Brazil were exclusively Christian. This is important for a sense of a rapport between Christian and non-Christian radicalism in Freire, which also distinguishes between reactionary forms of the same. The key, in this particular context, is the acceptance of the development of 'science and technique' as an aspect of human liberation, while still seeing the human being or 'man' as the author of his own liberation (rather than technology).

At the root of Freire's affirmations and denegations is once again the issue of power and especially reciprocity between teacher and student. What constitutes radicalism, Freire says, its identifying mark, is a rejection of the 'palliatives of "assistencialism"' (Freire, 2005a, p. 12). ('Assistencialism' is the term used in Latin America to describe policies of financial or social assistance which attack the symptoms, rather than the causes, of social ills.) This point of course has resonances with Freire's whole critique in *Pedagogy of the Oppressed* of 'false charity'. As a further point of affirmation of Christian progressivism, Freire cites in a later footnote the example of 'Pope John XXIII': 'development should not involve aid which involves disguised forms of colonial domination, Christianity and social progress' (Freire, 2005a, p. 17). Freire is associating here with a Christian progressivism. He is, in this context, citing what he sees as a progressivist papacy or papal injunction, at the heart of orthodox Catholicism. The discussion in this section finishes with a further reference to the importance of critical consciousness: 'Conscientization, *Conscientizacao*, [which] represents the development of the awakening of critical awareness, must grow out of critical educational effort' (Freire, 2005a, p. 15). This important emphasis yet again on the connection or inter-dependency between critical consciousness per se and critical educational consciousness should not be overlooked with regard to the ongoing sense of a symbiosis between education and the political.

Closed society and democratic inexperience: an analysis of Chapters 2 to 4 of *Education as the Practice of Freedom*

The second chapter of *Education as the Practice of Freedom* (Freire, 2005a) is entitled 'Closed Society and Democratic Inexperience'. We have discussed Freire's development of his thematics in Chapter 1 of the former text, in the context of the analysis of 'A Society in Transition', which looked at the specifics of Brazil but also at the wider context of the social dynamics in the analysis of epochal shifts and the possibilities of education to seek to understand and transform society. In Chapter 2, Freire is especially interested in what impedes the possibility of the actual operationalization of democracy. Here, he cites the 'lack of democratic experience; this has been and continues to be one of the major obstacles to our democratisation' (Freire, 2005a, p. 19). The impact of the colonization of Brazil by Portugal was especially relevant, which prevented the experience of self-government: 'Experience in self-government might have afforded us an exercise in democracy, but the conditions of our colonization did not favour this possibility. In fact, Brazil developed under conditions which were hostile to the acquisition of democratic experience' (Freire, 2005a, p. 19). This description is not just useful for an understanding of *Education as the Practice of Freedom*. It also helps us to understand better the background which remains somewhat implicit in *Pedogogy of the Oppressed*. It also raises a question which will run through *Education as the Practice of Freedom* and especially Freire's early texts. To what extent is this a singular Brazilian experience or to what extent is it universalizable beyond the specifics of the Brazilian context?

Freire refers to the 'democratic inexperience' as causing a 'habit of submission'. It also allows Freire to reintroduce the concept or theme of 'adaptation' which will be central throughout his earlier work and which he here contrasts with what he terms 'integration': 'this habit of submission led human beings to adapt and adjust to their circumstances, instead of seeking to integrate themselves with reality' (Freire, 2005a, p. 21). This is hardly surprising, Freire says, although obviously disappointing. Humanity does not simply develop the capacity for integration with reality in a simple or natural way. Rather, such integration involves the need for an initiation into the very ethos of democratic living and political organization. It also involves a need for critical consciousness which itself struggles under non-democratic regimes:

> Integration, the behaviour characteristic of flexibly democratic regimes, requires a maximum capacity for critical thought. In contrast, the adapted human being, neither dialoguing nor participating, accommodates to conditions imposed upon him or her and thereby acquires an authoritarian ... frame of mind.
>
> (Freire, 2005a, p. 21)

Here, we see the basis laid for Freire's more sophisticated elaboration of this problematic in *Pedagogy of the Oppressed*.

In this essay, Freire moves between a more conceptual and political analysis and a broader historical sweep which concerns the particular historical development of Brazil as a country. With regard to the specific historical development of Brazil, Freire notes 'during the 16th to 19th century, Brazil was a society which lacked almost all forms or expressions of individual or family status except the two extremes: master and slave' (Freire, 2005a, p. 27). This is a phrase or concept which is taken, Freire acknowledges, from Gilberto Freyre, from the text *The Mansion and the Shanties* (cited in Freire, 2005a, p. 27). In this context, we see how Hegel's master–slave dialectic works in history, according to Freire, and we have seen the theoretical discussion of this in *Pedagogy of the Oppressed*, whereas *Education as the Practice of Freedom* analyses the more specific empirical context of Brazil. What is lacking, then, are the constituents for a proper society which would favour what Freire will later call *problem-posing education*. In this context, he emphasizes the lack of a proper conducive context for dialogue:

> The proper climate for dialogue is found in open areas, where human beings can develop a sense of participation in a common life. Dialogue requires social and political responsibility. It requires at least a minimum of transitive consciousness which cannot develop under the closed conditions of the large estate.
>
> (Freire, 2005a, p. 21)

Again and again, commentators have drawn attention to one of Freire's key themes being the overcoming of what is termed, by Freire himself, the 'culture of silence' (for example, Elias, 1994, p. 19). Freire makes explicit reference to this in this section, where he speaks of the genealogy of Brazil's 'mutism': 'herein lie the roots of Brazilian "mutism"; societies which are denied dialogue in favour of decrees become predominantly "silent"' (Freire, 2005a, p. 21). It should be noted that silence does not signify an absence of response, but rather a response which lacks a critical quality.

Another of Freire's key themes relates to the issue of the master–slave dialectic, and this foregrounds the whole problematic of freedom and authority. Here, the theme of authority and especially 'external authority' is foregrounded explicitly: 'the centre of gravity in Brazilian private and public life was located in external authority and power. Introjecting this external authority, the people developed a consciousness which housed oppression, rather than the free and creative consciousness indispensable for authentically democratic regimes' (Freire, 2005a, p. 22). In this context a few key concepts are already introduced. The concepts of *external authority* and *power* here introduced are developed in *Cultural Action for Freedom* (Freire, 1977), in terms of Freire's concept of *director societies*. Second, the concept of *introjection*, which refers to the internalization of the image of the oppressor as dominating, thus generating a feeling of 'fear of freedom' (this indicates the complex polarity which authority remains in with freedom). Introjection is a concept which Freire seems to have developed from psychoanalysis, perhaps directly from Freudian thought or mediated through Erich Fromm (Fromm, 2001). It is a dual concept which refers to an individual but also to a societal unconscious which inculculates and oftentimes dominates.

Third, there is the concept of consciousness which 'housed' oppression. In Chapter 1 of *Pedagogy of the Oppressed*, Freire develops this idea of the complex relation between consciousness and authority. One example which we have already discussed in our analysis of the latter text is the issue of how the oppressed can desire to become the oppressor, even when (or especially when) they are free of the oppressor. This also relates to the enigmatic relation which exists between the master and the slave in the master–slave dialectic. Fourth, there is a free and creative consciousness. This shows the importance of conscientization but it also raises the issue of false consciousness and whether such a free and creative consciousness is actually possible under current conditions. Fifth, there is the concept of 'authentically democratic societies' and this is obviously what Freire's work aims at, a kind of radical democracy connected to a similar emphasis in contemporary political philosophy, for example, the work of Chantal Mouffe (Mouffe, 2005) and also to be found in specific kinds of anarchist political thinking (Irwin, 2010b–c).

Unfortunately, Brazil comes in on the naïve side of each of these issues, as Freire observes:

> Brazil never experienced that sense of community, of a participation in the solution of common problems which is instilled in the popular

consciousness; and transformed into a knowledge of democracy. On the contrary, the circumstances of our colonization and settlement created in us an extremely individualistic outlook; as Vieriea said so well, 'each family is a republic'.

(Freire, 2005a, p. 23)

This issue of individualism once again brings us back to the binary or either/or opposition between materialism and idealism, and that between subjectivism and objectivism: in each case, Freire wishes to posit a *both/ and possibility*. What is significant for Freire is that often, from a formal viewpoint, there can be an attempt to inaugurate democracy but this formalism fails to take account of the informal lack of experience which lies under the formal claims: 'it was upon this vast lack of democratic experience, characterised by a feudal mentality and sustained by a colonial economic and social structure, that we attempted to inaugurate a formal democracy' (Freire, 2005a, p. 24). Central to this feudal structure for Freire was a whole psychology of fear and failure: 'upon a feudal economic structure and a social structure within which men were defeated, crushed and silenced, we superimposed a social and political form which required dialogue, participation, political and social responsibility, as well as a degree of social and political solidarity which we had not yet attained' (Freire, 2005a, p. 24). We can see how this analysis connects very clearly to Freire's description in *Pedagogy of the Oppressed* of what he calls the whole pathology of sadism and masochism, but what this analysis of the Brazilian situation allows us is an empirical grounding for the analysis of a theory which can seem very abstract. Whereas Sartre (Sartre, 2003), for example, sees such a pathology of sadism and masochism in the very structure of human relationships, Freire sees it rather as conditional upon the context in which one is working. Thus, what this latter approach of contextualism also allows is a sense that the situation can be transformed, and in some cases, radically transformed.

The contingency of oppression

In other words, what Freire seems to be allowing for here is the sense both that oppression and anti-democracy are contingent trends, and that as contingent they can be transformed and overcome. Within the context of Brazilian society specifically, Freire is looking to explain *the resistance to democracy* which seems to be such a feature of his society. Here, the discussion is not merely abstract but is based on the events leading up to 1964 and the military coup. As Freire says elsewhere, the very fact of a military coup is already a sign that the process of democratization was actually working. In other words, it was working too well and had to be stopped, cut at the joints. The elite in Brazil were scared and responded in the only way they knew how, by destroying the very basis of democracy as it had started to develop (Gadotti, 1994). But what Freire is also aware of here is how successful his approach to democracy had been in Brazil. In other words, the military coup of 1964 gives Freire and the democracy movement in Brazil much to be proud of, in the movement's pushing of the boundaries or, perhaps more accurately, much to be hopeful about, in terms of the very real possibilities of future revolutions and transformations in Brazil and beyond, a hope which sets the scene for Freire's future work post-1964.

Returning to his theme of how the colonial past stunted the growth of democracy in Brazil, Freire states: 'obviously these conditions did not constitute the cultural climate necessary for the rise of democratic regimes. Before it becomes a political form, democracy is a way of life, characterised above all by a strong component of transitive consciousness' (Freire, 2005a, p. 24). In this context we see how Freire combines historical analysis with an analysis of the various forms of consciousness which accompany these developments. *Transitive consciousness* refers to a positive form of critical consciousness which can only be achieved once democracy has become a way of life and dialogue has become embedded in the society. Freire describes the previous states of consciousness in the society as, first, *intransitive*, which corresponds to a very negative state of societal affairs, which is recalcitrant to democracy; and, second, *naïve consciousness*, which does represent a move beyond intransitive consciousness, but only just.

Freire is tracing how a crisis began to occur in Brazilian society: 'until the split in Brazilian society offered the first conditions for popular participation; precisely the opposite situation prevailed; popular alienation, silence and inaction' (Freire, 2005a, p. 26). This is an important statement of concepts: 'popular alienation, silence and inaction'. However, a break began to occur in this blanket homogeneity, spurred by economic changes: 'then finally major economic changes began to affect the system of forces which had maintained the closed society in equilibrium; with the end of that equilibrium, society split open and entered the phase of transition' (Freire, 2005a, p. 26). This 'phase of transition' provides the very impetus for Freire's own work. Freire locates the key paradigmatic point of this transition in Brazil in the 1920s, although obviously this already succeeds a significant indus-trialization in the nineteenth century:

It was in this century, however, beginning in the 1920s and increasing after the Second World War, that Brazilian industrialisation received its strongest impulse. At the same time, the more urbanised areas of the country grew rapidly ... the country had begun to find itself, the people emerged and began to participate in the historical process.

(Freire, 2005a, p. 26)

The people emerged and Freire also emphasizes here 'the historical process', that sense of an open history which allows for change and transformation.

Education vs. massification

In Chapter 3, Freire develops the theme of 'education vs. massification'. We have seen already how central education is for Freire in terms of a politicization of 'the people'. Massification also has the opposite effect, keeping people submerged in a kind of ideological haze. But what Freire also wants to suggest here is that economic progress alone, or what he calls 'industrialization' or 'modernization', is not simply the reason for the change in Brazilian popular consciousness. In fact, Freire suggests that this process of technological change or modernization can often have the opposite effect, reducing people to a much more dominated consciousness. 'Certainly we could not rely on the mere process of technological modernisation to lead us from a naïve to a critical consciousness; indeed, an analysis of highly technological societies usually reveals the "domestication" of man's critical faculties by a situation in which he is massified and has only the illusion of choice' (Freire, 2005a, p. 30). This discussion is important in a number of respects. In the first instance it critiques the view that all the Third World needs to do is become like the West. Therefore, it critiques a developmentalist perspective based simply on the ideology of the 'director societies' (or the consciousness of the colonizer) and Freire will return to this issue in more detail in both *Extension or Communication* (Freire, 2005b) and *Cultural Action for Freedom* (Freire, 1977). Second, this acts as a critique of the Western society itself and its technologizations which connects as we know with the thematics of the Left in theorists like Marcuse, in texts such as *One-Dimensional Man* (Marcuse, 2002). Third, in terms of this analysis, Freire recognizes that often the societies can seem to constitute a change or a revolution, as there is a rhetoric of 'choice' surrounding the situation. However, this is merely, he says, often the 'illusion' of choice. This also connects with the thematic of 'false consciousness' which we associate with Marcuse and others and the aforementioned themes of massification or 'adaptation', which are central to the conceptual framework of these early texts. Initially, in a footnote, Freire makes clear that this quarrel is not with technology itself. Freire also clarifies in this context – and this is very significant – that he should not be understood to be making an essentialist point about the negativity of technology (footnote 3: 'by this I do not mean to say that technology is necessarily massifying' (Freire, 2005a, p. 30)). Freire makes the implications of this point clear for the relation between humanity and technology: 'the answer does not lie in the rejection of the machine but in the humanization of people' (Freire, 2005a, p. 31). Thus such a process of humanization does not preclude accelerating modernization and this is a paradigmatic statement from Freire. What Freire also wants to foreground, in this context, is the distinction between a more reactive attack on technology or the modern society which he calls (Freire, 2005a, p. 32) 'naïve rebellion', and what he refers to as a more 'critical intervention' (Freire, 2005a, p. 32).

Education which reinforced the problem

With regard to *Education as the Practice of Freedom*, we can now look at the very title itself. How can education truly be a practice of freedom, given all the aforementioned problems which Brazil faced? However, rather than education being a process which resists or fights such domestication, could it be possible that education actually can become complicit in the very process by which critical consciousness becomes submerged and stultified? As Freire starts by observing here, 'nothing threatened the correct development of popular emergence more than an educational practice which failed to offer opportunities for the analysis and debate of problems, or for genuine participation; one which not only did not identify with the trend towards democratisation but reinforced our lack of democratic experience' (Freire, 2005a, p. 32). This is a paradoxical and somewhat tragic situation – *education, which is meant to be a process of self-realization and self-development, becomes the very opposite*. Education reinforces the problem of the trend towards decreasing democratization. This is, in reality, a travesty: this education is not an education in an authentic sense at all. Once more, Freire refers to the need for 'popular participation', the connection to the kind of popular revolution which Sartre had made famous. Often, as Freire will reiterate again in *Pedagogy of the Oppressed*, the revolution can end up using the methods of banking education in seeking to assert a problem-posing solution; banking becomes the supposed means to a better end, but this is a tragic and fatalist contradiction for the process of education itself. That is, for Freire, even in a transitional phase, banking education or its methods must never be used. 'We cannot enter the process as objects in order later to become subjects.' Rather, what is required is a new kind of education; one 'which would lead human beings to take a new stance towards their problems; that of intimacy with their problems, one oriented towards research instead of repeating irrelevant principles; an education of "I wonder" instead of merely "I do"... vitality' (Freire, 2005a, p. 33).

Of course, not only are these problems often not recognized, but people blame the wrong thing completely for what has been happening. Here, as Freire suggests, theory or the tendency towards theorization in education and politics has been blamed, as if the problem for Brazil was that its people and its philosophers were 'too theoretical'. For Freire, this connects with a misunderstanding of what he terms a Brazilian 'verbosity'; 'critics of the Brazilian taste for verbosity have customarily accused our education of being "theoretical", mistakenly equating theory with verbalism' (Freire, 2005a, p. 33). This identification of verbosity with theory is radically mistaken for Freire.

> On the contrary, we lacked theory; a theory of intervention in reality; the analytical contact with existence which enables one to substantiate and to experience that existence fully and completely; in this sense, theorising is contemplation (although not in the erroneous connotation of abstraction or opposition to reality). Our education was never theoretical precisely because it lacked this bent towards substantiation.
>
> (Freire, 2005a, p. 33)

This is a subtle and provocative statement and one which is also tied in with Freire's critique of so-called activism as not properly involving itself in an authentic 'praxis', which we discussed above.

Verbalism and lack of dialogue

Freire goes on to develop this point and thematic in more detail. 'Our verbal culture corresponds to our inadequacy of dialogue, investigation and research; as a matter of fact, I am increasingly convinced that the roots of the Brazilian taste for speeches, for easy words, for the well turned phrase, lie in our lack of democratic experience' (Freire, 2005a, p. 33). Why?

> The fewer the democratic experiences which develop through concrete participation in reality to critical consciousness of it, the more a group tends to perceive and to confront that reality naively, to represent it verbosely; the less critical capacity a group possesses, the more ingenuously it treats problems and the more superficially it discusses subjects.
>
> (Freire, 2005a, p. 33)

This is a radical critique of the appearance of dialogue in the Brazilian tendency towards verbalization. It also gives the lie to those who would see Freire as too 'populist', one of the main criticisms made of him in Brazil, for example (Torres, 1993). Here, in his early work, we see his radically critical spirit, which he applies not simply to those who oppress, but to the entire resources of the ordinary culture of Brazil. Again, Freire finishes with a reference to the revolution's connection to a thematic of 'love', indeed education's integral connection to such a *love*: 'education is an act of love and thus an act of courage; it cannot fear the analysis of reality or under pain of revealing itself as farce, avoid creative discussion' (Freire, 2005a, p. 33).

So how was Brazil to get beyond this verbalism towards true dialogue? Despite Freire's radical criticisms of much of the existing education, he also pinpoints several good examples of pedagogical practice, which he associates interestingly with the possibilities of institutional life at third level, specifically in the university. This will also connect with a whole theme of university life and politics which we see in Lyotard (Lyotard, 1993) and which connects Freire to the May 1968 events. We have seen how Freire marks this on the first page of Chapter 1 of *Pedagogy of the Oppressed*. He will return to this topic explicitly in his discussions regarding university life at the University of Mexico which begin in 1984 and which were published in English in 1994 (Freire *et al.*, 1994). The problem here, as always for Freire, is that we have the right goal but the wrong kind of education to get us there. So often the residues of the banking system remain in our mentality towards education and politics, even (or especially) when we think of ourselves as transformative. Under the aspect of transformation, we often reinforce the problem if we have not chosen the right method of pedagogy. This is because banking education or education for domination (even if its underlying intention is transformative) is anti-democratic and reinforces what Freire calls 'massification' or lower levels of consciousness. 'The existing form of education simply could not prepare human beings for integration in the process of democratisation; because it contradicted that very process and opposed the emergence of people into democratic life' (Freire, 2005a, p. 33).

Modernization

So what are we to oppose to this? Freire is clear that this must involve an acceptance of a certain level of modernization: 'it was essential to harmonise a truly humanist position with technology by an education which would not leave technicians naïve and uncritical in dealing with problems other than those of their own speciality' (Freire, 2005a, p. 33). True humanism, or perhaps *radical humanism*, is thus not in itself anti-technological. Freire is not just speaking in the abstract but also gives examples of two institutions in Brazil which he looks upon favourably in this regard. This is especially significant, as it is how Freire distances himself from the unequivocal or generalized critique of institutionalized education which we see, for example, in the work of Ivan Illich (Illich, 1971). It is also relevant for our purposes because it involves a focus on third-level education, often a level of education neglected by educationalists and educational theorists: 'along these lines I mention two experiments of the greatest importance in university and graduate instruction; the ISEB and the University of Brasilia; both efforts were frustrated by the military coup of 1964' (Freire, 2005a, p. 34).

Freire now delineates what he sees as two important consequences of this more revolutionary approach to education at these two specific institutions in Brazil, which demonstrate his conviction that such a problem-posing education is possible at institutional level, even under severe constraints in the society, as in the case of Brazil and as he has already outlined. 'Two important consequences emerged; the creative power of intellectuals who placed themselves at the service of the national culture, and commitment to the destiny of the reality those intellectuals considered and assumed as their own' (Freire, 2005a, p. 35). We see here a theme of the public role of intellectuals, a thematic to which Freire will return in his text on the universities (Freire *et al.*, 1994). Two aspects to his concern are evident. First, that there is in itself the worthy intervention of intellectuals in the public culture, which is a significant development. Second, that once intellectuals become involved in the very definition of a reality, they leave their institutional submersion behind and become active problem-posers, who see their professional and personal destinies intertwine. This is significant from the point of view of Freire's previous critique of the way in which education can often serve as a bulwark for the reinforcement of the status quo (a theme which bell hooks takes up in her provocative image of intellectuals as 'misery pimps') (hooks, 1994).

Third worldism and imported models of cultural invasion

This becomes especially significant for Freire here because he mentions that much discourse on Brazil, even in Brazil, depends on what he terms 'imported models of cultural invasion'. The University of Brasilia seems to have avoided this pitfall: 'thinking of Brazil as subject also characterised the University of Brasilia which deliberately avoided the importation of alienated models' (Freire, 2005a, p. 35). 'Thinking of Brazil as subject' rather than as object of 'false charity': this, then, is crucial for an understanding of Freire's critique of developmentalism, even though he is often associated with the very same approach. Paul Taylor, writing on Freire, especially takes up this theme in his analysis of his own disenchantment with his work in development education in the Third World (Taylor, 1994). The importation of alienated models is the key to understanding why Freire has such a problem with these approaches, and this is a theme which we also find in Fanon (Fanon, 1986a). Freire praises the specific Brazilian institutions he mentions for their approach to education, implicitly viewing them as problem-posing. Why? Because they avoid not simply the importation of foreign models but also what he calls here 'technism', which refers to a reductionistic approach to technology.

The latter eschewal of 'technism' is not the same as rejecting the use of technology altogether. Quite the contrary in fact, as Freire explicitly says that his affirmed institutions had technician graduates: 'it did not seek to graduate verbose generalists nor to prepare technician specialists; but rather to help transform the Brazilian reality, on the basis of a true understanding of its process' (Freire, 2005a, p. 35). This technology and modernization (perhaps even *postmodernization* (Lyotard, 1986)) can transform reality in positive ways, so long as technology and modernization are not divorced from humanization. This is also a problematic which goes beyond intra-educational issues, or a question of intellectuals speaking to themselves. This is an example of how universities can play a very positive role in the development of public space and in the politicization of the society. 'The influence of these two institutions can be understood in terms of their identification with the awakening of the national consciousness, advancing in search of the transformation of Brazil; in this sense, the message and the task of both continue' (Freire, 2005a, p. 35). The last phrase seems especially important: 'the message and the task of both continue'; that is, this process is not nearly at an end. Freire will return to this thematic explicitly in the first pages of *Pedagogy of the Oppressed*, when he invokes the student movements and demonstrations.

Education is not a miraculous process

Of course, Freire is always aware of his own positioning being hardly neutral here and he is also conscious that his position might be seen as overly romanticized. In a footnote, he takes up this issue of 'utopianism' which is a complex issue in Freire's work. 'I am aware that education is not a miraculous process capable by itself of effecting the changes necessary to move a nation from one epoch to another' (Freire, 2005a, p. 36). 'Education is not a miraculous process' – we should bear these words in mind. Not only does Freire acknowledge here that education cannot work miracles but he goes further in acknowledging that education on its own cannot really expect to effect any real social or political change (or even any real educational change per se).

> Indeed, it is true that by itself education can do nothing, because the very fact of being 'by itself' (i.e. superimposed on its context) nullifies its undeniable power as an instrument of change. Thus, one cannot view education as an absolute value nor the school as an unconditioned institution.
>
> (Freire, 2005a, p. 36)

Another theme recurs, in this context, which has been significant especially in the earlier part of *Education as the Practice of Freedom*, and which will recur in *Extension or Communication* and *Pedagogy of the Oppressed*. That is, the distinction between the animal and the human.

In a footnote, Freire takes up this issue in a way which is important in a number of respects. Freire's primary concern here is with the concept of education and the critique of specialism, but among other things we can see the influence of neo-Thomism in this context on Freire, in the case of Jacques Maritain (Maritain, 1943). Freire notes:

> As Jacques Maritain has pointed out, if we remember that the animal is a specialist and a perfect one, all of its knowing power being fixed upon a single task to be done, we ought to conclude that an educational program which would only aim at forming specialists ever more perfect in ever more specialised fields, and unable to pass judgement on any matter that lies beyond their specialised competence, would lead indeed to a progressive animalisation of the human mind and life.
>
> (Freire, 2005a, p. 36)

This is taken from Maritain's influential book *Education at the Crossroads* (Maritain, 1943): the 'progressive animalisation of the human mind and life'. For Freire, humanization can only take place for humans, by definition. This is because of the chasm which separates the animal from the human, in Freire's eyes.

This question leads into Freire's final chapter in *Education as the Practice of Freedom,* 'Education and Conscientização'. Freire is here preoccupied with the specific aspects of the Brazilian context in the 1960s from which his work emerged:

> My concern for the democratisation of culture within the context of fundamental democratisation required special attention to the quantitative and qualitative deficits in our education. In 1964, approximately four million school age children lacked schools; there were sixteen million illiterates of fourteen years and older. These truly alarming deficits constituted obstacles to the development of the country and to the creation of a democratic mentality.
>
> (Freire, 2005a, p. 37)

These are indeed 'alarming deficits' in anyone's language and they also demonstrate how raising the theme of literacy couldn't but also connect with the wider socio-political reasons why so many people were illiterate. Thus, there was then a real need for what Freire calls 'conscientization' or 'conscientização'. Freire distinguishes in this context between an authentic 'critical consciousness' and two other forms of consciousness which can often prevent the achievement of critical consciousness (he has mentioned these before, but with a slightly different sense): 'Critical consciousness is integrated with reality; naive consciousness superimposes itself on reality, and fanatical consciousness whose pathological naivete leads to the irrational, adapts to reality' (Freire, 2005a, p. 39).

Huxley's art of dissociating ideas

These glaring issues of a lack of critical consciousness and an empirical context of deprivation and extreme illiteracy and lack of schooling or education led Freire to evolve the radical method which he proposed in the early 1960s. 'We began to prepare material with which we could carry out concretely an education that would encourage what Aldous Huxley has called the "art of dissociating ideas" as an antidote to the domesticating power of propaganda' (Freire, 2005a, p. 49). This is a telling image from Huxley: education as 'the art of dissociating ideas'. What Freire wishes to do here is to show up the oftentimes identification of education as ideology or propaganda, an education which fails to call into question its own presuppositions. This identification fails to call up or judge what Freire calls the 'deceit' in this kind of 'education', which of course is not really education at all. 'Education and propaganda: at the same time, they are preparing themselves to discuss and perceive the same deceit in ideological or political propaganda' (Freire, 2005a, p. 49). Freire links Huxley's sense of a dissociation of ideas to the very notion of democracy, here understood as a radical version of democracy: 'they are aiming to dissociate ideas; in fact, this has always seemed to me to be the way to defend democracy not a way to subvert it' (Freire, 2005a, p. 49). This notion of a democracy defended by deconstruction or dissociation is very close in spirit to what Derrida refers to as the democracy 'to come' (Derrida, 2000) or what Mouffe has referred to as a 'radical democracy' (Mouffe, 2005). 'One defends democracy by leading it to the state Mannheim calls "militant democracy"; a democracy which does not fear the people, which suppresses privilege, which can plan without becoming rigid, which defends itself without hate, which is nourished by a critical spirit rather than irrationality' (Freire, 2005a, p. 49). This dense statement needs unpacking in terms of its revealing elements, especially as this section constitutes the end of the *Education as the Practice of Freedom* text.

Radical democracy

We will look at several elements in turn. First, there is the simple emphasis on democracy itself and its connection to education. Certainly, as we have seen, Freire does not naïvely believe that education alone can bring about this democratic change or progress, but he does believe that education as a political process can instigate change in political terms and indeed is indispensable to such change. *Education is thus not a sufficient condition but is a necessary condition for the bringing about of democracy.* By referring to militant democracy, Freire seems to be distinguishing lesser versions which might claim the democratic mantle but which don't deserve the title. In reality, perhaps he means simply a democracy which genuinely lives up to its name, that is, 'rule by the people'.

Freire makes the point that often the attempt to 'dissociate ideas' may be seen as a threat to democracy. We see this among other places, for example, in the case of Socrates. Philosophy is often at odds with democracy but Freire seems to be saying here that this is only because democracies are often not properly democratic at all. This distinguishes Freire's thought from those elements of leftist thought which would shun democracy, and here he is reiterating a point he makes clearly in *Pedagogy of the Oppressed*, where he brings together the need for a subversion of the oppressor, with a move away from the oppressor consciousness which would seek to 'impose' a new solution. Rather, the new politics must be genuinely democratic: *otherwise, one simply has an inversion*. Freire's way of describing this is not coincidental; a 'democracy which does not fear the people'. The theme of fear runs through his work and also 'the people' is a concept which he sees as crucial with regard to the emphasis on 'participation'. Moreover, he says that this democracy must suppress privilege – this demonstrates the continuing importance of the socio-economic redress in Freire although this may not become the determining instance. Second, this militant democracy must involve 'a plan without becoming rigid'. Thus we are not dealing with a completely capricious philosophy. Third, it must be a process 'which defends itself without hate' (Freire, 2005a, p. 49). Again, the emphasis on love rather than hate is important in Freire. Finally, Freire's emphasis on critical consciousness remains undiminished, and 'which is nourished by a critical spirit rather than irrationality' (Freire, 2005a, p. 49).

Culture circles in pictorial form

It is worth noting that Freire includes a significant Appendix in *Education as the Practice of Freedom*. In this Appendix, he includes the drawings he used in the original 'culture circles' in Brazil. In the first case, it is interesting that the original drawings were done by Francisco Brenand but were taken from Freire during the military coup. Those included in the newer edition were drawn by another Brazilian artist, Vincente de Abreu, who is himself described as being now in exile. This tells us something important about the Brazilian context from which Freire's work derives. The final picture in the series is meant to exemplify the culture circle itself, where participants come to recognize themselves, at least if the process has been properly successful. This is the tenth and final picture in the process: 'a culture circle in action' (Freire, 2005a, p. 75). Freire describes the discussion around this picture vividly. The discussion pictured involves a 'synthesis of the previous discussions on seeing this situation, the culture circle participants easily identify themselves' (Freire, 2005a, p. 75). This self-recognition is important, as previously the discussants believed themselves to be alienated from such a dialectic or philosophical discussion. In addition, we see here the sense of the concept of 'culture' itself which plays such an important part in Freire's analysis.

In this tenth picture of the culture circle, Freire notes that: 'they discuss culture as a systematic acquisition of knowledge and also the democratisation of culture within the general context of fundamental democratisation. The democratisation of culture has to start from what we are and what we do as people, not from what some people think and want for us' (Freire, 2005a, p. 75). Therefore, a little like postmodernism (Drolet, 2004) (an element of postmodernism that is often underestimated), the emphasis on popular culture is primarily a question of undermining the powerful hegemony which elite culture (especially aesthetic elite culture in modernism) exerts. It is also a way of involving or allowing the people's culture to emerge. Thus the concepts of militant democracy, of the people and of culture, become indissociable.

What this also allows for is a much more organic and involved definition of *literacy*, as constituted by politicization and a deepening of existential perspective, thus moving beyond the narrow technicism of much literacy and emancipatory education; 'literacy only makes sense in these terms, as the consequence of human being's beginning to reflect on their own capacity for reflection' (Freire, 2005a, p. 76). This also connects *Education as the Practice of Freedom* directly to the next text we will discuss, *Extension or Communication* (Freire, 2005b), a discussion of which follows in Chapter 4. This latter text is again much concerned with the issue of pedagogy and democracy, and the way in which supposedly emancipatory pedagogy is often delivered in an approach that favours transmission or 'extension'. In *Extension or Communication*, Freire makes a particular connection between this approach and development education in the Third World, here agrarian reform in Chile. There is thus a powerful critique of developmental politics in Freire's work, as, for example, Paul Taylor points out clearly (Taylor, 1994). In the following chapter we will thus address the *Extension or Communication* text in relation to the most important text to be written immediately after *Pedagogy of the Oppressed*, Freire's *Cultural Action for Freedom* (Freire, 1977).

CHAPTER FOUR

From *Extension or Communication* to *Cultural Action for Freedom*

Introduction – from Fanon to Freire

In this chapter, I will focus on two texts which succeed Freire's 'first text', *Education as the Practice of Freedom* (Freire, 2005a), and which respectively pre-date and succeed *Pedagogy of the Oppressed* (Freire, 1996a). The first text we will look at here is *Extension or Communication* (Freire, 2005b) which was written almost simultaneously with *Pedagogy*. As with the latter text, this shorter work demonstrates a change which has taken place in Freire's work, specifically during his time in exile from Brazil, since 1964. Here, we see the move from reformism to revolution, and also a foregrounding of education as key to the process of political transformation. Later, Freire will deny this reading of his early work, but there is an undeniable forcefulness here, which is distinctly different and more moderated in the later texts.

The second text I will look at in this chapter is a book which reinforces this view of the early, post-exile Freire as a revolutionary thinker of education and politics. *Cultural Action for Freedom* (Freire, 1977), written after the worldwide acclaim which greeted *Pedagogy*, is a more minor text, but in its principled stances it mirrors and reinforces the earlier work. If anything, it may be seen to clarify and intensify some of the ambiguities which may have caused some confusion in *Pedagogy*. This reinforcement of radicalism is captured in the Preface by Coutinho, which places Freire's work firmly in the tradition of Frantz Fanon and Albert Memmi (Coutinho, 1977). If there was any doubt before, there is no doubt now – Freire's pedagogy politicizes the relationship between Third and First worlds, and its advocation of literacy should not be seen as some useful literacy pedagogy for underdeveloped regions of the world. Rather, if anything, Freire's work speaks more profoundly to the First world, to those who would wish to keep political injustice reinforced, often under the cover of piecemeal educational reform. Coutinho's message, deriving from Fanon (Fanon, 1986b) and Freire, is unequivocal – Freire's critique of the banking system and banking mindset goes to the roots of the Western existential malaise (Coutinho, 1977). In this respect, Coutinho's Preface continues and develops Sartre's infamous Preface (Sartre, 1986) to Fanon's *The Wretched of the Earth* (Fanon, 1986b), which appeared to justify, if not eulogize, the use of violence against colonizing forces.

Contextualizing Freire's agrarian work in Chile

An analysis of Jacques Chonchol's Preface to *Extension or Communication* (Chonchol, 2005) allows us to contextualize the significance of this often overlooked piece of work in Freire's *oeuvre*, a text which Elias describes as short but underestimated in its importance (Elias, 1994). The context as always is crucial for Freire and the Preface is written in the realization that Freire's work in this text develops out of a specifically Chilean situation (Chonchol, 2005). The Preface is written by a Chilean educationalist (one should also note Freire's work with Antonio Faundez as similarly elaborating on Freire's Chilean connections) (Freire and Faundez, 1989). Chonchol clarifies this context: 'in this essay, Paulo Freire the internationally renowned Brazilian educator who recently lived and worked in Chile, analyses how technicians and peasants can communicate in the process of developing a new agrarian society' (Chonchol, 2005, p. 80). The background context for the work is thus the history of developmental projects in rural agrarian Chile, and Freire has a lot of critical words to say about the underlying philosophy of these developmental projects. As always with Freire's work, there is a strong connection between reflection and action, between theory and the empirical context for practice, and here we see a strong relationship between *Education as the Practice of Freedom* and *Extension or Communication*, both of which mix the theoretical and empirical elements more carefully and successfully perhaps than *Pedagogy of the Oppressed*, which is more overtly theoretical. Chonchol does not hide the difficulty of Freire's approach:

> Freire's thought is profound and at times difficult to follow but penetrating; its essence reveals a new world of truths, relations among

these truths, and a logical ordering of concepts. We perceive that words, their meaning, their context, the actions of men, their struggle to dominate the natural world and to create their culture and their history form a totality in which each aspect has significance not only in itself but in function of the whole.

(Chonchol, 2005, p. 81)

This holism is central to Freire's thought as we know, not least in the very holism of the concept of praxis itself. As we have seen with Freire's earlier work, education here as a process is not understood in isolation from the other processes which influence our lives, especially the political processes. Chonchol sees education as functioning in a 'synthesizing role' in Freire's work, by which he means the way it brings together the various common parts which other thinkers separate out. In *Pedagogy of the Oppressed* Freire refers to the 'axial' structure of his thought, the way it combines aesthetics, ethics and politics. Here, for example, we can compare and contrast Freire's approach with Kierkegaard's three-tiered system of understanding which has affinities but also significant disaffinities with that of Freire, placing as it does the religious at the culmination of the axial dialectic (Kierkegaard, 1992). As Chonchol notes: 'More than just analysis of the educational task of the agronomist, the present essay seems to me to be a profound synthesis of the role Paulo Freire attributes to education understood in its true perspective, that of humanizing man through his conscious action to transform the world' (Chonchol, 2005, p. 81). So this essay is exemplary in this respect in moving between the particular and the general, but the essay is also useful, as it is written around the same time as *Pedagogy of the Oppressed* (also written in Chile) and so the comparison is apt and helpful. Freire's initial focus here is on the very semantics of the term 'extension'. He looks at 'extension' from various points of view according to Chonchol. 'Freire begins by analysing the term "extension" from different points of view; the linguistic meaning of the word, a criticism based on the philosophical theory of knowledge, and a study of the relations between the concepts of extension and cultural invasion' (Chonchol, 2005, p. 81). We shall see in our analysis of *Cultural Action for Freedom*, a slightly later work, how this earlier analysis of the concept of 'cultural invasion' sets the scene for the later critical analysis of the same topic.

Agrarian reform and change

The key to this analysis is Freire's specific focus on agrarian reform, which, despite his acknowledgment of its best intentions, is dealt with very critically by Freire. As Chonchol (2005, p. 81) notes,

Subsequently he discusses agrarian reform and change, demonstrating the profound opposition which exists between extension and communication; the agronomist-educator, like teachers in general, must choose communication if he genuinely wants to reach men; not by being abstract, but by being concrete, within a historical reality.

These emphases are not new in Freire. The emphasis on a critique of abstraction, the emphasis on concrete change and concrete description, runs consistently through his work, early to late, and takes its cue from Marx's 'Theses on Feuerbach' (Marx, 1992a). The attempt to connect to people's deeper humanity: that is a process of humanization. In addition, the emphasis on a 'historical reality'; again this historical reality is the very real context of agrarian reform in 1960s Chile. Freire makes a key distinction between 'extension' as the term has been used in Chile and in development approaches more generally and the concern for 'communication'. We have seen how later, in *Pedagogy of the Oppressed*, the Freirean emphasis on 'extension' is replaced and extended by a more general category of 'banking' education and politics, but we may say that 'extension' as the term is used here is a subset of the banking problem. It exemplifies all the same characteristics.

Freire is intent on offering a radical and unequivocal critique of the concept of extension (and development) in Latin America, notwithstanding the often good intentions of the protagonists concerned. As Chonchol observes: 'reading this essay makes us realize the poverty and limitations of the concept of agricultural extension which has prevailed among us and many other Latin American countries, in spite of the generosity and good will of those who have dedicated their lives to this good work' (Chonchol, 2005, p. 82). This also is not some partial or externalist critique. We realize, in no uncertain terms, that it is a critique which is directed at the very failure of the projects to achieve their own stated intentions (similar to the literacy programmes in Brazil). The failure of the projects is often blamed on the lack of intelligence or willingness to change among the peasants themselves. Freire is keen to emphasize where the real blame lies, as Chonchol outlines: 'we can see how their failure to achieve more lasting results was due, in some measure, to their naive view of reality but more commonly to the marked attitude of superiority and domination with which the technician confronted the peasant within a traditional agrarian structure' (Chonchol, 2005, p. 82).

Here, we have a key confrontation between the technician and the peasant which we have seen replicated in *Pedagogy of the Oppressed* in what Freire calls *the teacher–student contradiction*. We know that this relation bears a distinct resemblance to Hegel's *master–slave dialectic* (Hegel, 1979) and Freire is explicit in his debts to this Hegelian structure of thinking. Rather than the actual content of the approach itself (although Freire will have criticisms to make of this too), Freire focuses primarily on the relation (or *lack of relation* in an authentic sense) between teacher and student. Rather than any authentic dialogue, we are faced here with an objectification of the student, in this case the rural peasant, who is turned into a 'thing': 'Freire shows you how the concept of extension leads to actions which transform the peasant into a thing; an object of development projects which negate him as a being capable of transforming the world' (Chonchol, 2005, p. 82). This is thus no accident of the process. The very concept of extension itself leads inevitably to the reification or objectification of the peasant.

Freire's early work in Chile

For Chonchol, we must see Freire's early work on extension in Chile as part of a wider discourse which Freire is seeking to instigate and develop on the whole process of education per se. Already, in this early context, we see the embryo of the later concept of banking education. For Freire, says Chonchol, 'knowing is not the act by which a subject transformed into an object docilely and passively accepts the contents others give or impose on him or her' (Chonchol, 2005, p. 82). In other words, education is not banking education; this latter is not worthy of the name of education. And although Freire is focused on the concept of extension here and doesn't use the concept of banking, we can see how the former becomes an example of the latter, in the language of *Pedagogy*. In addition, what is paradigmatic in relation to *Extension or Communication*, from the point of view of education and politics, is the discussion of technology and its relation to the evolution of modern and postmodern society, a theme which Freire turns to again but which also connects him to the wider leftist discourse on technology, which goes from Marcuse's rather negative approach (Marcuse, 2002) to thinkers like Lefebvre's (Lefebvre, 2002) more ambiguous relation to it. As Chonchol observes, 'in addition, Freire emphasises that from a humanistic and scientific perspective, one cannot focus on technical capacitation except within the context of a total culture reality' (Chonchol, 2005, p. 82). Two aspects are worthy of note in this context: first, the emphasis on holism and the need to see technology not as a specialization but as something which must be connected to our whole vision of the world. Our relation to technology must be consistent with humanistic values. Second, however, there is the very acceptance of a tendency to 'technical capacitation'. Again, this marks a difference from other thinkers on the Left (and some on the Right), who see technology as an evil in itself.

For Chonchol, this represents a crucial aspect of *Extension or Communication*, which he concludes by saying has two main threads to follow. First, 'I would like to stress the importance of Freire's criticisms of the concept of "extension" as cultural invasion; as an attitude contrary to the dialogue which forms the basis of an authentic education' (Chonchol, 2005, p. 83). This is foundational for an understanding of Freire's Third Worldism, which he returns to, for example, in *Cultural Action for Freedom*, discussed below. Second, 'also fundamental to Freire's analysis of the relationship between techniques, modernisation and humanism is he shows how to avoid the traditionalism of the status quo, without falling into technological messianism' (Chonchol, 2005, p. 83). Chonchol here is naming an important point. Much of leftist thinking falls into a 'traditonalism of the status quo' when it comes to the issue of technology and media – it is arguable (as we shall see in Chapter 7) that this fate befalls certain aspects of contemporary critical pedagogy (Giroux, 2000). Thus we can say that this kind of leftist thinking possibly fails the test of progressivism; it fails to open up to the positive possibility of some elements of these technological developments. By the same token, Freire is not sympathetic to 'technological messianism' which we might associate with a more technocratic vision. This subsumes the human to a technological future vision (one example is futurism) and of course we know that this can certainly lead to (although it is not exhausted by) a semi-fascistic vision which turns the human into an object among others. Chonchol quotes Freire in a powerful way on this in summation: 'as he quite correctly affirms, while "all development is modernisation, not all modernisation is development"; thus we should distinguish between the positive and negative elements of modernisation' (Chonchol, 2005, p. 83). Where this leaves the postmodern we will return to in later chapters. We should also note the time and location of Chonchol's piece on Freire – 'Jacques Chonchol; Santaigo de Chile; April 1968' (Chonchol, 2005, p. 83). The Chilean context is one we have already commented on and, in addition, the year, 1968, is highly symbolic, with all its political ramifications. This text wasn't published in English for several years to come, significantly after *Pedagogy of the Oppressed*, and yet it had been used in Chile in its Spanish version to significant effect. Let us now look at an analysis of the text itself.

Extension or Communication: analysing the text

The text of *Extension or Communication* contains three main chapters. A footnote clarifies the very meaning of the term 'extension' as it is going to be used in the essays. 'Rural extension; designates the educational and technical assistance efforts of outside agencies acting through extension agents or extension workers to extend or transmit to peasants' knowledge designed to improve farming practices' (Freire, 2005b, p.100). There are several elements of this definition which we can already see as significant. First, Freire refers to 'educational and technical assistance'. This is important, since it shows that these two elements, of education and technique, are distinct but very much related in the effort to develop rural areas in Chile. The technical or technological elements are key to modernization but we have already seen how Freire has both affirmed these elements, while also warning against them. We must keep the distinction between education and technical assistance clear, even though, in the projects themselves, the two are often confused (i.e. education becomes defined as technical assistance predominantly). Second, Freire refers to the efforts of 'outside agencies'. Often the work is planned from outside, whether that means, in this case, outside Chile involving international assistance (a commonplace in development education) and/or possibly planned outside the rural areas, perhaps in the department of agriculture in the local urban area. Third, the projects are designed to transmit or extend peasant knowledge. Transmission or extension, as technical-pedagogical concepts, obviously give a very particular sense of what is going on here. In Freirean terms, going back to *Education as a Practice of Freedom*, this is *education as domination*. Certainly the intention is good, designed to improve farming practices, but the educational methods are suspect. 'It appears that the act of extension in whatever sector it takes place is ... mechanical transfer' (Freire, 2005c, p. 89). As we have seen in *Education as the Practice of Freedom*, this is not education in any authentic sense of the term but is rather a dominating process masquerading as education. There is no consciousness-raising, but simply a depositing of information which involves no participation by the peasants themselves. The process is one-way only, from the powerful to the powerless. Second, it is not only the methodology that is at fault in this situation. If we look at the education in a total context, we see that the 'externalist' source of the knowledge is also highly problematic. Freire refers to this as a form of 'cultural invasion' and here his criticisms strike to the very heart of what development education is often about (we might argue that the radicality of Freire's words in this context, *their vehemence*, has often been lost). It may also be argued that the relative marginalization of *Extension or Communication* as a text might be grounded in the fact that its targeting is much more direct. Developmental efforts in Chile are the target but, by implication, also development education as such. Whereas the theoretical words of *Pedagogy of the Oppressed* seem to strike a similar note of critique, they do not seem to be directed so angrily at development itself. In this measure, combining a reading of *Pedagogy of the Oppressed* with *Extension or Communication* helps us to gain a more authentic sense of what *Pedagogy of the Oppressed* is really saying and how its words can often be misinterpreted and their true radicality diluted somewhat. 'Cultural invasion, manipulation etc. in whatever sector it takes place means that those carrying it out need to go to "another part of the world" to "normalize it", according to their way of viewing reality, to make it resemble their world' (Freire, 2005b, p.89). This is also a theme which Freire takes up in *Cultural Action for Freedom* and it bears a significant similarity to the works of Fanon (Fanon, 1986b) and Memmi (Memmi, 1975), both of whom Freire mentions consistently throughout this early period.

It is also interesting to think about how this explicit discourse of Third Worldism continues in Freire's work, where it is perhaps sidelined (if not rejected *tout court*) in some other thinkers' work post-1968. Here, Kristin Ross's work on May 1968 and its 'afterlives', in France most especially, is very revealing (Ross, 2004). These two elements are then interrelated in Freire's critique, first, the sense of the distortion of the educational process itself, and second, its very externalist aspect, its domination 'from outside', from the First World in effect. The term *extension* thus comes to signify both transmission, as a mode of distorted pedagogy, and it comes to signify precisely cultural invasion, the extension, in other words, of the First World's dominion of power.

> Thus, in its field of association, the term extension has a significant relation to transmission, handing over, giving, messianism, cultural invasion; manipulation etc; all these terms imply actions which transform people into 'things' and negate their existence as beings who transform their world. As we shall see, they further negate the formation and development of real knowledge. They negate the true action and reflection which are the objects of these actions.
>
> (Freire, 2005b, p. 89)

Cross-referencing to Pedagogy of the Oppressed

The cross-references to *Pedagogy of the Oppressed* in this context are very notable. Here, in the specific situations of agrarian extension in Chile, one has the rudiments of the distinction between banking education and problem-posing education which Freire will develop more whole-heartedly in *Pedagogy of the Oppressed*, which he must have been simultaneously writing alongside this text. Already, he is moving towards a concept of *teacher–student contradiction* which he develops in a footnote: 'with regard to the overcoming of the educator–educatee contradiction this produces, there no longer exists the educator of the educatee nor the educatee of the educator but the educator–educatee and educatee–educator' (Freire, 2005c, p.100).

But if such a contradiction can be overcome, how might this look? Here, in this text, we can see that the contradiction in itself, in being reinforced through extension, has had terrible consequences for the failure of development, while such failure often runs the risk (mistakenly or at least overly simplistically) of being blamed simply on the native peoples themselves for being unintelligent, lazy or resistant to change. But what would liberation mean for these peoples and how might it be properly achieved, against all the negative lessons of extension? 'Liberation implies the role of the educator is communication and not extension' (Freire, 2005b, p.100). Thus, rather than banking education, we need problem-posing (in the language of *Pedagogy of the Oppressed*).

A discussion of magic

Freire, of course, understands the predicament which education in contexts of deprivation faces. He makes this clear in his discussion of rural mores in Latin America, especially in a fascinating discussion of magic and religious beliefs concerning weather conditions and crops. These peasants remain 'dependent on prayers and priests rather than actions' and Freire asks 'what can be done from the point of view of education in a peasant community which is at such a level?' (Freire, 2005c, pp. 94–95). Again, showing the interesting interconnectedness of his early texts, Freire namechecks both *Education as the Practice of Freedom* and *Cultural Action for Freedom* in his discussion of an answer to this thorny problem (Freire, 2005b, p.101). Certainly, Freire does not want to have to affirm such beliefs and he acknowledges the negative impact which these beliefs about magic have on the peasant's life and community, insofar as they cause them to refuse to take 'action'. They induce a passivity and a belief that external forces will remedy the situation. However, although Freire acknowledges that the beliefs need to be 'replaced' (Freire, 2005b, p. 95), he disavows the attempt to get rid of them by the method of 'extension': 'the answer cannot lie with those extension agents who, in their relations with the peasants, mechanically transfer technical information' (Freire, 2005b, p. 95).

Freire now enters into an interesting discussion of the nature of the magical beliefs themselves which shows him to be already a subtle thinker concerning myth and its relation to *logos*: 'magic thought is neither illogical nor pre-logical; it possesses its own internal logical structure and opposes as much as possible any new forms mechanically superimposed' (Freire, 2005b, p. 95). In order to understand the nature of people's beliefs, then, we must first undertake what Freire will call a more 'generative' critique of their existing views, but second, this must be done in dialogue with the people. Any simple attempt using a transmission or an extension model to change people's beliefs runs the risk of a simple external compliance with no internalized change. As Freire makes clear elsewhere in the essay, what will happen most likely then is that the magic beliefs will remain and be used to reinterpret the content of the 'extension programme' in their own way. Thus, the efforts of the extension programme are bound to fail as the peasants will continue to return to their superstitious traditions and give only give superficial adherence to the new practices which are being inculcated. Thus, no real new knowledge or wisdom is acquired in such a situation; this is no re-education: 'knowledge is not extended from those who consider that they know to those who consider that they do not know; the effort required is not one of extension' (Freire, 2005b, p. 99).

Critical consciousness

Here we see the links to *Education as the Practice of Freedom*, if the effort is not to be one of extension. It is rather to be one of critical consciousness: 'the effort required is not one of extension but of *conscientização*; if it is successfully carried out it allows individuals to assume critically the position they have in relation to the rest of the world' (Freire, 2005b, p. 99). For Freire, then, the problem with extension is that, although it claims to be in tandem or in harmony with the goals of humanism, in reality and in its effects it actually contradicts the humanistic mission of education. Indeed, Freire thinks that, even from a semantic viewpoint, this contradiction is evident because the semantics of extension emphasize the duality of teacher and student and the passivity of the learner, in this case 'the peasant'.

In an interesting footnote (Freire, 2005b, p.101), Freire uses another example of how simple extension involves an imposition on people's beliefs which will backfire from a constructive humanistic viewpoint. It fails in terms of its process but it also fails in terms of its results. He recounts the story of a priest in Peru who, when arriving at the Catholic church he has been assigned to, is shocked by some of the practices of the local Catholic peasants. In particular, he is outraged by the positioning of the figure of St James and his horse within the church which the priest views as wholly superstitious. He also observes the people praying not just to the statue of St James, but to the horse. The priest resolves to change this state of affairs, as he is convinced that this is 'false' religion or idolatry. Thus he undertakes to remedy the situation himself by extension and he has the horse and the St James figure placed well away from the church. The peasants are outraged by what they see as an act against their own beliefs, but moreover they are worried about the implications of going against the 'demons' they imagine to be present in the statues of St James and the horse. They thus angrily attack the church and destroy many of the more orthodox figurines inside and reinstate their own effigies. The priest is then hounded from the village (Freire, 2005b, p.101).

This is an excellent example of what Freire means by 'extension' and also shows up its complete failure to change anything in a progressive manner. However ridiculous the beliefs may be, simple extension or trans-mission education will do nothing to effect real change. This example is also interesting because, in many respects, it shows something surprising. One might have expected the peasantry to go along with the priest's actions as an authority figure. Imagine that this latter adherence had taken place. Although this would have been viewed by the priest as a victory for 'extension' education (note how the priest was an external figure, presumably from a larger rural or urban area, more 'advanced' in its beliefs), one can none-the-less imagine that the people would have still trusted in their horse and St James statues. Thus, no real internalization of the change would have happened and the victory would have been merely pyrrhic. Interestingly, in the case cited above, the people revolt angrily and violently. Rather, than this being seen as an outbreak of savagery which is presumably how the extension priest saw the situation, we might see it as a development of a more than merely intransitive consciousness. They refuse to bow down to their oppressor in a completely passive way. Rather, the people, however naïve, show a certain critical awareness in the defence of their own beliefs.

In many respects, the priest practises what Freire in another footnote calls 'training', which he opposes to proper or authentic education. 'The critical conception of the process does not use the term "training" with reference to people; "trees are cultivated, animals are trained, people are educated", says Kant' (Freire, 2005b, p.122). This again shows a certain enlightenment element in Freire (the reference to Kant), which we also see in his very notion of a critical consciousness. This is an example of what Freire calls 'cultural invasion'. What he highlights in this essay is that this cultural invasion is not always that of a colonizer from outside. It may often occur in the context of a national programme insofar as one area where the political structures and administration are centralized can set up the process of 'extension', which is then applied to all areas under state control. Moreover, one can say that often, in such instances, many of the teachers sent out to 'train' the people will be themselves external figures, with no local knowledge. This of course is an ongoing problem, even today.

Cultural Action for Freedom: the heterogeneity of early Freire

We began Chapters 2 and 3 with a specific rationale. We wished to look again at the overemphasis which *Pedagogy of the Oppressed* receives as a text, to the detriment of Freire's other texts. When we look at Freire's *oeuvre,* we see an immensely challenging and varied corpus which is anything but homogeneous. But, crucially, we can also say that this heterogeneity exists in Freire's work from the very beginning and this is nowhere more apparent than in the very first period of his textual production. This is true whether we look to *Education as the Practice of Freedom*, to *Extension or Communication* or to the text we come to now, *Cultural Action for Freedom* (Freire, 1977). Unlike the other two texts, which may be said to precede *Pedagogy of the Oppressed*, *Cultural Action for Freedom* immediately succeeds the latter.

The *Cultural Action for Freedom* text was written as a series of essays in the wake of Freire's sudden fame as a result of *Pedagogy of the Oppressed*, when he takes up a visiting professorship position at Harvard in the early 1970s. Thus, once more, we need to take into account the context of the work for a proper understanding of its meaning and significance. With both of the other early texts, we may say that they provide a fuller empirical picture of the background of *Pedagogy of the Oppressed* which, as a text, is much more obviously theoretical as well as being quite condensed and somewhat didactic in its approach. There is a rhapsodic and theoretical element to *Pedagogy of the Oppressed* (perhaps 'prophetic' is the word) which is absent from the two earlier texts. This is both a strength and a weakness of *Pedagogy*. With *Cultural Action for Freedom*, we can say two things about its context: (1) As the output from the Harvard context, it is dense and theoretical, although it also lacks the rhapsodic edge of *Pedagogy of the Oppressed*. Thus, it is not as concerned with specific empirical elements as are the first two texts, namely *Education as the Practice of Freedom* and *Extension or Communication*. (2) However, it does involve a theme of Third Worldism which was very present in the early texts and especially in *Extension or Communication*. Although this appears in *Pedagogy of the Oppressed*, it is not so clearly stated. It is interesting that, at Harvard, Freire should become so explicit and unequivocal about the relation between director societies and the Third World countries, a thematic which connects Freire to the evolution of the later discussion concerning 'multiculturalism' and 'interculturalism'. Perhaps this is also an effect of being in America and witnessing the power of the First World so forcefully. This conception of a Third Worldism in Freire also makes an explicit connection to the work of Frantz Fanon (Fanon, 1986b), whom we have mentioned several times already in relation to Freire's early work. Fanon's work becomes especially crucial in relation to the thematic of *Cultural Action for Freedom* and, before looking at the latter text in detail, I will evaluate the significance of these thematics in Fanon's work, in his two key texts, *Black Skin, White Masks* (Fanon, 1986a) and *The Wretched of the Earth* (Fanon, 1986b), respectively.

The seminal work of Frantz Fanon: from *Black Skin, White Masks* to *The Wretched of the Earth*

Frantz Fanon's *Black Skin, White Masks* (Fanon, 1986a), originally published in 1952, and *The Wretched of the Earth* (Fanon, 1986b), origi- nally published in 1961, have emerged as two of the most influential texts within the debate about the relationship between First and Third worlds. However, it is perhaps a signal of some of the protracted difficulties at the heart of this debate that Fanon has come to be used by theorists at opposite ends of the philosophical spectrum. In the first case, his work initially came to prominence through his advocation as a 'developmentalist revolutionary'. Here, in simple terms, his philosophy was seen as anti-colonial and tied to Fanon's own struggles during the Algerian revolution. The key Fanon text cited in this interpretation was *The Wretched of the Earth*, published just before Fanon died at the age of 36. This reading of Fanon continues to be an influence to the present day in the intercultural debate, most especially through trends in neo-Marxism.

In the 1980s however, an earlier text by Fanon, virtually ignored by the revolutionary interpretation, was taken up by post-colonial and postmodern discourse, his 1952 work *Black Skin, White Masks*. This new reading of Fanon tends to play down the revolutionary dimension of Fanon (and most especially his advocation of violence) by more or less ignoring *The Wretched of the Earth*. On this reading, Fanon's contribution to inter-culturalism has less to do with class politics and race or ethnic equality and more to do with issues of 'cultural identity', most especially the issues of racial and sexual identity. The question becomes one then of whether we can bring about some kind of dialogue between these two Fanons: to what extent is it possible to reconcile the divergent strands in Fanonist thought, in what measure can we make the two Fanons one? In addressing this question, I want to also suggest that the problems at the heart of the inter-pretation of Fanon represent a microcosm of macro-theoretical problems which continue to plague attempts at intercultural dialogue or resolution, and which we have seen present throughout our analysis of Freire's work.

Early Fanon – Black Skin, White Masks

Homi Bhabha has commented that Fanon reveals with 'greater profundity and poetry than any other writer … the question of cultural identity' (Bhabha, 1986, p. xxxv), and it is in the extraordinarily lyrical and passionate *Black Skin, White Masks* (Fanon, 1986a) that this expression finds its most intense formulation. As well as being his most poetic work, this text is also Fanon's most explicitly philosophical, and it is not surprising that postmodernist thinkers have found it so seductive. Like the later *Wretched of the Earth* (Fanon, 1986b), the backdrop to *Black Skin, White Masks* (Fanon, 1986a) is the psychopathology of colonialism, in this case specifically the experience of being black under French rule in Martinique.

Fanon's experience of Martinique is of a highly complex and layered system of racial hierarchy and 'race prejudice' (Fanon, 1986a, p. 9) where the three main categories of white, mixed race and black are organized in descending order of status and power. Fanon tells a related joke: three men arrive at the gates of heaven and are greeted by St Peter, a white man, a man of mixed race and a black man. What do you want most, St Peter asks? Money, says the white man. And you? Fame, says the man of mixed race. St Peter turns to the Negro, who says with a wide smile, 'I'm just carrying these gentlemen's bags' (Fanon, 1986a, p. 49). Although Fanon himself only realizes this system of stratification when he leaves Martinique for France (as growing up in Martinique this system operated as a kind of social unconscious), he retrospectively traces its influence on the Martinician psyche which now comes to symbolize the psyche of the colonized (although as we will see, there are important differences within the colonized themselves, between, for example, the Afro-Caribbeans and the Africans).

This Manichean structure – 'black or white, that is the question' (Fanon, 1986a, p. 51) – for Fanon is not the result of an essentialist truth of dual race but rather the symptom of a pathology of identity which results from political and social colonization. Although he recognizes the cultural power which comes with identification with the white race – 'one is white as one is rich as one is beautiful as one is intelligent' (Fanon, 1986a, p. 51), he also asserts the nonessentiality of such racial categories, whether white or black: 'The Negro is not, anymore than the white man' (Fanon, 1986a, p. 231). This critique of identity, written in 1952, means that Fanon is already anticipating many of the later deconstructions of humanism of thinkers such as Foucault (Foucault, 2004) and Derrida (Derrida, 1978).

'Man is a no': later Fanon and The Wretched of the Earth

To conclude my analysis of Fanon, I want to briefly outline how one might consider the relation between the structure of analysis we have seen Fanon outline in *Black Skin, White Masks* and the analysis of his later text, *The Wretched of the Earth*. As I have already stated, these texts are often seen as being in conflict with each other, and are said to represent two supposed versions of Fanon, the younger subtle theorist of identity and the later revolutionary advocate of anti-colonial violence, and perhaps even racial essentialism. Here I want to make three main points.

First, the reception of *The Wretched of the Earth* (Fanon, 1986b) was greatly influenced by the vehement Preface which Sartre wrote for it and which led to Sartre becoming 'the most hated man in France' (Lacey, 2000, p. 10). Sartre sought to defend what many saw as the extremity of Fanon's work by claiming that 'only violence can destroy violence' and describing such violence as 'man re-creating himself' (Sartre, 1986, p. xlvi). Fanon's work, Sartre claimed, could demonstrate to the West its own pathology, that in fact it 'was estranged from itself' (Sartre, 1986, p. xlvii). While supposedly well intentioned, Sartre's Preface none the less had the effect of greatly simplifying the meaning and implications of Fanon's work. Although it is true that Fanon does justify anti-colonial violence in the text, this justification is highly contextualized and qualified by a wider phenomenological and psycho-pathological analysis, an analysis that seems to drop out of the Sartrean interpretation altogether. This interpretation also has the effect of creating an acute difference between the earlier *Black Skin, White Masks* and its concerns with identity and *The Wretched of the Earth* which has been reduced to a defence of violent anti-colonialism.

Second, anything but a superficial reading of *The Wretched of the Earth*, however, shows a great continuity between Fanon's earlier and later concerns. Certainly there is a contextual difference. In 1952, Fanon is working in France (having fought in the Second World War for the resistance) and is sensitive to the questions of racial identity and racial hierarchy present in his society in Lyons. By 1961, Fanon was working as a psychiatrist through the horrors of the Algerian War, forcing him into exile in Tunisia. By this time, his consciousness of French imperialism was intense, as was his desire to free North Africa of the ruthless colonial forces and settlers. This led him at the very beginning of the text to affirm 'violence' (Fanon, 1986b, p. 28) as a necessary part of the struggle and to express disdain for the Western expression of a need for self-restraint on behalf of the colonized (Fanon, 1986b, p. 33). But his reasons for this disdain are quite specific and relate to what he sees as a Western moral hypocrisy and double standard: 'The violence with which the supremacy of white values is affirmed and the aggressiveness which has permeated the victory of these values over the ways of life and thought of the native mean that, in revenge, the native laughs in mockery when Western values are mentioned in front of him' (Fanon, 1986b, p. 33). Fanon is thus justifying violence here not as active but as *reactive*. This certainly represents a change in emphasis from *Black Skin, White Masks*. There, in conclusion, he had warned against a certain psychology of reactiveness on behalf of the colonized: 'Man's behaviour is not only reactional. And there is always resentment in a *reaction*. Nietzsche had already pointed that out in *The Will to Power*' (Fanon, 1986a, p. 222; emphasis in original). It is clear that his experience of Algeria led him to consider that reactiveness of this kind was inevitable and justifiable, at least to some extent. However, this is not his final word on the topic in *The Wretched of the Earth*.

Third, reading the first half of *The Wretched of the Earth* exclusively suggests that Fanon radically changed his philosophical position from *Black Skin, White Masks*. His approach seems now to become subject to the very Manicheanism he lambasted in his earlier work; black vs. white, colonizer vs. colonized, the oppressor's violence vs. the reactive violence of the oppressed. This binary world however is complicated as Fanon develops his argument. 'Racialism and hatred and resentment – "a legitimate desire for revenge" – cannot sustain a war of liberation' (Fanon, 1986b, p. 111). The 'primitive Manicheanism' (Fanon, 1986a, p. 115) must be overcome towards a much more ambiguous future of contradiction and what Fanon refers to as a bewildering 'semi-darkness': 'The clear, unreal, idyllic light of the beginning is followed by a semi-darkness that bewilders the senses ….The barriers of blood and race-prejudice are broken down on both sides' (Fanon, 1986b, p. 111). Racial essentialism and the binary oppositions of Manicheanism are therefore broken down not by a clear light of truth, but by ambiguity and confusion; truths now become only 'partial, limited and unstable' (Fanon, 1986b, p. 117). At the very conclusion of *The Wretched of the Earth*, Fanon calls for 'new concepts' and a new humanity (Fanon, 1986b, p. 251), as this ambiguity and confusion can no longer be made sense of by the old binary oppositions of race and essence. To this extent, and through a very different route, Fanon has ended up at a similarly vertiginous point to *Black Skin, White Masks*.

While his torrid experiences during the Algerian War may have given Fanon's words a new vehemence and extremity, leading him to justify bloodshed and violence in the name of freedom, he only does so with great reserve and qualification. His fundamental vision, early to late, remains one of *anti-essentialism*, or more positively of an existentialist freedom sensitive to the distortions of colonialism and imperialisms of all kinds, which distort the individual and collective on a psychic level, leading to pathology, sadism and masochism. The only escape route is to undo the colonial logic, which afflicts and assimilates oppressor and oppressed alike, and to construct a different kind of space, an intercultural space. For Fanon, this space is only visionary, it remains to be created. In his work as a psychiatrist, his battles as a revolutionary and his writings as a thinker, Fanon sought to remove at least some of the most insistent and invidious barriers to the production of such interculturality.

There are clear connections between Fanon and Freire's work, most especially in relation to the Third Worldist critique which they address to colonial societies and conflicts. I want to suggest here that Fanon's work also remains relevant to our analysis of Freire insofar as it exemplifies an irreducible dimension of *conflict*. As David Lacey has suggested, Fanon writes that 'man is a yes' but he also writes that 'man is a no' (Lacey, 2000, p. 505): 'no to scorn for man. No to the indignity of man. No to the exploitation of man. No to the murder of what is most human about men: freedom' (Lacey, 2000, p. 505). It is this resounding no (as well as a rather more subtle yes) which is one of the greatest echoes from Fanon's life work, and it is a shrill cry which I think we should try not to forget in our sometimes over-complacent attempts to synthesize difference. It is also a No which we will hear resounding throughout Freire's work.

Freire as a voice from the third world

In his Preface to *Cultural Action for Freedom* (Freire, 1977), Joao da Veiga Coutinho (Coutinho, 1977) looks in detail at the very question of Third Worldism from the specific perspective of Freire's work. 'Here is a voice from the third world which is so often spoken of but itself seldom speaks; its message is today being heard and finds an echo among those sectors of the first world which, for one reason or another, feel attuned to the third' (Countinho, 1977, p. 7). This sums up perfectly my point above, although we should not lose sight of the fact that Freire is firmly placed in the First World context when he writes these pieces, albeit only through an enforced exile. We should also note that much of Freire's work after 1970 will be through his work with the World Council of Churches. This again should not be seen as irrelevant to his work, especially if we take account, for example, of Guinea-Bissau (Freire, 1978), and the history of the church when it comes to development work. Coutinho places Freire's work here directly in a new counter-tradition which goes back to Fanon's aforementioned *The Wretched of the Earth* (Fanon, 1986b):

> something has happened since Frantz Fanon wrote *The Wretched of the Earth*, when that book appeared in the early sixties. In Fanon, said Sartre, the third world has found itself and is speaking to itself. In the voice of Paulo Freire, the third world still disdains to address itself to the managers of the first.
>
> (Countinho, 1977, p. 7)

Countinho also foregrounds crucial points made by Freire in relation to the status of education, what he calls 'the inherent ambivalence of education – both conditioning and conditioned' (Countinho, 1977, p. 9) Since, as Freire reiterates in many texts, from his perspective, education is never neutral, neither for domestication nor for freedom (Countinho, 1977, p. 9). This challenges the educator to take a stance; the key to this process according to Countinho is what he terms, after Freire, 'problematization': 'an act of subversion or overdetermination' (Countinho, 1977, p. 9). Again, this foregrounds the paradigmatic role played by the 'revolutionary educator', where the effort of problematization is enabled by a context of dialogue. Against all the pessimism of the oppressed, all their masochism, as well as the sadism of the oppressor, Freire, says Countinho, is pointing to the possibilities of transformation and a new reality: 'there are people speaking of a new language to redefine the reality in which we live' (Countinho, 1977, p. 9).

Cultural action for freedom: the text itself

Freire's text *Cultural Action for Freedom* (Freire, 1977) is an amalgamation of two texts written during his period at Harvard in the early 1970s. It comes after *Pedagogy of the Oppressed* (Freire, 1996a) and so provides an interesting sense of the aftermath of that seminal text. It also shares the significant emphasis on a theoretical approach to education, which was the great strength of *Pedagogy of the Oppressed* (Freire, 1996a), while it also connects with the more explicit thematic of literacy which we saw advanced in, for example, *Education as The Practice of Freedom* (Freire, 2005a). Freire begins by clarifying his educational stance: 'one of the basic aims of this work, where the process of adult literacy is discussed, is to show that our option is "for man". In other words, there is a clear emphasis on humanism' (Freire, 1977, p. 13). Freire also delineates how this humanism (which as we have seen is a radical rather than traditional humanism) is therefore 'an act of knowing and not of memorisation' (Freire, 1977, p. 13). Freire has already spoken in earlier texts about the relationship between education and technology. Here he makes clear again his critique of technicism owing to its tendency to reductionism:

> This act can never be accounted for in its complex totality by a mechanistic theory, for such a theory does not perceive education in general and adult literacy in particular as an act of knowing; instead it reduces the practice of education to a complex of techniques, naively considered to be neutral.
>
> (Freire, 1977, p. 13)

In line with a reading of education and society by theorists from critical theory such as Marcuse (Marcuse, 2002), Freire clarifies that this technicism is 'the means by which the educational process is standardised in a sterile and bureaucratic operation' (Freire, 1977, p. 13). This bureaucratization of education and of society is something to be opposed strongly. Again, Freire is interested in the process by which a society becomes alienated while at the same time seeking a way out of this impasse: 'Authentic thought-language is generated in the dialectical relationship between the subject and his concrete historical and cultural reality; in the case of the alienated cultural processes characteristic of dependent or object societies, thought-language itself is alienated' (Freire, 1977, p. 13). So the dialectic between subjectivity and objectivity is what is required to generate authentic thinking in the society but, because this dialectical harmony is lacking in other dependent societies, their whole thought becomes 'alienated'.

In a footnote (Freire, 1977, p. 14), Freire clarifies how this relationship (which connects with the aforementioned theme in Hegel (Hegel, 1979) of the master–slave dialectic), can be made sense of in the context of the relation between the colonizer and the colonized, or more generally the relation between 'metropolitan' and 'dependent' societies. Freire also refers to the former as 'managing societies' and they do not escape the process of alienation:

> These managing societies in their turn usually suffer, as is natural, from the contrary illness; they are convinced of the infallibility of their thought, and for this reason find it normal that it should be piously followed by the dependent societies; in saying this we merely underline an obvious fact.
>
> (Freire, 1977, p. 14)

The alienation of the dependent societies and the lordly manner of the metropolitan societies

In the relationship between metropolitan and dependent societies, 'the alienation of the latter corresponds to the lordly manner of the former' (Freire, 1977, p. 14). Again there is clear reference here to Hegel's master and slave dialectic. As always with Freire, he wishes to complicate what at first seems to be the relative simplicity of this reading of society: 'in either case however, one must refrain from absolutising the statement for just as among the alienated there are those who think in a non-alienated manner, there are unlordly denizens of the metropolises; in both cases, for different reasons, they break with the norms of their respective contexts' (Freire, 1977, p. 14). There is then always the possibility of 'breaking with the norms of one's context'. This is an optimistic view and points towards the possibility of transformation: the status quo is never absolute in Freire. Thus, Freire wishes to present a picture here of not simply the dependent society of the Third World but the metropolitan society of the First World as potentially vulnerable. Yes, the societies give the appearance of 'unshakeable stability': however, forces within these societies can lead to change and transformation. We might point to the recent 'revolutionary' forces, in Egypt and the wider Middle East, of democratization as a paradigmatic example. 'There we also see the emergence of the most depressed popular sectors; which previously did not exist as problems, hidden as they were in their society's affluence. As they emerge, these groups make their presence felt by the power structures' (Freire, 1977, p. 14).

Student movements

Freire here makes an interesting reference to the student groups, whom he has also cited on the first page of Chapter 1 of *Pedagogy of the Oppressed*: 'student groups which for a long time concentrated on purely academic demands gradually come to share the restlessness of the oppressed groups; the same happens to the most progressive amongst the intellectuals' (Freire, 1977, p.15). Clearly, Freire is here affirming the student movements and progressivism while joining the two together. The student movements are an example of progressivism at work in metropolitan society, and within these societies, in a *process of transition*, to invoke his chapter heading from *Education as the Practice of Freedom*, progressive intellectuals can also play a key political role as public intellectuals: 'thus the entire scheme of metropolitan societies begins to be called into question' (Freire, 1977, p. 15). However, Freire later notes the specificities of these societies, their very specific process of development and evolution. These metropolitan societies are distinctive insofar as the process of change in them is quite different from so-called Third Worldist societies, for Freire. For example, these metropolitan societies are very capable of 'absorbing dissent': 'it is true that in speaking of the process of social change within these societies, one has to take into account their greater capacity for absorbing dissent' (Freire, 1977, p.15). Freire makes a specific reference to Herbert Marcuse's (Marcuse, 2002) work here and states that it is the advanced technology of these societies that alters their capacity for dealing with dissent.

'Marcuse has repeatedly called attention to the fact that this techno-logical power is able to transform many of these protest movements into mere manifestations of folklore' (Freire, 1977, p. 15). Again, this is significant for the foregrounding of the student movements but also the sense that these movements are incapable of real and revolutionary change. Freire, however, acknowledges here that this issue of protest and of the relation of the society to the protest is not his main subject, but a digression: 'This point however is not part of our subject, nor can it be adequately dealt with in a footnote' (Freire, 1977, p. 15). This discussion develops from what Freire has said about the specific context of colonization in, for example, *Education as The Practice of Freedom*, where he spoke about the lack of democratic experience from which Brazilian society has suffered in the effort to develop a new kind of progressivism. Again, here, Freire wants to delineate a colonial specificity, although his discussion is more generalized rather than specific to Brazil: 'in either case, there is a funda-mental dimension to these societies resulting from their colonial phase; their culture was established and maintained as a "culture of silence"' (Freire, 1977, p. 16). Again and again we see this as Freire's target, the 'culture of silence' – how we can work politically and educationally to subvert this 'culture of silence'. Freire describes this here as a 'twofold pattern'.

The alienated society and the director society

As Freire notes (Freire, 1977, p. 16), 'externally, the alienated society as a whole as the mere object of the director society, is not heard by the latter. Meanwhile, within the alienated society itself, the masses are subjected to the same kind of silence by the power elites' (Freire, 1977, p. 16). This is *massification* and *objectification* as Freire understands it. As we have seen, however, this process is rarely complete. There will always be some pockets of resistance but when there is a resistance to this, when the resistance breaks out, there is a powerful reinstating of power from the oppressors: 'when the popular masses are able to break their submissive silence, the power elites violently attempt to arrest the process. The director society takes it upon itself to do so' (Freire, 1977, p. 16). Here, Freire seems concerned with the colonized society itself. When there is a resistance movement developed in this dependent society, often the power elites will call upon the 'director society' to kill off the resistance. Again, there are clear resonances between this discussion and the critical analysis which Fanon undertakes of these situations in *The Wretched of the Earth* (Fanon, 1986b) (or indeed in Memmi's *The Colonizer and the Colonized* (Memmi, 1975)).

For Freire, this is also a matter of the people's consciousness which, while rebelling, still remains at the level of 'naïve rebellion' or of 'naïve consciousness'. None the less, the repressions undertaken by the forces of the oppressor are significant. As Freire notes,

> The repression used to return the masses to their silence is preceded and accompanied by a myth-making effort to identify as diabolical all thought-language which uses such words as alienation, domination, oppression, liberation, humanization, and autonomy; to counter this effort among a well-intentioned but naive population.
>
> (Freire, 1977, p. 16)

This is propaganda and Freire calls for 'demystifying work', which will show what the rulers really stand for. Again, there is a specific emphasis on the Third World, although the point seems more generalizable: 'De-mystifying work is necessary to show what the words really stand for; the expression of objective, socio-historical and political categories whose dramatic character in the Third World allows no one to be neutral' (Freire, 1977, p. 16). Freire connects his own genealogy as a thinker to this breaking with the 'culture of silence'; this was the very genesis of Freire's own educational theory: 'At a time in Brazil when the "culture of silence" was being exposed for what it was, I began, as a man of the Third World, to elaborate not a mechanical method for adult literacy learning, but an educational theory generated in the womb of the culture of silence itself' (Freire, 1977, p. 16). This is a revealing phrase, indicating the paradigmatic power of Freire's notion of the 'culture of silence'. As Coutinho made clear, then, Freire is irrepressibly a 'man of the Third World' and his effort, his educational theory and praxis, is not seeking to be the voice of the Third World as much as to be one of the 'instruments of that still faltering voice' (Freire, 1977, p. 17), which, of course, is an attempt to overcome the very 'culture of silence'.

At this point, Freire acknowledges the key influences on his work and we will come to these below, but what he also makes clear is a key thematic of *Cultural Action for Freedom*. We can certainly be influenced by other thinkers and thinkers from another part of the world (here Freire is acknowledging the influence of First World theorists on this Third World approach) but what we must beware of is a form of 'cultural invasion'. The perspective being critiqued is the view put forward in some development circles of a simple transposition of one programme from the First World to the Third World, or indeed vice versa (if we take Freire's own programme). Freire warns in this context of the need for an emphasis on cultural specificity; the programme 'cannot be simply transplanted' (Freire, 1977, p. 17) – the thinking developed here is not free of the influence of other thought; that would be impossible, but confrontation with our particular world has taught us *the impossibility of simple transferability from one culture to another*. That is, that 'any ideas coming from another part of the world cannot be simply transplanted; they must first be submitted to what Professor Guerreiro Ramos calls a "sociological reduction"' (Freire, 1977, p. 17). This notion of *sociological reduction* points to the impossibility of simple transferability.

So, on the one side, we have a warning about the ultimate non-transferability of educational and political programmes, especially from First to Third World. This latter view has been the tradition, for example, in literacy primers or indeed in the process of extension that Freire has castigated in both *Education as The Practice of Freedom* but also in *Extension or Communication*. At the same time, change is beginning to be radicalized within the Third World itself: 'nevertheless, the emerging Third World is rapidly becoming conscious of its plight. ... Thus, the fundamental theme of the Third World – implying a difficult but not impossible task for its people – is the conquest of its right to a voice, of the right to pronounce its word' (Freire, 1977, p. 17). 'A difficult but not impossible task'; Freire adopts a very personal tone, referring to himself as 'a man of this world': 'as a man of this world, who has already lived some significant, if not excessively traumatic, experiences for having presumed to have a voice in the culture of silence' (Freire, 1977, p.1 8). Freire has himself faced these situations existentially and politically – this is his context, he is a man of the Third World. His experiences have been 'significant if not excessively traumatic'. We think of his imprisonment and exile. He tells us that, in this situation, he has 'only one desire' (Freire, 1977, p. 18). Here, he distinguishes between wholly silenced cultures and 'cultures which repress the voice'. In both incidences, presumably the dependent and the director societies, Freire wishes that his thinking 'coincides' with the 'unrest of all those ... who are struggling to have a voice of their own' (Freire, 1977, p. 18).

Cultural action for freedom is adult literacy

Freire next makes clear what he is really designating as 'cultural action for freedom'. He clarifies that, in essence, he is talking about the 'adult literacy process' (Freire, 1977, p. 21), but Freire's understanding of literacy is broad and humanistic. In an important statement, Freire reiterates the key link between education and philosophy or theory: 'All educational practice implies a theoretical stance on the educator's part; this in turn implies an interpretation of man and world' (Freire, 1977, p. 18). Freire is critical of what he terms a 'mechanisitic mentality', which we have seen him castigate in his discussion of society and technology. Interestingly, he distinguishes Marx from this position of mechanism or reductivism, although some (especially those who might link with Christianity) would seek to critique

Marx and the following neo-Marxism for precisely its reductive materialism. Here Freire states his disagreement with this reading of Marx (Marx, 1992a–b). Clearly, for Freire, Marx is not materialist in this technicist sense. Rather, this technicism represents, for Freire, a vulgarization of the potential of the Marxist tradition, and we can say that this issue or problematic also has relevance with regard to the wider concern of an increased emphasis on technicism and instrumentalism in education.

Marx's critique of technicism

Freire notes, apropos of Marx, on mechanism and reductionistic versions of materialism: 'A mechanistic mentality which Marx would call "grossly materialistic"' (Freire, 1977, p. 22). He also establishes a direct and important link between illiteracy and the culture of silence which draws his reading of literacy together with his critical and political theory of the world; as he puts it elsewhere, 'reading the word and reading the world'. 'Contemporary illiteracy as a typical manifestation of the culture of silence' (Freire, 1977, p. 25). Again, this connection between the problem of illiteracy and the deep and broadly defined socio-political problem of the 'culture of silence' takes us beyond narrow definitions of the problem of literacy or indeed narrowly defined supposed solutions to the latter.

Freire invokes a distinction which Jean-Paul Sartre (Sartre, 2003) had made famous between 'beings for themselves' and 'beings for another', the latter referring to the objectification that befalls humanity (and which we have seen thematized in others' work, such as that of Marcuse (Marcuse, 2002)). Rather than being marginal, Freire argues that it is the people's being 'beings for another' which constitutes the central problem:

> in reality, they are oppressed human beings within it [the society].
> Alienated beings, they cannot overcome their dependency by incorporation into the very structure responsible for their dependency. There is no other road to humanization – theirs as well as everyone else's – but authentic transformation of the dehumanising structure.
>
> (Freire, 1977, p. 28)

'Cultural action for freedom', then, as Freire understands this process, is the evolution of a problem-posing education as against the banking education system of the past, which has maintained and reinforced the 'culture of silence'. Now, instead of being a passive object, the individual learner moves beyond oppression towards action: 'interpreting illiterates as men oppressed within the system – the literacy process, as cultural action for freedom, is an act of knowing in which the learner assumes the role of knowing subject in dialogue with the educator' (Freire, 1977, p. 28). We can break down the phrase 'cultural action for freedom' into its most significant aspects.

'*Culture*', as we know, has been a recurrent term of importance for Freire. *Action* refers to moving beyond passivity. Finally, *freedom* refers to the move beyond a reductionist notion of liberal freedom to a genuine freedom, which is grounded in a dialectic between subject and object and indeed between freedom and authority. As Freire puts it, we must see 'the adult literacy process as an act of knowing' (Freire, 1977, p. 29).

Literacy and humanization

We have already seen in our earlier discussion of *Education as the Practice of Freedom* that Freire's conception of literacy must, first, critique a more narrowly defined understanding which sees literacy as simply a literalist interpretation of reading the alphabet. For Freire, literacy is only possible or only worthy of the name when it involves an authentic critical awareness and a reading of the world as well as a reading of the word. 'As an event calling forth the critical reflection of both the learners and educators, the literacy process must relate speaking the word to transforming reality, and to the human being's role in this transformation' (Freire, 1977, p. 31). In other words, literacy is primarily or fundamentally a process of humanization and of transformation of reality. It also, as Elias, for example, reminds us, depends crucially upon a well-worked-out theory of epistemology, a theory of knowing (Elias, 1994). As in *Pedagogy of the Oppressed*, but perhaps especially in *Extension or Communication*, Freire uses a paradigmatic theory of knowing which eschews both idealism and materialism or objectivism and subjectivism, instead opting for a dialectical approach, which owes something to both Hegel and Marx. There is in this dialectical approach an 'indisputable unity' between subjectivity and objectivity: 'a theory of knowing; subjectivism and idealism come into play. When the subjective-objective unity is broken, we recognize the indisputable unity between subjectivity and objectivity in the act of knowing' (Freire, 1977, p. 31).

Freire describes the existence of two interrelated contexts. 'The adult literacy process as an act of knowing implies the existence of two interrelated contexts. One is the context of authentic dialogue between learners and educators as equally knowing subjects. This is what schools should be – the theoretical context of dialogue' (Freire, 1977, pp. 31–32). The second context is definitely extra-school: 'the second is the real, concrete context of facts, the social reality in which human beings exist' (Freire, 1977, p. 31). This again shows how for Freire, following Dewey, among others, there must be a critique of the isolationism of the school in traditionalist education. Here, we can refer once again to Dewey's *Experience and Education* (Dewey, 1973), where he cites the need to move away from traditionalism and, as one example, the traditionalist tenet of keeping the school as an isolated institution set off from the rest of society. To this extent, Dewey agrees with the progressivist critique of the school. However, he also significantly is critical of what he sees as the excesses of progressivism. We will return to this point below.

Freire now returns to his original question in *Cultural Action for Freedom* of the issue of the relation between the director society and the dependent society, and the issue of how colonization or even post-colonized alienation might be resolved. What Freire is attacking here is not simply the colonizer and its violence. Rather more significantly, he is interested in the very process by which the director societies move towards a supposed process of post-colonization. In this very process, however, where they seem to be acting as 'liberators' of the originally colonized countries, something else is taking place. Freire, of course, is not simply talking in the abstract here but is referring to real processes of countries becoming independent (in *Education as the Practice of Freedom*, for example, he refers to Brazil's becoming independent from Portugal). In letters to Guinea-Bissau (Freire, 1978), he speaks in detail of his work in this former Portuguese colony in Africa. What is wrong with the hegemonic approaches in this decolonization is that their 'salvation' of the dependent country is a sham:

> Salvation of the third world by the director societies can only mean its domination, whereas in its legitimate aspiration to independence lies its utopian vision; to save the director societies in the very act of freeing itself; in this sense the pedagogy we defend is a utopian pedagogy; to be utopian is to engage in denunciation and annunciation.
>
> (Freire, 1977, p. 39)

Thus, the fake salvation is replaced by a proper liberation which will liberate not simply the oppressed peoples but also the oppressor (and there is an attempt to avoid the circle of violence which Fanon describes in terms of the oppressed becoming the oppressor, etc. in *The Wretched of the Earth*) (Fanon, 1986b)). This then leads to what Freire rather unproblematically refers to as 'freedom'.

Once more there are several references back to the earlier *Pedagogy of the Oppressed*, most notably to the discussion in the Preface. This highlights the issue concerning the relation between 'radicalization' and 'sectarianism'. As Freire makes clear, utopianism is on the side of radicalism: 'utopia is linked to radicalization not sectarianism; built on the future etc' (Freire, 1977, p. 41). This is important, as often we might think that utopianism, in its very nature, is linked to a more dogmatic approach on the Left which isn't grounded in a historical process. But Freire's conception of utopianism is specific; it *denounces and announces*. It denounces the banking system and the mindsets of domination in oppressor and oppressed alike. It announces a future pedagogy but one that can only be forged in a creative moment, invented by inter-subjective beings (Freire, 1977, p. 41). Here, we see a number of Freirean themes converge and one image for the way in which

Freire's thought works is the image of the *matrix*, a complex interplay of various approaches and influences. We see the theme of education itself connect with the issue of utopianism, with the issue of radicalization and with the notion of cultural action, the latter which Freire claims is synonymous with what he means by authentic education. Moreover, Freire now extends his analysis to speak of the relation between conscientization (which we have seen approached, for example, in *Education as the Practice of Freedom* in detail) and cultural action, and cultural action itself becomes identified with conscientization; 'Cultural action as conscientization; conscientization refers to the process in which human beings, not as recipients but as knowing subjects, achieve a deepening awareness both of the socio-cultural reality which shapes their lives and of their capacity to transform their reality' (Freire, 1977, p. 51). More terms emerge from this juxtaposition: *knowing subjectivity*, *socio-cultural reality*, and *transformation*. This is precisely the Freirean matrix of problem-posing pedagogy which also breaks down the distinction between politics and education. In developing his theme here, which is a reiteration of a thematic in *Pedagogy of the Oppressed*, Freire once again returns to an existentialist framework of the specificity of humanity, which allows him to foreground humanism.

Conscientization recognizes that consciousness is conditioned

Freire reiterates a number of thematics from his earlier texts, especially concerning the relation between existentialism and the human/animal divide. He simultaneously foregrounds, however, the limits of human consciousness. As Freire notes, 'conscientization is possible only because human being's consciousness, although conditioned, can recognize that it is conditioned' (Freire, 1977, p. 54). This is crucial – 'can recognize that it is conditioned'. Once more, Freire moves constantly between the particular and the general, and in this discussion of conditioning he returns to the theme of Brazilian society, and more generally to what he terms 'Latin American society' (in which he includes the South American experience) and their very process of conditioning. He refers to the experience of a 'closed society' which again is a reference back to his theme of closed societies and the lack of democratic experience which he thematizes in Chapter 2 of *Education as the Practice of Freedom*. To conclude this chapter, I will explore Freire's more developed analysis of the Latin American situation in this later context.

Latin American societies as closed societies

As Freire notes, 'Latin American societies were established as closed societies from the time of their conquest by the Spanish and the Portuguese when the culture of silence took shape' (Freire, 1977, p. 61). So, for Freire, there is a direct correlation between colonization and the closure of a society. In this context, Freire is first concerned to delineate the specificity of the colonized experience. However, he also wants to claim that similar patterns are at work in metropolitan societies, which seem, on the one hand, to be not so closed. However, on the other hand, Freire makes clear that he thinks these metropolitan societies often have a greater capacity to 'subdue dissent' and thus 'absorb resistance'. They are also more than likely to have a greater capacity to hide the very nature of the oppression of their citizens, this oppression or massification being not as obvious as in dependent societies. This is because many of the societies operate under the auspices of a liberal democratic regime whereas many dependent societies are under the rubric (as was Brazil) of a military dictatorship. As Blake *et al.* (Blake *et al.*, 2003b) discuss, one of the difficulties here is the inherent ambiguity of liberalism and especially the problem that this liberal ambiguity is felt more forcefully (and with more tragic results) by dependent societies. This is because the appearance of liberalism does not have to be maintained by the director society in its colonies, to the same extent as in the home country.

One significant question which Freire addresses here is whether revolution is easier to achieve in a dependent society. Certainly, Freire does point to the complex processes of assimilation which have only been enhanced by the growth of contemporary technologies in the West most especially (here there is a great deal of connection with Marcuse's thematic). However, Freire's comments on Latin American societies (here written in 1973) suggest that Latin American societies have struggled considerably with the possibility of a democratic transition. We will return later to how these societies have changed in the intervening years and the implications thereof, especially in the Brazilian context when we look at Freire's own political and educational efforts following the return of democracy there (O'Cadiz *et al.*, 1998). However, Freire does acknowledge that there is one Latin American society already in 1973 which shows itself to have moved beyond 'closure': 'with the exception of post-revolutionary Cuba, these societies are still closed societies today' (Freire, 1977, p. 71).

The extraordinary level of cross-referencing continues with Freire referring back to the key distinction between sectarianism and radicalization which he initially referred to in his earlier texts but which receives its fullest elaboration in *Pedagogy of the Oppressed* in the Preface (Freire, 1977, p. 71). Similarly, there is a related reference back to Freire's conceptions of 'biophilia' and 'necrophilia' (Freire, 1977, p. 73), which is borrowed explicitly with regard to Erich Fromm. He follows with a critique of gregariousness (Freire, 1977, p. 74), which he previously looked at in his analysis of the specifics of Brazilian society in his 'Society in Transition' section of *Education as the Practice of Freedom*. There, he connected this pejorative sense of gregariousness with his critique of the structures of Brazilian society, and its manifestations of a deep cultural unconsciousness of repression and alienation. This was manifested, for example, in a tendency towards verbalism (which despite appearances to the contrary) was, for Freire, radically anti-dialogical. He also develops the point in this later context with a critique of the right-wing approach to education and politics as being fundamentally (that is, *de jure*) incapable of what he terms 'utopianism' (Freire, 1977, p. 76). He returns to this theme in his lectures at the Institute of Education in London in the early 1990s (Freire, 1995b), and we will follow up the implications of this in Chapter 5 in our discussion of the relationships between progressivism and utopianism.

The value of philosophy

Significantly, Freire returns to the value of the discipline of philosophy itself in the elaboration of an approach to liberation; *'philosophy is the matrix of the proclamation of the new reality'* (Freire, 1977, p. 77). This is an important intervention in the discussion concerning the relationship between philosophy and *praxis* where many might consider that *praxis* actually moves to a 'transcendence of the very need for philosophy' (Freire, 1977, p. 77). We have already seen this discussed in a related manner in Balibar's discussion of Marx's complex relationship to the need to overcome philosophy (first elaborated in 'Theses on Feuerbach' (Marx, 1992a)). With Balibar (Balibar, 2007), we already have a sense that this critique of philosophy actually and paradoxically leads to a renewal of philosophy as a discipline. We have seen a similar dialectic elaborated in Blake *et al.* (Blake *et al.*, 2003b) with regard to the genealogy of the philosophy of education. Where managerialism develops its hegemony over more theoretical approaches, there follows in reaction an actual *renewal of theory*, against all the odds (Blake *et al.*, 2003b). This renewal of theory which takes place in the 1990s in the philosophy of education sets the scene for the emergence of Freire as a key figure, to be included in what might be termed the 'continentalist' turn in the philosophy of education. Here we can see why. Freire explicitly sees philosophy as the 'matrix'. And if philosophy is indeed the proclaimer of the new reality, it is the need, not just in Latin America, but throughout all emerging democracies, for this proclamation to be heard that most concerns Freire in his conclusion to *Cultural Action for Freedom*.

The liberation of Latin America

As Freire (1977, p. 81) notes,

> We have spoken of the challenge facing Latin America. In this period of transition we believe that other areas of the Third World are no exception to what we have described though each will present its own

particular nuances. If the paths they follow are to lead to liberation, they cannot bypass cultural action for conscientization.

In Freire's own words, 'other areas are no exception', so these findings are generalizable, although Freire does acknowledge the culturally specific nuances, and also, if there is hope of liberation, it can only come about through conscientization: 'it cannot bypass'. Here is a warning that Freire puts out to all the newly emergent independent nations of the Third World: 'one cannot enter the process as objects in order later to become subjects'. This is a lesson or warning which Freire will himself have to ambiguously and conflictually face in his work, for example, in Guinea-Bissau (Freire, 1978) and later in Brazil itself when he returns as education minister. It is also an ambiguity which Antonio Faundez, for example, explicitly challenges Freire on in the text *Learning to Question* (Freire and Faundez, 1989) and which O'Cadiz and colleagues take up in their text *Education and Democracy* (O'Cadiz *et al.*, 1998).

Freire ends appropriately with a question: 'What is the next step for an educator who believes that learning to read and write is an act of knowing (who also knows that this is not as for Plato an act of remembering what has been forgotten)?' (Freire, 1977, p. 86.) The message is clear: whether his reading of Plato is correct or not, Freire is opposing any apriorism in epistemology, and especially in the way in which such epistemologies might ground a politics. Truth must be forged in action, in true *praxis*, and this is also the only way that liberation can be achieved; problem-posing education and political process 'cannot be bypassed'.

PART TWO

Impacts and legacies – from Freire's return to Brazil to critical pedagogy

CHAPTER FIVE

On Freire's *Pedagogy of Hope: Reliving Pedagogy of the Oppressed*

Freire's 'actual process of reflection'

In *Pedagogy of Hope: Reliving Pedagogy of the Oppressed* (Freire, 1992), Freire calls for an attempt to 'explain and defend progressive postmodernity' (Freire, 1992, p. 4), saying his book 'will reject conservative, neoliberal postmodernity' (Freire, 1992, p. 4). But he also makes clear that this represents a continuity with his earlier work: 'The debates in which I shared in the 1970s are as current today ... fear of freedom ... the tyranny of liberty and the tyranny of authority ... the urgency of the democratization of the public school' (Freire, 1992, p. 14). Only a radical politics, he claims, not a sectarian one, however, can truly provide the conditions for an authentic democracy (Freire, 1992, p. 14). Again stressing the need for an awareness of the dynamics of power in liberatory education, he says, 'these peasants know more than we do' (Freire, 1992, p. 32). At the same time, however, 'a respect for the peasants' ingenuousness does not mean that an educator must accommodate to their level of reading the world' (Freire, 1992, p. 36). The bridge here must always be *dialogue*.

Freire speaks movingly of the need to 'stir my memory and challenge it', 'to show you the actual process of my reflection, my pedagogical thought and its development; the consistency between word and deed, not paralysis but consistency which still allows me to change position' (Freire, 1992, p. 53). For Freire, this is a permanent process of search which requires patience and humility. In our dealings with others, he tells us, at times, we find ourselves lacking these virtues. Instead, we must cultivate an inter-subjective process of becoming vulnerable, which he describes as a 'virtuous' process (Freire, 1992, p. 53). The mark of a true educator is the ability to dialogue with educatees in a mode of reciprocity, which may paradoxically lead him or her to decree his or her own 'death' as an educator. It is only through such a 'death' of the authority figure that the authentic birthing of education can emerge (Freire, 1992, p. 53). This latter may be regarded as a paradigmatically 'progressivist' view in education, where the latter ideology is regarded as a critique of teacher-centred traditionalism and an affirmation of more student-centred approaches. This notion of progressivism as student-centred is certainly one aspect of the progressivist philosophy and connects Freire very clearly to it. However, in the following section I want to look at a more complex reading of progressivism which will also allow us, in connecting Freire's work to the latter, to present a more nuanced picture of Freire's own later thinking.

Freire and progressivism

In an important essay, 'Progressivism' (Darling and Nordenbo, 2003), written by John Darling and Sven Erik Nordenbo, the authors demonstrate a crucially nuanced understanding of what progressivism means and has meant in its various incarnations, and it is an analysis which bears directly on Freire's own work. Freire engages with progressivism, in its various modes, throughout his work, for example, in his later declaration in *Pedagogy of Hope: Revisiting Pedagogy of the Oppressed* (Freire, 1992) that his work constitutes 'a progressive postmodernity' (Freire, 1992, p. 4). The latter part of the statement regarding postmodernity has received all the attention and we will see the significance of this below. However, we should not lose sight of the significance of the first part of the statement: a 'progressive' postmodernity.

Often, progressivism has been misunderstood as constituting a specific set of ideas regarding child-centredness and a subversion of teacher authority; it has come to be associated with a rather vulgarized interpretation of John Dewey's work, most especially his early thought. Quite aside from the fact that Dewey himself explicitly critiques such a position in his *Experience and Education* (Dewey, 1973), what such a view also loses sight of is the very meaning of progressivism as a philosophy of education per se. Darling and Nordenbo address this problem head-on. According to the latter, 'Progressivism or *Reformpedagogik* arises in contexts in which major educational crises exist in the form of significant gaps between existing arrangements and perceived societal and cultural needs ... such crises have occurred three times in the modern history of education' (Darling and Nordenbo, 2003, p. 288). They locate the first of these crises in the 'the second half of the eighteenth century and around the beginning of the nineteenth' (Darling and Nordenbo, 2003, p. 288) and mention Rousseau and Humboldt specifically. The second crisis occurs in the last decade of the nineteenth and the first third of the twentieth century when 'a new interest in the nature of the child took its point of departure' (Darling and Nordenbo, 2003, p. 288). This is the moment when the whole emphasis on 'child-centredness' became so prominent and it is this particular moment which tends to give the definitive reading of what progressivism entails. Significantly, however, Darling and Nordenbo don't stop there. According to their reading of educational history, there is a final moment of progressivism, 'the period from the 1960s onwards in which it is a commonplace to think of things as being in crisis' (Darling and Nordenbo, 2003, p. 288). This period coincided with the publication of Freire's earliest work, which we have analysed closely in the first four chapters. Thus, according to Darling and Nordenbo's criteria, the publication of *Pedagogy of the Oppressed* (Freire, 1996a) takes place exactly at the time when the development of progressivism has reached its newest stage. This then would seem to point towards an understanding of Freire as a progressive thinker. We will develop this complex issue below.

However, Darling and Nordenbo (Darling and Nordenbo, 2003, p. 288) complicate their picture of progressivism once they have introduced this threefold historical distinction between the Rousseauist, child-centredness and late 1960s phases. Developing the logic of this conception, they argue that progressivism cannot be associated with a particular set of fixed or stable doctrines. Although related, as we have seen, the three delineated phases of progressivism foreground the distinctiveness of each of these theoretical approaches within progressivism, related but different. There is no one essential progressivism derivable from this analysis. This is an important point because it leads to a fundamental redefinition of what progressivism involves:

> We argued above that progressivism is not just a name for a distinctive body of opinions about educational theory. The kind of progressivism we are talking about has to be related to the historical situation from which it arises, and we accepted that progressivism arises in contexts in which major educational crises exist, that is, that each crisis provokes its own kind of progressivism.
>
> (Darling and Nordenbo, 2003, p. 306)

At least two points are worth noting here for our purposes. The historical situatedness of each of the various moments of progressivism points to our own need to understand the specifics of Freire's time, most especially here his arrival on the scene of late 1960s counter-cultural political and educational theory. Second, there is a sense that we can expect more crises. Indeed, I would question whether Darling and Nordenbo's designation of a third phase of the late 1960s onwards is itself too unilinear. While a useful designation, it perhaps occludes key revolutionary elements of trans-formation at various points since the 1960s, or how the current situation in the year 2011 cannot be understood under the same thematic as this supposedly last, third phase.

Darling and Nordenbo do go some way towards this analysis in outlining how the latest aspects of progressivism have a distinctiveness in terms of the challenges which progressivism now faces. Whereas previously progres-sivism was the revolutionary movement, now it seems that it has become the new hegemony: progressivism seems to be the accepted creed across educational discourses and cultures, especially with regard to the emphasis on child-centredness and individualism. However, Darling and Nordenbo question the cogency of such a view: all is not as it appears. Beneath the veneer of a progressivist ascendancy lies the hegemony of materialism, which instrumentalizes education. Here, it is hardly the individual who is in the ascendant at all; quite the contrary. What makes matters worse is that, under the veneer of dominance, progressivism appears to have lost its way and power. 'Now ... educational theorists have more and more turned ... [to] technicalities about how to turn the learner into an efficient tool of the economic system ... the individual is now to be regarded as a loser' (Darling and Nordenbo, 2003, p. 306). This is a very interesting argument. From a Freirean perspective, it perhaps gives us the impression that Freire *is* a progressive and to be intimately associated with the late 1960s social and revolutionary movements. However, on this view, the quandary his philosophy and others like it now face is that although they appear to have become hegemonic, they have lost a great deal of power. In other words, progressivism since the late 1960s, and Freire's philosophy as an example, have been a failure in the longer term (despite all the appearances and rhetoric to the contrary).

Finally, it is worth noting that while progressivism cannot be reduced to a specific set of doctrines or definitive ideas, there are clear characteristics in common between the various movements. And whereas Darling and Nordenbo locate progressivism as finding its feet initially in the eighteenth century, they also provide a more far-reaching historical trajectory for the understanding of the other periods or paradigms of thought opposed to progressivism. This historical analysis also allows certain indispensable elements of progressivism to emerge. In line with an old distinction in logic, we might say that these are necessary but not sufficient conditions for progressivism. Developing their own narrative, Darling and Nordenbo distinguish between three periods of educational understanding, three phases of educational trends and approaches (Darling and Nordenbo, 2003, p. 298). First, they identify the paradigm of traditional, objective truths for the sake of salvation in another world, which is associated with a premodern perspective. Next there is the Renaissance paradigm, objective truths for the sake of this world (Darling and Nordenbo, 2003, p. 298). Then, thirdly, a contestation of the mimetic principle itself: knowledge is now seen as a personal acquisition obtained by learning from experience and, from the early twentieth century, this is called 'progressivism' (Darling and Nordenbo, 2003, p. 298). Here, the aim for the student is to be transformed into a new person or, as is sometimes said, brought to true humanity by virtue of his or her achieved experience: the emphasis is on individuals and their personal growth (Darling and Nordenbo, 2003, p. 299). Of course, this is not necessarily the last phase and we will see later how some commentators posit a further intensification of this position in a postmodern moment (Kearney, 1988).

A more problematic and potentially damaging idea, introduced by Darling and Nordenbo in summation, is that 'if progressivism is taken to its logical conclusion, it results in the renunciation of the educational enterprise itself' (Darling and Nordenbo, 2003, p. 302). This calls the validity of progressivism into question and, for our purposes and by implication, the philosophy of education of Freire into question. Certainly, 'antipedagogy' is one example of a progressivism which goes all the way in this regard. Freire, however, sees his project as fundamentally about renewing the very value and meaning of education rather than seeking such ultimate destruction in a more nihilistic version of his thinking. However, the question remains: Can any education worthy of the name be salvaged from the deconstructive project which progressivism undertakes in opposition to traditional education? This was also Martin Buber's point (Buber, 2002) when he said that a distinction between the teacher–student relation and the friendship relation must be maintained for the sake of the distinctiveness and integrity of education. We will have to see below whether Freire holds this line or whether the accusation of a kind of educational nihilism (grounded in a radical progressivism) is a valid one to launch at Freire.

The hermeneutic context of *Pedagogy of Hope*

One of the most interesting things about *Pedagogy of Hope: Reliving Pedagogy of the Oppressed* (Freire, 1992), as a text, is that it is directly and explicitly set up as a readdressing of the exact topic and history of *Pedagogy of the Oppressed* (Freire, 1996a). This seems an acknowledgement (if it was needed) that *Pedagogy of the Oppressed* is Freire's most important work. However, as we have tried to show in this book, this should not lead to a neglect of the other texts. Freire's *Pedagogy of the Oppressed* stands as a distillation of his earlier work and anticipates much of his later work, although there are tensions throughout. Even the earlier work, while providing a lead-in to the key text, is hardly always consistent with it in tone or purpose and, as we have seen in Chapters 1 and 2, there are key differences between, for example, the content of *Pedagogy of the Oppressed* (Freire, 1996a) and the content of *Education as the Practice of Freedom* (Freire, 2005a), *Extension or Communication* (Freire, 2005b) and *Cultural Action For Freedom* (Freire, 1977).

Moreover, we know something else about *Pedagogy of Hope: Reliving Pedagogy of the Oppressed* as a text in terms of its original *raison d'être* which casts light on this hermeneutic issue. Freire tells us in his lectures at the Institute in London (Freire, 1995b) that *Pedagogy of Hope: Reliving Pedagogy of the Oppressed* (Freire, 1992) was originally intended as an introduction to *Pedagogy of the Oppressed* (Freire, 1996a) to accompany a new edition of the work in the 1990s. As he wrote this text however, he began to realize that it was not simply an introduction to *Pedagogy*; it was, as he says, 'a new book' (Freire, 1992, p. 42). This is significant, since it shows that, for Freire, although each of his works builds on the last, there is also a forward propelling progressivism which sets out to contextualize each new work in its specificity, both politically and temporally. Twenty years have elapsed since *Pedagogy of the Oppressed* was written and so this new context requires a kind of new thinking, 'new ways' (Freire, 1992, p. 42). Thus *Pedagogy of Hope: Reliving Pedagogy of the Oppressed* serves two purposes at once. In the first instance, by excavating some of the personal-existential and social-political context around *Pedagogy of the Oppressed*, it deepens the analysis of that latter text, which is perhaps Freire's most obviously theoretical text. Second, by revisiting the latter, it questions its assumptions and perhaps points to some of its errors.

The personal existential style

What is so powerful about *Pedagogy of Hope: Reliving Pedagogy of the Oppressed* is that it does this both theoretically and existentially, with a rich seam of existential analysis and references to social and educational situations. This is in line with Freire's development of a multiple array of writing styles to exemplify the complexity of the project he is engaged in, whether it be spoken books, shared or co-authored books, books in the forms of letters regarding political work, or letters to his niece, as his later thought develops (Freire and Faundez, 1989; Freire, 1996b). In *Pedagogy of Hope: Reliving Pedagogy of the Oppressed*, as in several other texts, extensive notes are provided by Freire's wife, which again adds to the personal-existential sense of what is going on. So this is the hermeneutic context for *Pedagogy of Hope*. But what does the book actually say more formally?

The subtitle of the book captures immediately what Freire is driving at: *Reliving Pedagogy of the Oppressed*. This is a 'reliving' and it is so, as Freire makes clear from the beginning, because 'The debates in which I shared in the 1970s are as current today' (Freire, 1992, p. 4). Freire makes reference explicitly to the 'fear of freedom' debate which is a key part of *Pedagogy of the Oppressed* (Chapter 1), a fear that afflicts both oppressor and oppressed alike (Freire, 1992, p. 4). There, the reference is to Erich Fromm but also to Sartre and Fanon, and we again see the complexity of Freire's influences, his 'eclecticism, or drawing from many wells' as John Elias puts it (Elias, 1994, p. 3). In talking of the 'fear of freedom', Freire of course also implicitly makes clear that one of his paradigmatic ideals is freedom itself, which, as was suggested earlier, could be seen as problematical. What kind of freedom are we talking about here? Is this not a liberal rather than a socialist or communitarian notion?

Given that the original *Pedagogy of the Oppressed* was written in 1968, when the claims of freedom were at their strongest, it is interesting that Freire returns to this theme in *Pedagogy of Hope: Reliving Pedagogy of the Oppressed*, 20 years later, and revisits it. But Freire's work provides the possibility of a slightly different reading here. Freire refers to a simultaneous 'tyranny of liberty and the tyranny of authority' (Freire, 1992, pp. 14–15), where both are seen as polar opposites. Instead we should, Freire intimates, be looking to a dialectical understanding of the relationship between freedom and authority. More empirically and practically in contexts of education, Freire is also keen, now in 1992, to point to how the politics of education has little changed. He asserts the continued importance of the theme of 'the urgency of the democratization of the public school' (Freire, 1992, pp. 14–15). Freire is here talking in the context of an ongoing battle through the 1970s and 1980s, thematized explicitly by Freire's followers in America, those who have developed his legacy, such as Henry Giroux in particular (Giroux, 2000), where the battle for public spaces became acute with a turn towards the New Right. This was made all the more contentious insofar as several of the key figures here had been ex-gauchists. Freire has been strongly connected to this issue which of course is also a question of the status of progressivism in American schools, and education more globally. As Darling and Nordenbo (Darling and Nordenbo, 2003) show, progressivism is a complex idea in education and politics, and there is certainly a backlash against the kind of progressivism associated with Dewey and thus Freire (who practices according to McLaren a 'new Deweyism' (McLaren,1989)) in the 1980s. Freire here makes clear that 'only a radical politics, not a sectarian one however, but one that seeks a unity in diversity amongst progressive forces, could ever have won the battle for a democracy that could stand up to the power and virulence of the Right' (Freire, 1992, p. 29). This is a clear statement of continuity with the earlier work and especially the famous Preface on sectarianism versus radicalization which I looked at in Chapter 1 (Freire, 1996a). Of course, as we saw in Chapter 2, this theme had already been developed clearly in Freire's early work (Freire, 2005a; 2005b). Can we see a difference in the tonality of this new affirmation of progressivism? Certainly much has changed since

1968 on this issue and perhaps the more explicit affirmation of a 'unity in diversity of progressive forces' marks this need to take sides in a stratified debate, in the USA most especially. What this also pinpoints, and this is a point reiterated by several critics, for example, Torres (Torres, 1993), is that although Freire's work is associated with revolution, it depends, owing to its progressivism and unequivocally democratic principles, on a parliamentary democracy to be a possibility. This is made clear in the later work although at times the tension between reformism and revolution in the earlier work is more intense (Quinn, 2010).

Similar themes emerge which were present in the earlier work but which are now reaffirmed through the description of an empirical context of education and politics: 'these peasants know more than we do' (Freire, 1992, p. 32). All the way through Freire's work there has been this questioning of the status of the 'expert' and the vehement critique of 'false charity' which we see in *Pedagogy of the Oppressed*. Again, in this context, we see the affirmation not of pessimism or of violence but rather of love (which anticipates Badiou among others): 'the genuine revolutionary is animated by feelings of love' (Freire, 1992, p. 34). The latter is a quotation from Che Guevara, who remains a key 'radical' hero for Freire. However, the critical edge of Freire's work survives and it is the subtle balance between respecting and also questioning and challenging the student that is most obvious in this context.

Respect not submission

As Freire notes, 'a respect for the peasants' ingenuousness does not mean that an educator must accommodate to their level of reading the world' (Freire, 1992, p. 36). That is, this is not submission to the student's word; the role of the teacher remains but as a questioner most of all, and Freire also stresses the role of 'dialogue' as constitutive (Freire, 1992, p. 36). We have already seen the importance of Fanon (Fanon, 1986b) for Freire's analysis in Chapter 4. Here in *Pedagogy of Hope* (Freire, 1992), it is not surprising to see Fanon again invoked in an important way: 'step back from the adherence of the oppressed to the oppressor, and localize the oppressor outside themselves as Fanon would say' (Freire, 1992, p. 39). And in a way that connects several important themes that we have been looking at; Freire tells us 'let us be postmodern; radical and utopian; progressive' (Freire, 1992, p. 40). We have seen how crucial the 'postmodern' is in Freire. We will return to this thematic in significant detail in Chapter 7, in relation to Freire's respective relations to the CCCS, the critical pedagogy movement and the whole politicization of education (Irwin, 2010b). With regard to radicalization, we can see the explicit reference back to the Preface of the *Pedagogy of the Oppressed* text.

While this work of *Pedagogy of Hope* obviously reiterates much of *Pedagogy of the Oppressed*, we should also be clear that, at a meta-level, this is definitely not just restatement: 'I wrote *Pedagogy* in 1967/1968; now in 1992, I want to look at it again, rethink it, restate it; and to do some new saying as well; by speaking of hope' (Freire, 1992, p. 39). That is, this new book involves itself in a 'new saying' which should not be underestimated. In some ways, what Freire is doing is drawing out elements which were present in the earlier work but which have been reinterpreted somewhat or reemphasized. For example, Freire speaks of the 'meeting between Erich Fromm and Ivan Illich' where Fromm described the shared practice of their work thus: 'this kind of educational practice is a kind of historico-cultural, political psychoanalysis' (Freire, 1992, p. 44). Of course, psychoanalysis is important in the early work but here, writing in the 1990s, this dimension of the work has become increasingly significant. I am thinking, for example (although Freire does not mention him here) of the importance of Lacan (and neo-Lacanianism) in much of the contemporary political discourse which dovetails with that of Freire, for example, the political theory of Mouffe and Laclau (Mouffe, 2005) or of Žižek (Žižek, 1994).

But, as always with Freire, we return from the high towers of theory to the concrete existential reality of lived experience and especially the lived experience of the student or the peasant. Freire reinvokes his insight from many of his meetings with peasants in Chile following his exile from Brazil; fear of freedom had marked each meeting, flight from the real, 'an attempt to tame the real through concealment of the truth' (Freire, 1992, p. 45). By the same token, this critique must be balanced with respect for the insights which each individual already has, a warning against the kind of teacher condescension which ruins genuine rapport and relation: 'the educator must not be ignorant of, underestimate, or reject any of the knowledge of living experience with which educands come to school' (Freire, 1992, p. 47). In an excellent example, one of his most evocative, Freire quotes a letter: 'an excellent letter from a group of workers in São Paulo; ' "Paul" they said, "keep writing – but next time lay it on a little thicker when you come to those scholarly types that come to visit as if they had revolutionary truth by the tail. You know, the ones that come looking for us to teach us that we're oppressed and exploited and to tell us what to do"' (Freire, 1992, p. 51). Once more, Freire returns to the question of what his meta-level hermeneutic sought to achieve; the need for memory is affirmed but not simply to reattest the past experience: 'stir my memory and challenge it; show you the actual process of my reflection, my pedagogical thought and its development; the consistency between word and deed; not paralysis but consistency which still allows me to change position' (Freire, 1992, p.53). At root, this is a perspective of radical philosophical interrogation: 'a permanent process of search which requires patience and humility; in our dealings with others; at times, we find ourselves lacking these virtues' (Freire, 1992, p. 53). It is a rethinking of the 'soul and body' of the previous text: 'in writing this *Pedagogy of Hope*, in which I rethink the soul and the body of *Pedagogy of the Oppressed*' (Freire, 1992, p. 55).

As so often with Freire, we are bordering on poetics in this context, as Gadotti brings out so well in his poignant book on Freire (Gadotti, 1994), and, all the while, what is being emphasized is 'the knowledge of living experience' (Freire, 1992, p. 57): 'challenge them to go more deeply into the meaning of the themes or content and thereby learn' (Freire, 1992, p. 57). *We thus have a restatement but also a revisiting.* Freire's work doesn't stay still, he refuses to simply agree with his previous sayings but rather than this being a gratuitous element of novelty, it responds to the changing context of politics and political life as well as existential changes. We will see that the importance of this goes beyond Freire's own internal understanding of his genealogy and also inspires the movement of critical pedagogy, insofar as McLaren says what is most powerful about Freire's work is his openness to reinterpretation and his call for such a thing to happen of necessity (McLaren, 1994). Indeed, this is an aspect which relates not simply to postmodern fragmentation but also to the original work of Marx, which, as Balibar has shown so well, already induces real change in the self-understanding of philosophical work (Balibar, 2007).

A matrix of Freirean texts

In this section, I want to look in more detail at the specifics of *Pedagogy of Hope*, which really does act as a kind of fulcrum for Freire's career and *oeuvre*, if we look at it as the hinge which joins together the early work with *Pedagogy of the Oppressed* at the centre and the later work, much of it published posthumously (Freire, 2005d, 2006). But unlike the latter myriad texts, *Pedagogy of Hope* was completed and published during Freire's lifetime and it also looks explicitly at *Pedagogy of the Oppressed* and the genealogy of the latter as central to an understanding of the evolution of this thought as a whole. As stated above, Freire had originally intended to write an introduction to *Pedagogy of the Oppressed* but ended up writing a new book (Elias, 1993, p. 3). We can take from this not simply that Freire felt the need to write something substantially new to explain *Pedagogy of the Oppressed* but also that he was intent on explaining the evolution of his thought since the latter. As well as seeking to answer criticisms of *Pedagogy of the Oppressed,* what makes Freire's thought so interesting (and here especially *Pedagogy of Hope*) is that he often articulates forceful objections to his own work. He is his greatest questioner and critic, and this is captured in the title, 'Reliving Pedagogy of the Oppressed'.

In referring to the book as 'reliving' the original text, we can already see the existential dimension of the book, which is a constant preoccupation of Freire as we know. Grounding the more complicated theoretical issues is the existential dimension. The context in which Freire is writing is now somewhat different from the earlier context of *Pedagogy of the Oppressed*.

There, his main target was the oppressor regimes, or 'director societies' and the way they were maintaining their oppression over developing society (or the 'Third World'). In addition, Freire wanted to lay claim to a certain *universalization effect* here in that it wasn't simply the Third World which was suffering from this predicament but the whole world, and his initial reference to the students' movements on the first page of *Pedagogy of the Oppressed* puts this more globalized perspective into stark relief. Now, as we have seen in our Introduction, for example, we are living in a world that is dominated by quite different educational and political concerns. There, developing a thematic which is powerfully elaborated by Blake *et al.* (Blake *et al.*, 2003b), we saw that the evolution of a 'managerialism' or what Fiachra Long has called the 'rubricist paradigm' in the 1980s and 1990s in education (especially in the UK) had led to a very different set of problems for education (Long, 2008). Indeed, paradoxically, the authors made the point that that this increasing instrumentalism in education had paradoxically led to what they called a 'renewal of theory' (Blake *et al.*, 2003b). In many ways, under the violence of the system of managerialism, the opponents of this new system have been forced to look to theory for greater resources in the attempt to try to draw a broader and enriched picture of education. Freire speaks of a 'pragmatic discourse' holding sway, *a neo-liberal pragmatism which is against dreams*: 'we are surrounded by a pragmatic discourse that would have us adapt to the facts of reality; dreams and utopia are called not only useless but positively impeding' (Freire, 1992, p. 11). Immediately, then, Freire is going on the offensive against this managerialism. Here, already, he is citing the importance of what we have previously described as a 'utopianism' in his work (Freire, 1995b). The connections between dream and reality, where the vision of education allows one to intervene in and change reality, rather than accept the reduced role for the utopian, Freire posits as a necessity for any pedagogy worthy of the name; 'after all they are an intrinsic part of any educational practice with the power to unmask the dominant lies' (Freire, 1992, p. 1). Significantly for our purposes in this chapter, Freire also explicitly links this option to what he terms 'progressivism'; 'but for me, on the contrary, the educational practice of a progressive option will never be anything but an adventure in unveiling' (Freire, 1992, p. 2).

We have already speculated as to the origins of this utopian drive in Freire; some of it seems Hegelian (Hegel, 1979), while some of it is Christian (Gutierrez, 2001). We also know that there was a certain utopianism in Marxism. 'I do not understand human existence and the struggle needed to improve it apart from hope and dream; hope is an ontological need' (Freire, 1992, p. 2). Again, it is clear that Freire is not interested in some kind of narcissistic hope here; or a hope or dream locked into a subjectivist framework. Rather he sees such hope as *ontological*, that is, connected to a much more organic sense of the relation between subject and world and thus against those cynics who would claim that the absence of hope is more true to our cynical human natures. Freire sees this kind of 'hopelessness' as distortion, again foregrounding his humanism, which he sees as a radical humanism. 'Hopelessness is but hope that has lost its bearings; and become a distortion of that ontological need' (Freire, 1992, p. 2). Let us not forget the title of the book – *Pedagogy of Hope*. Does this signal a more positive framework than the earlier work? Certainly the early work has its own affirmativeness, but one may wonder as to whether Freire's work has become more rather than less optimistic over the years. A good test case of this will be in the discussion of Freire's later practical-educational work in Brazil in the next chapter (O'Cadiz *et al.*, 1998). We also see the return to a language of emotion and passion, which we have seen recur throughout Freire's work: '*Pedagogy of Hope* is that kind of book, it is written in rage and love' (Freire, 1992, p. 2).

Progressive postmodernity

Freire seeks to contextualize this work in relation to the thematic of modernity and postmodernity and this is certainly a new emphasis in his later work. As Freire notes, 'it is meant as a criticism of sectarianism. It attempts to explain and defend progressive postmodernity and it will reject conservative, neoliberal postmodernity' (Freire, 1992, p. 4). As well as this more generalized thematic or framework, Freire also wants to look specifically at some of the issues surrounding the very gestation of *Pedagogy* itself. He makes the distinction between *Pedagogy of the Oppressed* as an oral form and *Pedagogy of the Oppressed* as a written text. This is interesting in itself, and broadens out the problematic of writing and speech as binary opposition in Freire which we have already seen Paul Taylor thematize (Taylor, 1994). If *Pedagogy of the Oppressed* was originally an oral work, then it bears a close resemblance even in its written form to some of the later 'spoken word texts' (Freire, 1992, p. 4): 'the first step I will take will be to analyse or speak of the fabric, the texture, the very strands, of the infancy, youth and budding maturity in which *Pedagogy of the Oppressed*, which I revisit in the book, came to be proclaimed, both in oral form and then in writing' (Freire, 1992, p. 4). A second step in this book, this new book, Freire tells us (after this first stage above of revisiting the genealogy of *Pedagogy of the Oppressed*) will be to look at *Pedagogy* itself, its written details, the textuality which is intimately connected to but distinct from the original spoken text. Freire will also look in this context at the stages of the book, both in terms of its publication and its reception (a famous reception; and he says he will also look at some of the more negative reactions to the book): 'Then in a second step in this present book, I shall return to *Pedagogy of the Oppressed*. I shall discuss some of its stages and analyse certain criticisms levelled against it in the 1970s' (Freire, 1992, p. 4). From there, Freire moves to a third stage. In this third stage, Freire wishes to follow the journeys or pathways out of *Pedagogy* or on which *Pedagogy* took him as an author. Here he wants to 'relive' but also he says crucially '*rethink*' some aspects of this process:

> In the third and final step of the book, I shall speak at length of the threads and fabrics whose essence as it were was *Pedagogy of the Oppressed* itself; here I shall practically relive – and basically shall actually be reliving – and as I do so, rethink, certain special moments in my journeys through the four corners of the earth to which I was carried by *Pedagogy of the Oppressed*.
>
> (Freire, 1992, p. 5)

However, as is clear from the phrase 'rethink', this will not be some nostalgia trip for Freire, or some unequivocal affirmation of his approach. Rather, Freire wants to also spell out some of his reservations or questions concerning his own work, and this, of course, is completely in keeping with his problem-posing method. For Freire, philosophy is '*problematization*'; 'perhaps, however, I should make it clear to readers that in taking myself back to *Pedagogy of the Oppressed* and in speaking today of the tapestry of my experience in the 1970s, I do not intend to wallow in nostalgia' (Freire, 1992, p. 5). Rather, Freire says this will be a 'reencounter'; 'instead my reencounter with *Pedagogy of the Oppressed* will have the tone of one who speaks not of what has been but of what is' (Freire, 1992, p. 5). This also connects with his understanding of the history of philosophy as a discipline; *philosophical understanding is historical through and through*. We have not moved very far from the original discussion which is still ongoing today: 'the facts, the debates, the discussions, the projects, the experiments, the dialogues in which I shared in the 1970s all bearing on *Pedagogy of the Oppressed*, seem to me to be as current as do others to which I shall refer; of the 1980s and today' (Freire, 1992, p. 5). This raises the interesting question of the relation between the earlier debates in the philosophy of education and the current debates. Indeed, the very nature of progressivism is also at stake in this context; that is, is the new managerialism really just another kind of traditionalism against which progressivism has always fought? Darling and Nordenbo (Darling and Nordenbo, 2003) put forward a view of progressivism which is context-specific, but as Freire notes, in education debates, some of the co-ordinates have remained significantly consistent from the 1960s and 1970s, through to the 1980s and 1990s. In many respects this is still the case in 2011. The debate around progressivism and traditionalism (dealt with so interestingly by Dewey in his *Experience and Education*) (Dewey, 1973), continues in different guises to the present day.

The politics of education and the primacy of experience

One of Freire's great strengths is his ability to take complex theoretical notions and exemplify their resonance in the context of a very particular situation, as well as vice versa: to take a particular practice and shows its resonance (and relevance) in theoretical argument. Here, he moves on to speak about the concept of a 'fear of freedom', connected to the work of Erich Fromm and Sartre among others (Fromm, 2001), and connects it to the existential experience of parents and children in rural Brazil and Chile (Freire, 2005a; 2005b). As Freire notes of this in terms of his own experience, 'my life with children and their parents and their fear of freedom; and what Sartre calls the connivance of the oppressed with the oppressors' (Freire, 1992, p. 11). Freire cites in this context Sartre's previously discussed (Sartre, 1986) 'Preface' to Frantz Fanon's *The Wretched of the Earth* (Fanon, 1986b). The reference here to the latter is significant, as it is an interesting question as to how much Freire wishes to affirm Sartre's Preface which is controversial to say the least, not least in terms of the question of its affirmation of violence. Freire is also not afraid to look at the complex fabric of texts and authors which are woven through his work: 'the tapestries and fabrics; of Marx, Lukács, Fromm, Gramsci, Fanon, Memmi, Sartre, Merleau-Ponty, Simone Weil, Arendt, Marcuse ... and so many others' (Freire, 1992, p. 11). We have already seen some of these authors in explicit interlocution in Freire's work, while there is an implicit dimension which connects with some of the authors more indirectly.

Freire explicitly thematizes this connection and seems to suggest that the dynamic for him works from the experience out to the theory. In other words, *the experience is primary and constitutive*, which befits his phenomenological approach: 'in this effort to recall moments of my experience – which necessarily, regardless of when they were, became sources of my theoretical reflection' (Freire, 1992, p. 11). We can see this phrase as paradigmatic for Freire: *experience as source of theoretical reflection*. This stands as a helpful paradigm for Freire's approach, for his methodology so to speak, although we also know that we must be cautious when we speak about his 'method'. One thematic we touched on earlier and which Freire returns to here to 'rethink', in *Pedagogy of Hope*, is a change which takes place even within the ambit of Freire's early work, from 1964 to 1970. We can trace this movement, which is not exactly oppositional but which does involve some element of transition, between the early writing of *Education as the Practice of Freedom* (and even *Extension or Communication*) and *Pedagogy of the Oppressed*. In the later text, Freire definitely adopts a more strident revolutionary tone and one feels (and Freire has clarified this issue in some interviews) that his experience of the military coup and exile in Brazil has caused a change in the relation between politics and education. This issue is dealt with explicitly in the later collections of essays from 1985, *The Politics of Education* (Freire, 1985), but it is implicit in *Pedagogy of the Oppressed*. There, education is politicized in a way that is not the case in *Education as the Practice of Freedom*, and even if this does happen in *Extension or Communication*, it is not as clear-cut as in *Pedagogy of the Oppressed*. In the later text one sees the development of a tone and a rhetoric which owes a lot to, and stands beside, the tone and rhetoric of Memmi and Fanon (Fanon, 1986b). 'The writing of *Pedagogy of the Oppressed*, the experience resulted in a learning process of real importance for me; for my theoretical understanding of the practice of political education' (Freire, 1992, p. 13). Freire here then foregrounds the *practice of political education*, whereas before education itself stood as autonomous of politics.

Certainly, in *Pedagogy of Hope*, it seems that the 'rethinking' of *Pedagogy of the Oppressed* marks several shifts: (1) Pointing to the radical connection between politics and education in *Pedagogy of the Oppressed*, which marks a distinction from his earlier work. (2) But the tone in *Pedagogy of Hope* itself rethinking *Pedagogy of the Oppressed* is more conscious of the disconnect or contentious relation between education and politics. If it is not less utopian, it is perhaps less synthesizing, more aware of the specific differences between genres of life. In addition, we can say that increasingly Freire's work shows an awareness of the different contexts of education and *praxis*. One cannot simply import solutions from one area to the next. Although *Pedagogy of the Oppressed* does already acknowledge this to some extent, it is perhaps a little too uncautiously nodding towards a generalized revolutionary pedagogy for all. This, paradoxically, is a view that Freire cautions much more strongly against in other early works such as *Cultural Action for Freedom* and *Extension or Communication*, where the very notion of 'extension' is linked to this attempted generalizability, and where Freire stubbornly speaks against this kind of 'cultural invasion'. This would seem to suggest that Freire's move from generalization to specificity is less a chronological than it is a textual development and more an example of how specific *Pedagogy of the Oppressed* is as a text in Freire's itinerary: more theoretical to be sure and less experientially grounded, but also more polemical, more deeply rooted in existential phenomenology, more radical, more simplifying also to some extent.

Dangers of 'a tyranny of liberty'

Freire here also explicitly thematizes another lesson he has learnt in this process of reliving *Pedagogy*: this political education of which he speaks runs many risks but one of the most important, if not the most important, is the question of democratic and popular accountability to the 'people'. This political education 'must as I have always asserted take careful account of the reading of the world being made by popular groups and expressed in their discourse, their syntax, their semantics, their dreams and their desires' (Freire, 1992, p. 13). 'The people's dreams and desires' must be listened to and cultivated. Freire also makes clear here that this is all the basis of what he calls a *'progressive' political education*. Once more we see the crucial significance of what Freire means by progressivism, and its connection between politics and education, which may vary over time and different contexts in Freire's work. We can wonder, for example, at a comparison between Freire and Dewey on this point. To what extent, for example, does Dewey's view of the relation between politics and education develop over time, and to what extent is Dewey's view progressivist notwithstanding the critique of progressivism, radical as it is, in a text like *Experience and Education* (Dewey, 1973)?

Again, one of the key nodes of this discussion revolves around the question of freedom and authority. In both politics and education, one of the main problems which progressivism faced and which led in many ways (for example, in the UK under Margaret Thatcher) to a managerialism, was the sense that the progressivist emphasis on freedom of the child or student had led to a decline in the value of teaching and to a kind of liberal (or neo-liberal to be more accurate) free-for-all with no substantive philosophy or understanding (we see this genealogy outlined forcefully, for example, in Blake *et al.*, 2003b.) Freire tackles this question head-on here in terms of a dynamic which he refers to as 'the tyranny of authority and the tyranny of liberty' (Freire, 1992, pp. 14–15). The tyranny of authority is clearly a Freirean theme from the beginning and we know how this connects, for example, with his thematic of sadism and masochism, but the tyanny of liberty is not such a key concept in *Pedagogy of the Oppressed*, although it is obviously implicitly there, for example, in the concern that once the oppressed become 'free' they will become like the oppressor. One of the problems which needs to be addressed here is the relationship between the fear of freedom and the 'tyranny of liberty'. How is it possible to remain fearful of freedom but also tyrannical about freedom?

Freire develops his point in more detail:

> As for the relationship between authority and freedom ... we also run the risk either of denying freedom the right to assert itself, thus exacerbating the role of authority; or else of atrophying the latter and thus hypertrophying the former; in other words, we run the risk of succumbing to the seduction or tyranny of liberty, or to the tyranny of authority; thus acting at cross-purposes; in either hypothesis, with our incipient democracy.
>
> (Freire, 1992, p. 14)

Again, the first nodal point is clear; if we exacerbate the role of authority we 'atrophy' freedom. Freedom doesn't exist and we build a whole series of obstacles to its achievements, seemingly insurmountable obstacles which

Freire outlines under the ambit of his thematic of freedom in *Pedagogy of the Oppressed*, for example. But on the other side, we also have a potential problem; 'or else of atrophying the latter [authority] and thus hypertrophying the former [freedom]' (Freire, 1992, p. 14). This is a less thematized version of Freire's thought, that is, the danger of 'hypertrophying the former[freedom]', of overemphasizing freedom, but it is as clear here as, and mutually dependent with, the critique of authoritarianism. We should also note that neither side of this dynamic consistutes a critique of the value per se, whether we are talking about authority as such or freedom as such.

If we 'atrophy' authority, we run the risk of 'hypertrophying' freedom, and it is clear that although one of Freire's major concerns is to develop an affirmative concept of freedom, he does not want to affirm the value of freedom per se in isolation (here we might cite *the dialectical character of Freire's thought*). Second, it is clear that although the analysis of the concept of authority in this context seems to give the impression of a critique of authority per se (which is often seen as vehement and unequivocal, and associated with Freire's critique of imperialism), this is not Freire's intention. Rather there is a real danger of all sources of authority being devalued in a society in 'transition' or in 'crisis', if all such authority 'atrophies', to use Freire's own terms. Thus, Freire is a theorist of freedom, of the need for freedom, but *also of the need for authority.* This reminds no one more than of Hegel (Hegel, 1979) and his discussion of the relation between freedom and authority, and indeed of the relation between the individual and society. Freire makes clear then, here in *Pedagogy of Hope*, that he should not be understood to be emphasizing freedom at the expense of authority: 'this was not my position then and it is not my position now' (Freire, 1992, p. 14). This is clearly a riposte to those who would accuse him of an excessive progressivism of freedom.

The question of a Freirean turn? – 'better foundations'

Freire also makes clear in this context that in a comparison between his earlier work and his later phase of work there is no clear 'turn' or line of demarcation, although there is perhaps a change of emphasis or context which leads to 'better foundations'. This connects integrally to Freire's paradigmatic theme of the 'democratization of the public school'. As he notes, 'And today as yesterday while on perhaps better foundations than yesterday, I am completely persuaded of the importance, the urgency of the democratisation of the public school' (Freire, 1992, p. 14). Thus the relationship between authority and freedom must bring about the democratisation of the public school rather than its annihilation (here we perhaps see a key difference with Illich (Illich, 1971)) or the usurpation of the teacher's role or the teacher's authority per se (as may often be suggested by the more vulgarized interpretations and critiques of progressivist education and pedagogy).

This is a key point. There is an undoubted scaremongering in some of the vehement critiques of progressivism which may be seen to be characteristic of a certain New Right tendency in education, especially since the Thatcher era in Britain (Bell, 1973). Thus, for example, a paradigmatic scapegoating of this theory suggests that it leads to the 'eradication of the teacher's role'. However, Dewey's own distancing from such a view in *Experience and Education* (Dewey, 1973) demonstrates the perennial nature of this criticism. Dewey contends that his own view actually represents a 'multiplied' and more complex role for the teacher, as opposed to any annihilation or denigration of the pedagogue. This is also, in the main, Freire's view in both theory and practice. We see the practical dimension of this view in Freire's work in Brazil, discussed in detail in Chapter 6, where the teachers really are understood as autonomous agents in the process of pedagogical transformation at ground level (O'Cadiz *et al.*, 1998). However, a key difference between Dewey and Freire on this point is that the former distinguishes such a view from progressivism which he seems happy to associate with the kind of vulgarized critique emanating from traditionalism. *Freire, on the other hand (and more cogently in my view), defends such a multiplied and complex role of the teacher precisely in the name of a progressivism.* That is, he clearly refuses to accept the terms of the traditionalist argument. This seems, on my interpretation, both more consistent and more potentially revolutionary in pedagogical terms and also in political terms. We can also see such a view developed in political terms in Freire's work in politics in the Brazilian context, as part of the Workers' Party, where he similarly defends a progressivist leftism against vulgarized critiques of straw man 'communisms' (O'Cadiz *et al.*, 1998).

Again, if we are talking of Freirean inter-texts here, Freire gives another useful reminder of this when he says that this very process of learning, the politics of education we might say, the relation between education and politics, authority and freedom, begins with his early work but reaches some kind of apex in *Pedagogy of the Oppressed*: 'This learning process, this apprenticeship is sketched in *Education as The Practice of Freedom* and becomes explicit once and for all in *Pedagogy of the Oppressed*' (Freire, 1992, p. 17). Freire then explicitly and unequivocally recognizes the singular importance of *Pedagogy of the Oppressed* in his itinerary.

A dialectic of experience and theoretical reflection

One of the most interesting and affecting aspects of *Pedagogy of Hope* is the way in which Freire's dialectic of experience and theoretical reflection, where we start with experience of the world and move to theorize and make sense of it, is emblematized in the very examples he gives from his personal experience of education. One such example, extremely powerful, is that from Recife (Freire, 1992, p. 17), when he speaks of the tensions he experienced in speaking to a group of peasants who were recalcitrant to his supposed expertise, here in the case of speaking to a group of people about authority and freedom, and in this instance the issue of corporal punishment on children. One man stands up and speaks against Freire's emphasis in a respectful but 'searing' manner. Freire had been critical of 'violent punishments' (Freire, 1992, p. 17) in the relation between adults and children. The man spoke about what he had heard and asked the question simply; 'Dr Paulo sir; do you know where people live?' (Freire, 1992, p. 17). As Freire notes, '[in] Recife; a man gave me the most clearest and most bruising lesson I have ever received in my career as an educator; I acknowledge how much I owe to the person described and not just to scholars; it seared my soul once and for all' (Freire, 1992, p. 17). In many respects this experience may be seen as 'generative', to use Freire's own terminology of the whole thematic of relation between the student and teacher, which returns again and again in a kind of haunting of any attempt to formulate a pedagogy of emancipation; 'we cannot enter the process as objects in order later to become subjects'. Thus, there is an indispensability of *subjectivization* in Freire's work: conscientization must begin with subjectivity and work from there, although this is obviously never a subject in isolation from the world.

But, perhaps even more importantly, there is a sense that the educator must constantly 'rethink, relive' in a way that reminds one of Husserl's original phenomenological idea of reactivation or 'rückfrage' (Kearney, 1986). There is a danger that the 'process' gets lost and the contents of education become reified and sterile as products, as Freire makes clear, for example, in his vehement critique of banking education in *Pedagogy of the Oppressed*. Also foregrounded here is the question of power in the relation between educator and educatee. This is a complex balancing act, as Freire has made clear in his example of the issue of the 'tyranny of authority and the tyranny of liberty', which he views as being in a kind of vicious circle or a fatalist co-dependency. On one side lies the problem of the educator who practises an authoritarian approach. On the other is the danger of the individual student experiencing or undergoing a 'tyranny of liberty' or freedom which does away with the authority or need of a teacher's role; that is, where the student is completely freed up from the teacher. At the same time, Freire recognizes that this balance is precarious and, if anything, should be weighted in favour (perhaps very much in favour) of freedom rather than authority. Thus Freire makes the point that, as the student grows in conscientization, the educator must contemplate his or her own demise in the service of the education 'process'.

Class knowledge and class analysis: an existential approach

We also know that Freire's analysis has been keenly felt in the whole dynamic of class analysis, as it has been understood in terms of education and politics. 'This is class knowledge I say now' (Freire, 1992, p. 18). We know that, in recent times, the emphasis on the concept of class analysis and the very concept of class per se has fallen away somewhat in the emphasis on gender and ethnicity, which has become more and more a part of education studies, and often under the influence of a supposed 'postmodernisation' of pedagogy. However, in the first instance this loses sight, for example, of a critique of the very concept of class (or the rigidity of such a notion) within the discourse of neo-Marxism itself, whether we look to the analysis of Mouffe (Mouffe, 2005), Lefebvre (Lefebvre, 2002), and the extended critique of class analysis (at least in its more orthodox form) in the work of the Birmingham CCCS, for example, through Hall and Willis (Hall, 1996a; Willis, 1981), discussed in detail in Chapter 7.

Here, we can say several things. First, that there has been a return to an emphasis on class in recent sociology of education, for example, in Bourdieu (Bourdieu and Eagleton, 1994). But Freire's work is perhaps closer to that of the Birmingham CCCS in its mixture of a Gramscian emphasis on class, with a simultaneous emphasis on the multi-layered and interdisciplinary importance of the concept of culture (Hall, 1996a; Willis, 1981). In terms of critical pedagogy (Giroux, 2000; McLaren, 1994), we can say that there is an analogous emphasis on class, which is also somewhat inflected with the 'postmodern turn'. But what is particularly striking about Freire's analysis here in *Pedagogy of Hope* is the way it works out from a series of stories from Freire's own life experience. His class analysis we might say is 'existentialist'.

As well as an existentialist emphasis, Freire also seeks to link this problematic to the whole theme of 'progressivism':

> it was the culmination of the learning process which I had undertaken long ago; that of the progressive educator, even when one must speak *to* the people, one must convert the 'to' to a 'with' the people. And this implies respect for the 'knowledge of living experience' of which I always speak, on the basis of which it is possible to go beyond it.
>
> (Freire, 1992, p. 19)

Freire also speaks here of an 'existential experience that had a noticeable influence on the development of my pedagogical thought and my educational practice' (Freire, 1992, p. 20). The key to the class analysis, in this context, is a radicalization of the teacher–student relation, not that the teacher authority is undone but that the teacher's authority takes its authority from the students' experience of that authority. Thus authority can only be derived democratically from the people's own assent to the teaching content given. Thus, in this case, Freire's initial reaction to the threat imposed by the reaction from the student is to reassert his expertise over against the ignorance of the student. In talking to his wife Elza on the way back from the Recife event, Freire recounts what he said: 'I thought I'd been so clear I said. I don't think they understood me' (Freire, 1992, p. 20). That is, I was right, they were ignorant; they just didn't have the intelligence to understand my real meaning. His wife's response turns this pedagogical approach on its head: '"could it have been you Paulo who didn't understand them", Elza asked and then went on; "I think they got the main point of your talk; they understood you but they need to have you understand them; that's the question"' (Freire, 1992, p. 19). This retort of Elza to Freire is worth repeating: 'they need to have you understand them; that's the question' (Freire, 1992, p. 19). That is, the teacher must first seek to understand his or her students if they wish to teach them anything. Moreover, *the students will often teach the teacher.*

However, this does not mean that there is no place for teaching; but that the teacher's role is not simply to be the authority over against the students. Rather, authority must be both shared (within reason) and also earned. This dialectic between authority and freedom, teacher and student, thus avoids the twin perils of the tyranny of authority and the tyranny of liberty. But rather than this being some key phrase which can be used as a formula, it must be reworked continuously in the dialectical interplay of educational and political contexts, in pedagogical situations but also within lived, 'existential experience'. This is not simply about education but also about the process of life itself, the flow of existence.

We have spoken of this issue before, where there are clear connections between Freire's understanding of education and his more general philosophical understanding of existential experience, a tendency that of course places Freire in a long line of existentialist thinkers from Sartre to Beauvoir (Sartre, 2007). As Freire notes, 'existential experience that had a noticeable influence on the development of my pedagogical thought and my educational practice' (Freire, 1992, p. 20) and we have seen this throughout the book, with especial reference to the connections to thinkers such as Erich Fromm. At this point of the book, he is excavating his own existential and very personal experience (in a book which seeks to provide a genealogy of the development of *Pedagogy of the Oppressed* as text). Let us remember that one of the drawbacks of that great book was the lack of the process showing in the book; it came to us as a finished product. But Freire, in looking back on his experience, recounts a negative tendency which we do not often associate with his work, a sense of sadness and depression: 'A sense of despair and sadness: I could see the depression coming. This lack of interest in the world, this pessimism' (Freire, 1992, p. 20). Of course, we tend to associate Freire with a critique, a relentless critique of pessimism, especially in *Pedagogy of the Oppressed* and also his whole critique of necrophilia and the 'fear of freedom'. However, we also have in Freire an emphasis on psychoanalysis. Freire significantly does not simply recount this episode as a period of depression. He also speaks about how he tried to overcome such despair; to seek, as he puts it, the 'why of this despair'.

'The why of this despair'

As Freire notes, 'in seeking the deepest why of my pain, I was educating my hope. I worked on my will, invented the concept of hope in which one day I would see myself delivered from my depression' (Freire, 1992, p. 20). He 'invented the concept of hope'; this is very significant for our overall reading of Freire, that his pivotal concept of hope should be formed from within his very native experience of pessimism. This problematic of pessimism is personalized by Freire but there is also an irreducibly socio-cultural (or socio-political) dimension to it, as it is integrally linked to the whole experience of Brazil, in the period of a 'society in transition', as Freire notes. What this section also highlights is the very existentialist nature, the personal nature, of the book *Pedagogy of Hope*, and we know that many of Freire's later works in particular also tend in this direction: towards a more personalized testimony and memory. We can also link this to Gadotti's extraordinary book on Freire (Gadotti, 1994). Here, Freire, as Gadotti will later, returns us to his very experience of childhood, in Jaboatão: 'I went to Jaboatão in quest of my childhood; I saw again the mango trees, the green frons; I saw before me my father dying, my mother in stupefaction; my family lost in sorrow' (Freire, 1992, p. 22). This return to his childhood and to memory is a kind of self-analysis by Freire, where he seeks out the reasons for his depression, for a sorrow which comes to him from he knows not where. Freire tries to seek out the genealogy of such despair and pain; 'I discovered the fabric of my depression. I unveiled the problem by clearly and lucidly grasping its why; I dug up the archealogy of my pain' (Freire, 1992, p. 22).

This very eloquent self-analysis does not work in isolation from Freire's broader understanding of his political and educational task; *the personal is always the political*;

> At the same time as I was struggling with my personal problem, I devoted myself to moving from my discourse about my reading of the world, to them, and moving them, challenging them, to speak of their own reading. Many of them had possibly experienced the same process I had lived through, that of unravelling the fabric in which the facts are given to discovering their 'why', to move from my reading to their reading.
>
> (Freire, 1992, p. 22)

Again, this is a question of power, of allowing others to be facilitated in their own voice rather than to be offered up (or to have imposed) my reading of their predicament and plight. Freire is also clearly here in line with Marx's original 'Theses on Feuerbach' (Marx, 1992a), that the knowledge itself of the problem is not enough; that is, philosophy is never enough. *The point is not to interpret the world but to change it.* But what Freire also makes clear in his reading of this dictum is that, without the interpretation, there could be no action again and again. That is, he rejects per se the value of activism understood in isolation from theory: 'in the domain of socio-economic structures, the most crucial knowledge of reality does not of itself alone effect a change in reality; but the revelation is a step in the right direction' (Freire, 1992, p. 23). This reading of socio-economic structures and the relation between theory and practice and, we might say also the relations between 'base and superstructure', has a lot in common with Gramsci (Gramsci, 1988): 'The revelatory gnosiological practice of education does not of itself effect the transformation of the world; but it implies it' (Freire, 1992, p. 23). This process requires courage and going beyond the paralysis which comes with the fear of risk: 'the word always attempted and never spoken, in the fear of being rejected, also means refusal of risk' (Freire, 1992, p. 23). This refusal of risk, much like the fear of freedom of which Fromm speaks, prevents us from becoming actors in the world. It is based, Freire says, on the very same kind of depression and sorrow which he himself suffered from, and here Freire links the journey of the soul with the nature of politics itself, especially what he sees as the nature of a utopian politics: 'we experience a tumult in our soul, utopia lost, a broken dream, the danger of losing hope' (Freire, 1992, p. 24). Again and again, Freire will speak to us of the need for *utopianism*, but a utopianism that is founded on an authentic hope and a hope invented to overcome a real and very existential despair.

The experience of exile

Another facet of his experience which Freire speaks of here is his experience of exile. Indeed, Freire speaks movingly of his 'preoccupation': 'A preoccupation [in exile] with the original context; how to wrestle with the yearning without allowing it to turn into nostalgia; how to invent a new way of living and living with others' (Freire, 1992, p. 24). We see the affirmation of an authentic yearning and preoccupation while also critiquing or distancing himself from a more nostalgic way of living, which he seems to see as pathological. This resonates with his earlier discussion in the Preface to *Pedagogy of the Oppressed* of the differences between sectarianism and radicalization. Sectarianism is a form of nostalgia, but avoiding nostalgia does not mean avoiding the past or one's own roots. Significantly here, Freire speaks of an *'education of longing'*; 'to live with it but to educate it too' (Freire, 1992, p. 24).

He develops this point in more detail: 'Basically it is very difficult to experience exile; to live with longing and to educate it too. The education of longing has to do with the transcendence of naively excessive optimism' (Freire, 1992, p. 24). In this context we see the invocation of transcendence, which we know has been a problematical term for Freire throughout his work. All the while, it is the critical spirit which Freire seeks to keep alive: 'Subjected to long interrogations, I reflected on the education of longing; it would be terrible to let the critical view be killed' (Freire, 1992, p. 24). All the while, he is reflecting on his experiences which are very personal. We can also locate these experiences in the general framework we have of Freire's biography. We know that his exile began in Bolivia and then continued in Chile. He speaks of his arrival in Chile: 'November 1964 – arrival in Chile; begins work with Jacques Chonchol' (Freire, 1992, p. 26), who would later become Minister of Agriculture in the Allende government, and who wrote the Preface to *Extension or Communication*, which we discussed in detail in an earlier chapter. When Freire goes back to Chile in the early 1970s, there has been the 'arrival of Christian democratic government' (Freire, 1992, p. 26). While the Chileans seem optimistic about the future, Freire is more sceptical and his fears are borne out as legitimate: 'September 1973: the Chilean armed forces staged a military coup; the perversity and cruelty then came crashing down on Chile in 1973' (Freire, 1992, p. 26).

Freire uses his experience of the Chilean situation and the failure of the revolution there to return to his more general problematic of the difference between sectarianism and radicalization. What would have worked there, he says, 'would have been only a radical politics; not a sectarian one however but one that seeks a unity in diversity among progressive forces' (Freire, 1992, p. 29). It was this kind of radical politics that could deal with 'the virulence and power of the Right' (Freire 1992, p. 29) and which could have won the 'battle for democracy' (Freire, 1992, p. 29). However, instead of this radicalization of politics, the Chilean situation depicted only what Freire sees as 'sectarianism': 'instead there was only sectarianism and intolerance; the rejection of differences. Tolerance was not what it ought to be, the revolutionary future that consists in a peaceful co-existence with those who are different, in order to wage a better fight against the adversaries' (Freire, 1992, p. 29). 'A peaceful co-existence with those who are different' – this was never achieved. This seems to be *tolerance* as Freire understands it, a kind of authentic multicultural tolerance.

As often with Freire, the thematic returns to the question of language and literacy: 'here is one of the central questions of popular education; that of language as a route to the invention of citizenship' (Freire, 1992, p. 30). We have also seen Freire mention repeatedly the problematic or concept of 'invention', here in the case of an 'invention of citizenship'. If we think of the age-old problematic of invention versus discovery, we can better understand the significance of this thematic in Freire's work: that we cannot simply rely on some kind of objectivist ontology in order to be able to discover a real and new citizenship. Rather, it must also rely on a subjective creativity and invention, never working in subjective isolation (or 'narcissism') but rather in a truly *dialectical* relationship with the objective. This dialectic for Freire, inherited as we have seen to some extent from Hegel (Hegel, 1979) and Marx (Marx, 1992a) especially, provides the material basis for the dreams or utopianism of the people.

A finer, less ugly world

As Freire (1992, p. 3) notes,

> I still have in my memory today, as fresh as ever, snatches of the discussions by peasants and expressions of their legitimate desires for the betterment of their world; for a finer less ugly world, a world whose 'edges' would be less "rough", in which it would be possible to love. Guevera's dream, too, 'for a finer less ugly world; in which it would be possible to love'.

The dialectic here between utopianism and political materialism or even pragmatism is powerful. What it also points to is a real democracy at the heart of Freire's work, a notion of radical democracy or what he sometimes calls democratic socialism (for example, this is the political ideology underlying his work with the Brazilian Workers' Party) (O'Cadiz et al., 1998)). This, in effect, is what *Pedagogy of Hope* means: a hope in the people's understanding and innate intelligence which refuses to be subdued or destroyed by the failures of government and authority; 'the peasants know more than we do' (Freire, 1992, p. 32). This 'reading' or 'writing' of the world is not simply a transcription of what is already there but also a *futural transformation*: 'the reading and writing of the word would always imply a more critical rereading of the world as a [prelude] ... to the rewriting – the transformation – of that world; hence the hope that necessarily steeps *Pedagogy of the Oppressed*' (Freire, 1992, p. 33). Significantly, Freire also links this issue and problematic here to the wider problematic of multiculturalism or interculturalism: 'respect for cultural differences; a criticism of "cultural invasion", of sectarianism, and a defence of radicalness, of which I speak in *Pedagogy of the Oppressed*, originated in Brazil and deepened in Chile' (Freire, 1992, p. 34).

Significantly, Freire makes a further connection to May 1968: 'in May 1968 came the student movements in the outside world; rebellious, libertarian; there was Marcuse, with his influence on youth' (Freire, 1992, p. 33). Freire uses this as a possibility of generalizing to a conclusion about his teaching methodology itself: 'respect for the student does not mean that the educator must accommodate to their level of the reading of the world ... the great political importance of the teaching act ... the students must take themselves as co-signing subjects' (Freire, 1992, pp. 36–37). *The students as co-signing subjects with the teachers*: this is a statement which goes to the very heart of Freire's enterprise and demonstrates the radical equality at the heart of his project which, for example, contrasts with more qualified understandings of this relation in thinkers such as Buber and Dewey, but which might also be related to the latter. By the same token, it may be seen to connect more readily with more recent radical work connected from continental theory to theory of education, most obviously the work of Jacques Rancière (Rancière, 1991).

Working with students: Freire's stories

So as to epitomize the pitfalls of this relation, at several junctures in his existential analysis in *Pedagogy of Hope*, Freire recounts stories of working with peasants in Brazil and Chile. Repeatedly, there was the retort from the peasants when asked to speak in their own voice 'that you know and I don't'. Freire turns this back into a question: 'why do I know and you don't?' (Freire, 1992, pp. 38–39). 'Because of the will of God', comes back the answer, after an ensuing discussion of the 'the relationship of God to the people'. And, subsequently, 'no God isn't the cause of this; it's the boss' (Freire, 1992, pp. 38–39). As Freire sees it, 'those peasants were making an effort to get beyond the relationship of oppressor to oppressed; in order to step back from the oppressor and to localise the oppressor outside themselves; as Fanon would say' (Freire, 1992, p. 39). Through this analysis, which is both existential and socio-political, Freire believes progress is being made in what we might term 'critical consciousness'; 'an understanding of the social relations of production; an understanding of class interests, and so on' (Freire, 1992, p. 39).

Freire reiterates here the dictum that 'the educator must not reject any of the knowledge of living experience of educands' (Freire, 1992, p. 47). This is an oft-cited and very significant view of his which shows once more his suspicion of the power relations which obtain between educators and educatees, and how his own work seeks to constantly transgress the elitism of this relation. Freire also gives us an interesting insight into the publishing genealogy of *Pedagogy of the Oppressed*. He tells us it was 'Pedagogy of the Oppressed written in Chile in 1967/1968, published in English in 1970, only published in Brazil in 1975' (Freire, 1992, pp. 50–52). The meta-level *raison d'être* of *Pedagogy of Hope* is to rethink not simply *Pedagogy of the Oppressed* but Freire's whole intellectual and educational trajectory. Freire tells us that this requires great 'patience and humility' (Freire, 1992, p. 53) as it involves a lot of 'changing position' (Freire, 1992, p. 53). This again we may say is emblematic of Freire's postmodernism rather than his modernism. One such example of a need to change position which Freire cites himself here is the problematical issue of 'sexism', which of course bell hooks (hooks, 1994) emblematically raises in her respectful but critical interlocution with Freire's early work. Indeed,we know that this has been a very complicated and contested element of some of Freire's reception, most especially in North America. Freire honestly and unequivocally makes clear in this connection his 'rejection of sexism' (Freire, 1992, p. 55) but in order to do so he had to 'rethink the soul and body of *Pedagogy of the Oppressed*', which, for many, was riven with a kind of sexism, albeit only in certain aspects of the language. Freire, however, makes clear here his view that language is not just some adjunct, but rather integral to his meaning:

> Language's aesthetic moment, it has always seemed to me, ought to be pursued by all of us, including rigorous scholars; there is not the least incompatibility between rigor in the quest for an understanding and knowledge of the world, and beauty of form in the expression of what is found in that world.
>
> (Freire, 1992, p. 59)

The ethics of education and the 'stimulation of the contrary view'

Freire now undertakes an analysis of the educational process itself, pointing out its tensions and also its directionality towards knowledge and insight. For Freire, this process of education is *inherently ethical*: 'what especially moves me to be ethical is to know that inasmuch as education of its very nature is directive and political, I must, without ever denying my dream or my utopia before the educands, respect them' (Freire, 1992, p. 65). This is the challenge – to be both directive and political, while also respecting the experience and autonomy of the educands, their position as co-signatories: 'to defend a thesis, a position, a preference with earnestness, defend it rigorously but passionately as well, and at the same time to stimulate the contrary discourse, and respect the right to utter that discourse' (Freire, 1992, p. 65). 'To stimulate the contrary discourse' – this is one of the emblems of Freire's discourse, which perhaps explains his constant recourse to dialogue, and to co-authored books and interviews where his work can be challenged more and there is thus a shunning of didacticism. *The stimulation of the contrary view* which is simultaneously accompanied by an affirmation of the directive and politicized nature of education is what marks out Freire's discourse as distinctive. It is also, Freire tells us, *'the best way to teach'* (Freire, 1992, p. 65).

Thus we may speak of the two-pronged nature of any political and educational enterprise or project:

> First the right to have our own ideas, even our duty to quarrel for them, for our dreams; and second mutual respect ... respecting them means on

the one hand testifying to them of my choice and defending it; and on the other, it means showing them other options, whenever I teach – no matter what it is.

(Freire, 1992, p. 65)

It is this 'stimulation of the contrary view' and 'showing other options' that is perhaps the most powerful aspect of Freire's work and which marks it out as truly democratic and 'radical' as opposed to 'sectarian', to use his own distinction (Freire, 1996a). Freire undertakes an analysis of education here that points to the need for an inter-connected pedagogy which doesn't just look to discrete units or specializations. Rather, in each case, in the case of each subject area, the teacher must also look to what Freire calls the 'historico-social cultural and political' frameworks: 'let it not be said that if I am a teacher of something [e.g. biology] that I must not "go into other considerations"; that I must only teach biology, as if the phenomenon of life could be understood apart from its historico-social cultural and political framework' (Freire, 1992, p. 65). This leads to Freire's famous phrase that a 'reading of the word is also a reading of the world'. For Freire, no education can be neutral; my ethical duty, as one of the agents of a practice that can never be neutral – the educational – is to express my respect for differences in ideas and positions. 'I must respect even positions opposed to my own; positions that I combat earnestly with passion' (Freire, 1992, p. 66). But Freire is careful here not simply to single out the right wing in education. Rather, he is also very critical of the Left, which he sees as often just as guilty of the sectarianism which he is critiquing. This sectarianism is founded in an arrogance and conceit.

The authoritarianism of intellectuals: proprietors of revolutionary knowledge

As Freire notes, one of his tasks is 'to criticise the arrogance, the authoritarainism of intellectuals, of left or right, who are both basically reactionary in an identical way' (Freire, 1992, p. 66). Both Left and Right seek to take property over knowledge; they seek to own it and simply deliver it predetermined in hand to the people. As we know, this is one of the key criticisms Freire makes of banking education, most especially in *Pedagogy of the Oppressed*; that is, the complete lack of democracy in education. These educators, or so-called educators, thus 'judge themselves the proprietors of knowledge, the former (left) of revolutionary knowledge; the latter (right) of conservative knowledge' (Freire, 1992, p. 66). This is an important passage Freire is citing from *Pedagogy of the Oppressed*, as it highlights the power dynamics in the relation between teacher and student which Freire tirelessly brings to light. Here, the issue is how the process of conscientization takes place, or more accurately, how, under the supposed ambit of conscientization, it doesn't take place and is stunted by an inadequate form of pedagogy. Thus there is a need to criticize the behaviour of university academics, Freire tells us, who claim to be able to 'conscientize' rural and urban workers without having to be conscientized by them as well: 'One must criticise an undisguisable air of messianism, at bottom naive, on the part of intellectuals, who in the name of liberation of the working classes, impose or seek to impose the "superiority" of their academic knowledge on the "rude masses"' (Freire, 1992, p. 66). This goes to the heart of the politics of the university and the relationships between teachers and students. It goes to the heart of the politics of knowledge and the knowledge economy. It also connects especially to May 1968 and, for example, to Lyotard's attack on the university (Lyotard, 1993; Irwin, 2010b). We see Freire return to this thematics of the university in his later work at the University of Mexico (Freire *et al.*, 1994). Given what he has already said about the Left and the Right, it is clear that this critique of 'messianism' is especially directed at such messianism on the Left, all so well intentioned but so destructive of any authentic notion of a democracy in education. This critique also extends beyond the university to embrace the very nature of being a public intellectual. The whole issue of 'liberation' of the working classes is foregrounded here, the rhetoric of liberation which can often mask ulterior motives of self-aggrandisement, and here we see connections between Freire and Nietzsche, among others (Nietzsche, 1998). Freire refers in this context to the 'superiority of their academic knowledge' and their need and desire to 'impose', again suggesting the authoritarianism at the heart of the desire to liberate. Freire also makes clear just how crucial this dimension is in his thinking; this critique of power. It is not something ancillary but at the very heart and foundation of his most famous book, *Pedagogy of the Oppressed*; 'this I have always done; of this I speak, and almost of nothing else, in *Pedagogy of the Oppressed*, and of this I speak now with the same insistence, in *Pedagogy of Hope*' (Freire, 1992, p. 66).

So here we see the link or another link between the two books and a continuity in Freire's work, early to late, manifested in this notion of the 'same insistence'. Once more, *power* is the key issue, this time the power of the universities and public intellectuals in the quest to liberate the working classes from their plight; the 'rude masses', as Freire refers to them. Many of his critics see the route to the defeat of such educational practices in the 'fantasy' (on Freire's terms, at least) of a denial of the political nature of education. However, this denial of the politics of education, this emphasis on the neutrality of education, the value of free education which we see manifested most hegemonically now in the emphasis on a new managerialism in more recent educational discourse (Blake *et al.*, 2003b), must be combated.

A postmodern progressivism/a postmodern Marxism

One of the more interesting aspects of *Pedagogy of Hope* (Freire, 1992), and something which does distinguish it quite forcefully from *Pedagogy of the Oppressed*, is Freire's new emphasis on the importance of an understanding of the distinction between the moderns and the postmoderns, where one might have expected Freire to emphasize the modernist aspects in favour of the postmodernist. The opposite is the case in *Pedagogy of Hope*. Here, for example, he says: 'in a like perspective – indisputably progressive, much more postmodern, as I understand postmodernity, than modern, let alone "modernizing" – to teach is not the simple transmission of knowledge concerning the object or concerning content' (Freire, 1992, p. 67). Thus, Freire is seeking to indicate his favoured notion of pedagogy, which must never be neutral but rather always political, and thus politically progressive. For Freire, it seems that this progressivism can only be postmodern rather than modern. *'Much more post-modern than modern'* – his words are unequivocal in this context although he does leave the important proviso; 'as I understand postmodernity'.

He is once again critiquing the delivery model or banking model of education. Here, he is indicating clearly that for this model to be overcome, (that is, for banking education to be overcome) requires a progressive postmodernism in education. This connects with a renewed model of teaching which Freire wishes to emphasize: 'teaching – again, from the postmodern progressive viewpoint of which I speak here' (Freire, 1992, p. 67). This then is a postmodern and progressive model of teaching, which Freire wishes to oppose to banking education and which he referred to in *Pedagogy of the Oppressed*, as a problem-posing method of education. 'Teaching is a creative act, a critical act and not a mechanical one … educands become the ever more critical subjects' (Freire, 1992, p. 68). Critical subjectivity is thus key to the very notion of education which must be a facilitation rather than an imposition. This is what constitutes the very sense of a progressive education and pedagogy.

One of the other powerful and recurrent elements of Freire's writings and educational practice is the interconnectedness within his work as a whole. Here, he now returns us to the specificity of another key text which we have discussed earlier, that is, *Education as the Practice of Freedom* (Freire, 2005a).

'My first book ... Education as the Practice of Freedom'

As Freire observes, 'but let us go back to my first book, *Education as The Practice of Freedom*, completed in 1965 and published in 1967' (Freire,

1992, p. 74). Significantly, Freire refers to this as 'his first book'. In this text, Freire outlines how certain thematics developed which were going to be formative for his later work: 'local as basis for universal, defence of common sense and popular knowledge which must be the starting point, but not their mythification' (Freire, 1992, p. 76). Again, the subtle point here is worth restating and clarifying: Freire works from a defence of popular knowledge and we should not underestimate how this runs counter to certain strains in emancipatory and Marxist thought, which tend to downplay the popular knowledge as false consciousness or ideology. However, Freire also qualifies here, in an important way, his emphasis on popular knowledge. While the popular culture and class and their integral knowledge is defended, this does not involve 'their mythification' (Freire, 1992, p. 76). In other words, just as one makes a mistake if one underestimates popular knowledge, so too one makes a mistake if one overestimates its power and insights. Freire is always also stressing the need for critique, as accepting knowledge at face value would be unphilosophical and is itself ideological in a negative sense. Freire also stresses here another emphasis which we foregrounded in his first text, *Education as The Practice of Freedom*, that is, an 'emphasis on the individual and subjectivity' (Freire, 1992, p. 76).

Freire goes on to draw some conclusions regarding the implications of class struggle, and our understanding of the very nature and importance of social classes in the struggle for liberation: 'class struggle and social classes are not the motor of history but they are one of the motors' (Freire, 1992, p. 76). This strikes the balance between, on the one hand, rejecting the view (sometimes attributed to postmodernism) that classes are dead, and second, also qualifying the more standard leftist view that social class is the motor of history.

Interestingly, Freire also takes a side-swipe at what he terms 'neoliberal' discourse, and of course this relates back to his constant critique of the Right, which goes back to his earlier work and especially the critique of the sectarianism of the Right in the Preface to *Pedagogy of the Oppressed*: 'the neoliberal discourses, with all their talk of modernity do not have the power to do away with social classes' (Freire, 1992, p. 79). Thus, social class is once again reiterated as one motor, but crucially not the motor of history. For Freire, this is not simply an abstract issue. He speaks of the supposed 'rise of capitalism's excellence' (Freire, 1992, p. 80) and asks 'what excellence is this?':

> 1990 World Bank report; some 30 million children under five years die every year of causes that would not be fatal in developed countries; some 100 million children throughout the world (almost 20 per cent of the age group) fail to complete their primary education. UNICEF [estimate that] ... if current tendencies are maintained more than 100 million children will die of disease and malnutrition in the decade of the 1990s.
>
> (Freire, 1992, pp. 80–81)

He also directs his ire specifically at 'Marxists' who he accuses of smugness and over-certainty: 'what is becoming needful is that Marxists get over their smug certainty that they are modern, adopt an attitude of humility in dealing with the popular classes, and become postmodernly less smug and less certain; progressively postmodern' (Freire, 1992, p. 82). In this critique of smugness, then, and an avowal of less dogmatism and more uncertainty, we have the basis of what Freire calls *a postmodern progressivism*. However, this is not a postmodernism without direction, the ludic postmodernism of which McLaren (McLaren, 1994) speaks (whether justifiably or not). Rather, this is an oppositional postmodernism which none the less affirms its own uncertainties and insecurities.

Freire also seeks to unpack the implicit philosophy underlying his own pedagogy, which he relates to existentialist ideas of the human. First, he affirms that 'in *Pedagogy [of the Oppressed]* a particular anthropology is implicit' (Freire, 1992, p. 82). In a distinction which he often spoke of in his earlier work and which is implicit in *Pedagogy of the Oppressed*, Freire returns here to key distinctions made famous by existentialism, most paradigmatically between the animal and the human but also between the concepts of 'living and 'existence'; 'again existentialism: I cannot understand human beings as simply living. I can understand them only as historically, culturally and socially existing. We step back from existence and seek to know about what we know, the untested feasible that requires us to fight for it' (Freire, 1992, p. 83). This *'untested feasibility'* can only be worked on by humans for whom existence is a project rather than something certain or cyclical. However, while animals merely live cyclically, for humans their existence is a problem, a project.

As always with Freire's work, he does not hide from opposition or criticism but seems to revel in such philosophical conflict or at least foreground the latter critique without difficulty. Here, he mentions one of the most significant criticisms from the Left with regard to his notion of subjectivity and we have already spoken about some of the age-old difficulties in Marxism with the very notion of the individual or subjectivity per se. 'The criticism of Freire's conception of subjectivity in the name of a liberation fatalism' (Freire, 1992, p. 86). This relates also to the whole question of the motor of history and messianism. In affirming these, certain aspects of the Left, Freire believes, have abdicated their historical sense, the sense of contingency, and have also erred on the side of objectivism. However dangerous the emphasis on subjectivity can be, none the less Freire seems to be suggesting that a subjective component of conscientization is not just indispensable but even primary. Again, we see the connections to the early Sartre most especially (Sartre, 2007). This is why Freire advocates what he terms a 'dialectical' understanding of oppression. 'Only in a dialectical understanding of how awareness and the world are given is it possible to comprehend the phenomenon of introjection of the oppressor by the oppressed' (Freire, 1992, p. 90). This notion of 'introjection' is, as we have seen, paradigmatic for Freire and relates to the internalization of the oppressor's characteristics by the oppressed, a point Fanon had made very clearly in his analysis of post-colonial struggle in *The Wretched of the Earth* (Fanon, 1986b), what Freire terms 'the latter's adherence to the former i.e. the oppressor; the difficulty that the oppressed have in localizing the oppressor outside themselves' (Freire, 1992, p. 90).

Unless this is done, the oppressed run the risk of simply repeating the mistakes and brutality of the oppressor against themselves and their peoples and this has been one of the major reasons for the failure of revolutionary struggle in so many countries. We have explored Freire's very interesting analysis of this in his own country of Brazil in *Education as the Practice of Freedom*. Here, he makes the dangers of a pitfall of the Left into dogmatics and sectarianism very clear: 'the discourse and dogmatic practices of the left are mistaken not because they are ideological, but because theirs is an ideology that connives with the prohibition of men's and women's curiosity, and contributes to its alienation' (Freire, 1992, p. 100). In seeking to liberate, the Left actually sometimes connives in alienation, and indeed we know this is also his critique of education. Sometimes education itself, supposedly the great process of humanization and emancipation, actually reinforces alienation. We also know that this is not to be understood in an exclusivist sense within the sphere of education. Educational alienation goes hand in hand with personal and societal alienation.

Inter-subjectivity

This is a key point in terms of not simply affirming subjectivity in isolation but also in affirming an inter-subjectivity: 'I do not authentically think unless others think' (Freire, 1992, p. 90). I simply cannot think for others or without others; it is this implicit dialogical character which unsettles authoritarian mentalities: 'dialogue must work against a consistent tendency to authoritarianism in the struggle against oppression' (Freire, 1992, p. 90). For Freire, it is this sentiment which connects his earlier and later pedagogies: '*Pedagogy of the Oppressed* first saw the light of day twenty four years ago, under the impulse of the sentiment with which, more touched by it and enveloped in it than before, I restate it in this *Pedagogy of Hope*' (Freire, 1992, p. 103). Here, we see the important question raised of Freire's development since the earlier *Pedagogy of the Oppressed*, and we already know that the very question of his early development is itself complex among the thicket of texts which came out in the late 1960s and early 1970s. We now have a clearer sense of what rethinking and recasting *Pedagogy of the Oppressed* 20 years later may mean for some of the tensions in the evolution of Freire's work. For a thinker so steeped in experience and so honest about his questions and self-critique, this is hardly surprising. A large part of his analysis to date in *Pedagogy of Hope*, he says, was concerned with the origins and genealogies of the text *Pedagogy of the Oppressed*. The origins and this process had remained somewhat occluded in the text itself. Now, in the final part of *Pedagogy of Hope*, Freire wants to develop the analysis of the stage which succeeded the publication of *Pedagogy of the Oppressed*. He begins to describe the process which developed out of the publication as follows:

> A great part of the first part of this book has centred on a grasp of certain of the tapestries or frameworks in which *Pedagogy of the Oppressed* took its origin. Now in the latter part of this volume, I shall speak of facts, occurrences, tapestries, or frameworks in which I have shared and am sharing and which have evolved around *Pedagogy of the Oppressed*.
>
> (Freire, 1992, p. 103)

Pedagogy of the Oppressed was published in New York in September 1970, and immediately began to be translated into various languages, as Freire makes clear: 'the book appeared at an intensely troubled moment in history ... a lively loyalty to the meaning of the May of 1968' (Freire, 1992, p. 104). Once again, he reiterates his interest in the 'the progressive postmodern, democratic outlook in which I take my position.' (Freire, 1992, p. 114), and here he links this question explicitly to the problematic of 'multiculturalism'. With regard to the question of multiculturalism, Freire says that there is 'the need for unity in diversity' (Freire, 1992, pp. 133–134). Freire also broadens out the discourse here to include an important intersection or multivalent fulcrum: 'the intersection of race, gender and class divisions and inequalities' (Freire, 1992, p. 136). Next, he speaks explicitly of multiculturality: 'the creation of multiculturality; thus it calls for a certain educational practice. It calls for a new ethics, founded on respect for differences, a unity in differences' (Freire, 1992, p. 137). Finally, he connects this thematic to the issue of religion in Latin America, and specifically the positive influence of the Liberation theology movement on his philosophical development:

> With religious groups the launching pad was the theology of liberation. Both the importance of that theology and the defeat it proposed of accommodation and immobilism through acceptance of the deep meaning of the presence of man and woman in history, in the world, – a world ever to be recreated.
>
> (Freire, 1992, p. 159)

We have also seen Freire foreground the place and importance of the university sector in this struggle and he again returns to this question in this context: 'The university; the universities in Buenos Aires; instruction and research both strove to avoid any dichotomy between them; the universities were beginning to encounter social movements, popular groups, also at the university itself' (Freire, 1992, p. 169). Thus the university, in encountering social movements, could no longer stay detached or value-free in relation to socio-cultural or political change. Like education more generally, the university is political through and through and thus never neutral. Freire develops this point about universities in relation to the whole question of popular decision-making in the political world. The university, Freire is saying, very clearly must not shut itself off from the wider society or the popular world or the popular classes. Quite the contrary, it must, in Sartre's phrase, be engaged.

The university and the popular classes

In an important way, Freire links his emphasis on universities here to the whole problematic of popular knowledge and popular participation, which has been such a recurrent theme throughout his work. As Freire notes, 'more than ever before, political decision making in a progressive mould, ought to be extended into populism, so that a university would place itself in the service of popular interest as well' (Freire, 1992, p. 168). This should not be done in an arbitrary way but only in a critical way. If the previous way of developing knowledge and the university subscribed to a banking model which compartmentalized and alienated, this new approach must be based on what Freire called, in *Pedagogy of the Oppressed,* a *problem-posing approach*. This radical approach must not simply be taken in relation to education but to society itself and the relations between various groups and parts of society: 'this would imply a critical comprehension of how university arts and sciences ought to be related with the consciousness of the popular classes, that is a critical comprehension of the interrelations of popular knowledge, common sense and scientific cognition' (Freire, 1992, p. 168). These interrelations and a critical rather than a passive understanding of these interrelations were, and are, key to developing the debate and moving it forward.

Freire here develops the concept of the university in some detail. He says that the university should have two basic concerns. First, 'the moment of the cognition of existing, already produced knowledge' (Freire, 1992, p. 169); second, 'and the moment of our own production of new knowledge' (Freire, 1992, p. 169). This is significant because, throughout his work, Freire refers not simply to the need for recognition or discovery of the truth but actual 'invention' or here 'production' of the truth which he often connects to creativity and the subjective component of knowing. This then becomes part of the subjective component of emancipation which, for him, as he often reiterates against more traditionalist Marxism, must break with objectivism as the key or motor of history. He refers positively to the university system in Buenos Aires which he thinks has tried to develop this relationship between university knowledge and the relation to the popular classes: 'in Buenos Aires, what was being done was to diminish the distance between the university and what was done there and the popular classes, without the loss of seriousness and rigour' (Freire, 1992, p. 170). Clearly, then, Freire is not advocating some kind of dumbing down (or instrumentalist relation) but a greater democratization, which will not involve the 'loss of seriousness and rigour'. Key and paradigmatic to all of this is not disciplinary specialism but an interdisciplinarity.

Inter-disciplinarity

As Freire notes, 'The quest for an interdisciplinary understanding of teaching; the progressive strategic dream' (Freire, 1992, p. 170). Thus *interdisciplinarity* is linked to progressivism and progressivist pedagogy and, of course, Freire's own educational and philosophical practice bears this out – his eclecticism is often noted and sometimes criticized by more disciplinary-minded scholars and thinkers. Therefore, for Freire, this form of pedagogy, is not just some kind of pipe-dream but has been borne out, for example, in Argentina and indeed in El Salvador to which he also explicitly refers, in its advocation of his thinking in a truly political sense. We can also relate this to Freire's 1990s work in the Ministry of Education in Brazil in the 1990s (O'Cadiz *et al.*, 1998), and we will return to a more detailed evaluation of this below. Here, he refers to El Salvador: 'the trip to El Salvador in 1992; the peace accord where *Pedagogy of the Oppressed* was a book of great import for the historical moment in which they were living' (Freire, 1992, p. 172). We have already seen Freire speak quite positively of postmodernity. Here, near the end of *Pedagogy of Hope*, he wants to reiterate this positive reading of a *postmodernist progressivist pedagogy* but he also wants to clearly and carefully differentiate it from a more reactive reading of postmodernity, as the end of history and the end of ideology: 'in no way however does this mean for a society with this sort of living experience of democracy, the inauguration of a history without social classes; without ideology, as a certain pragmatically postmodern discourse proclaims' (Freire, 1992, p. 175).

This kind of *pragmatically postmodernist* discourse then is not the one that Freire advocates. Against the pragmatically postmodern, as Freire calls it, he proceeds to assert what he sees as the opposite; 'in fact the truth is just the opposite or nearly the opposite: postmodernity as I see it, has a different, substantially democratic way of dealing with the conflict, working out its ideology, struggling for the ongoing and ever more decisive defeat of injustice, and arriving at a democratic socialism' (Freire, 1992, p. 175). Postmodernism, at least as understood in this more progressivist vein, thus amounts for Freire to the advent of a democratic socialism. Here, he reiterates that we must make key distinctions between a postmodernism of the Right and the Left: 'there is a postmodernity of the right; but there is a postmodernity of the left as well. Nor does the latter – as this is almost always insinuated, if not insisted – regard postmodernity as an altogether special time that has suppressed social classes, ideologies, left and right; dreams and utopics' (Freire, 1992, p. 175). Thus Freire is arguing in many respects against some of the elements of the critique of postmodernism that we have seen and will see in the next chapter, which has become synonymous with critical pedagogy and especially McLaren (McLaren, 1994). What Freire seems to be arguing for here is a much more strongly politicized postmodernism.

Postmodernity and the reinvention of power

As he notes, 'postmodernity of the left' (Freire, 1992, p. 175) seeks a 'reinvention of power – and not its mere acquisition, as with modernity'. Again this is very significant, as Freire seems to be dismissing modernity per se or in essence as a more acquisitive and a more banking system of education and of power in society and politics, while postmodernism presents a more positive possibility of 'reinvention', that key term of Freire's occurring again. He also makes clear here that such a postmodernity may involve the affirmation and recognition of social classes: 'this postmodern moment we are living in the 1990s is not a time so utterly special that it knows no more social classes' (Freire, 1992, p. 175). This brings the book to a close but the Afterword, by his wife and fellow philosopher Ana Maria Araújo Freire (written after his death), does add some interesting contextualization to the equation: 'the ban the prohibition imposed on him and on so many other Brazilians; which by way of paradoxical reaction, led him to write *Pedagogy of the Oppressed*; the book that disallows all of the ban forms reproduced in Brazil down through the centuries and indicates the possibility of personal liberation' (Araújo Freire, 1992, p. 180). Here, she seems to see the prohibition (and exile) as central to the inspiration behind the writing of *Pedagogy*, and she also makes the connection to the present *Pedagogy of Hope* in an organic way: 'it is all brought to completion in the present *Pedagogy of Hope*' (Araújo Freire, 1992, p. 180).

For Araújo Freire, it seems that this is a triangle: 'my reading of the world, whose orientation is in terms of this triangle; prohibition, liberation and hope' (Araújo Freire, 1992, p. 180). Yes, there is prohibition but there is also the possibility of liberation for which we must keep hope alive. And, as we have seen again and again in Freire's work, that liberation and the process by which it takes place must be constantly rethought if the very process of liberation, paradoxically but tragically, is not simply to reiterate and reinforce the very problems it set out to solve.

CHAPTER SIX

From the Workers' Party to the Education Secretariat in São Paulo

Paulo Freire and the Brazilian context in the 1990s

Any book which seeks to do justice to Paulo Freire's philosophy must mingle and integrate the theoretical and practical elements of his legacy. Any merely intra-theoretical analysis will fail to do justice to the complexity of Freire's work. By the same token, as he often reiterates, any simple understanding of his work as exclusively an activism would be similarly flawed. One very interesting instance of Freire's practical educational and political practice, which may be understood alongside other very clear practical ventures, for example, his work in Guinea-Bissau (Freire, 1978), was his work in Brazil in the Education Ministry. This took place in the early 1990s, a decade succeeding Freire's return to Brazil and São Paulo, after his enforced exile of 20 years. The Brazilian context of education and politics will be the primary focus of this chapter, as it provides a powerful example of Freire's consistent commitment to the practical implementation of his philosophical ideas, alongside a fascinating test case of whether such ideas are still relevant and applicable in the real world. We will see how his co-founding of, and participation in, the *Brazilian Workers' Party (Partido dos Trabalhadores* or *PT)* is integral to an understanding of his thinking and how the very challenging social and educational context of São Paulo both enables and undermines certain aspects of Freire's vision. But, as those who have worked closely with Freire over the years insistently proclaim, throughout such difficult times it is Freire's character, and the philosophy it encapsulates, which remains resilient and inspiring. As Jonathan Kozol observes with regard to the Guinea-Bissau situation (Freire, 1978), 'the character of Paulo Freire, a character full of warmth, of humble attitude and militant fervour, all in a single man and oftentimes expressed in a single word or phrase' (Kozol, 1978, p. 2). We might remember here Freire's oft-quoted epigram from Che Guevara: 'let me say, with the risk of appearing ridiculous, that the true revolutionary is guided by strong feelings of love'. Moacir Gadotti's wonderfully lyrical text on Freire, *Reading Paulo Freire: His Life and Work* (Gadotti, 1994) also captures this sense of how Freire as philosopher and educator cannot be separated from Freire as person: a vivid presence of dark and light, of joy and righteous anger, which mirrors the great complexities and ambiguities of his own homeland (Torres, 1994, p. ix).

This is nowhere more apparent than in this final stage of Freire's life and work, developing from the moment of his return to Brazil in 1980 and coming to a close with his death in 1997, when he was still working on his final, unfinished and highly charged text *Pedagogy of Indignation* (Freire, 2004). In his 'Letter to Paulo Freire', included in the latter work, (Andreola, 2004, p. xxxvii), the Latin American philosopher Balduino Andreola provides an interpretation of the specificity of Latin American philosophy and its phases, which can help us to contextualize this later period of Freire's writings. Drawing on the work of the Argentinian thinker Gustavo Cirigliano, Andreola speaks of initially three phases of Latin American thought: 'pre-time (aural-oral period of great mobilisation … which preceded the dictatorships), counter-time (period of repression, arrests, exiles and executions) and … the dis-time or time of asynchrony … the time that affected all those who returned from exile during the long, dark night of the military regimes' (Andreola, 2004, p. xxxvii). Understood in this way, we can see Freire's work as occupying each of these phases in turn: some of the early work originates in the 'pre-time', the key work such as *Pedagogy of the Oppressed* is developed during the 'counter-time' and the later work is contextualized by the phase of 'dis-time'. Exploring Freire's work with the *Partido dos Trabalhadores* and at the Secretariat in São Paulo, we thus need to take account of this period of work being subject to rather different forces, socio-cultural and political, than the previous work, what we can call a 'dis-time', a time of asynchrony, which is emblematic of the rather enigmatic period in Brazil, and Latin America more generally, which followed the time of repression and dictatorship. However, Andreola introduces a further complication. Drawing on Cirigliano's work on Freire's *Pedagogy of Hope*, Andreola cites Cirigliano's observation that 'Paulo Freire has broken with dis-time because he has not lost his word, and that is a feat in our continent' (Andreola, 2004, p. xxxvii). Freire is thus seen as exemplary of a Latin American philosopher who has managed to move to a new period, where he has developed a progressivism which refuses the 'intellectual retreat' (Andreola, 2004. p. xxxvii) of many of his compatriots. This chapter will seek to explore this understanding of Freire's work in the context of both his political involvement in the Workers' Party and his subsequent work at the Education Secretariat. In the first case, I will explore some of the political background to Freire's involvement in the Brazilian Workers' Party which then provides the basis of his work at the Education Secretariat in São Paulo.

The Workers' Party

In their excellent book, *Education and Democracy: Paulo Freire, Social Movements and Educational Reform in São Paulo*, O'Cadiz, Wong and Torres (O'Cadiz *et al.*, 1998) look in detail at Freire's work during this period from both a theoretical and a practical perspective, and I will draw on this work extensively in this chapter. Torre's work especially (Torres, 1993; Freire and Torres, 1994; Torres, 1994) has focused in depth over the years on Freire's theoretical approaches and so he is well placed to analyse the relation between theory and practice during Freire's later political involvement in Brazil. Even the acknowledgements tell a tale in this book, being evocative and unusually personalized towards Freire as an individual. First, Pia Linquist Wong acknowledges how '*Pedagogy of the Oppressed* changed the way I thought about the educational process' (O'Cadiz *et al.*, 1998, p. xi) '[and] showed me that formal learning can indeed be a joyful and transformative act'. She also speaks of her newborn child whose birth makes her 'more determined than ever to do what I can to make this world [in the words of Paulo Freire], "less ugly, less cruel and less inhumane"' (O'Cadiz *et al.*, 1998, p. xii). Similarly, her co-author Pilar O' Cadiz states that 'finally, I would like to express my eternal indebtedness to Paulo Freire for providing me – since I first read *Pedagogy of the Oppressed* 17 years ago – with the philosophical foundation of a critical-utopian outlook on living, learning and knowing' (O'Cadiz *et al.*, 1998, p. xiii). We have seen throughout how this notion of a '*critical utopian outlook*' permeates Freire's work. O'Cadiz also makes reference to Freire's concept of being a parent, in this case in relation to the situation of her daughter's autism:

> Having finished this book one year after my youngest daughter Cala was diagnosed with autism, I believe that my Freirean foundation provides an enhanced perspective on how to seek at all times new ways in which to teach and learn with my daughter. Under these circumstances, Freire

would point to the obvious, to the eternal conflict between our being and acting in the world.

(O'Cadiz *et al.*, 1998, p. xiii)

This again shows the existential depth, both the practical and theoretical dimension to Freire's philosophy, and their constant symbiosis. Freire, for example, explicitly engages what he terms the 'ethics of parenting' in his last text, *Pedagogy of Indignation* (Freire, 2004, pp. 10–13). O'Cadiz goes on:

Knowledge is co-created among men and women in the world: knowledge is power and power can liberate. This is because we know not only with our minds – the neurological makeup of our organic brains – but with our bodies, our sense, our soul, with the history of those who came before us and with a vision of what we imagine the future to be.

(O'Cadiz *et al.*, 1998, p. xiv).

This integrated vision of Freire's work gives the lie to those who would see his work as too abstract, or too cerebral. This book is co-authored by Carlos Alberto Torres, a noted scholar of Freire, who makes mention of Moacir Gadotti's book on Freire (also built on a lifelong collaboration). 'In my many dialogues with Moacir, I have learned philosophy and pedagogy but he has also taught me that, as the book of Proverbs said, "when there is no vision, the people perish"' (O'Cadiz *et al.*, 1998, p. xv). This highlights the clear connection between Freire and Gadotti during the practical years of educational and political policy in São Paulo, from the participation in the Workers' Party to the involvement at the Education Secretariat. As Torres observes, 'I acknowledge here Moacir Gadotti, a man of vision, who as Freire's Chief of Staff at the Secretariat of Public Education in São Paulo, was responsible for many of the wonderful experiences that we critically analyse here' (O'Cadiz *et al.*, 1998, p. xv). We will refer to Gadotti's own powerful existential and political interpretation of Freire (Gadotti, 1994) throughout this chapter, and Gadotti was actually one of the co-founders of the Workers' Party alongside Freire, although he had to sign the founding documents for Freire, as the latter was still in exile. As Torres notes in his Foreword to Gadotti's text, 'in the acts of creation of the party on February 10, 1980, Moacir Gadotti signed in representation of Paulo Freire who, from Geneva, had enthusiastically adhered to the newly created mass party' (Torres, 1994, p. xi). This interconnectedness of both texts and people, of ideas, movements and friends, what we have termed the *Freirean matrix,* is evident all through our reading of Freire.

Given that we have already looked in detail at the relation between *Pedagogy of the Oppressed* and *Pedagogy of Hope*, as the former is 'relived' in the latter, almost 20 years later, it is fitting that O'Cadiz *et al.* begin their book with a chapter entitled 'From a *Pedagogy of the Oppressed* to a *Pedagogy of Hope'*. Our own chapter here will look in detail at Freire's work through the early years of the 1990s in São Paulo, most especially through the lenses of O'Cadiz *et al*.'s complex methodology. These three theorists and educational practitioners worked closely with Freire on the São Paulo project and provide a fascinating close-up glimpse of this huge project in action. With Torres' contribution, we have a connection to the wider scholarship on Freire, as Torres is now one of his most respected commentators and interlocutors. The work of O'Cadiz *et al*. is also exemplary in retaining a critical distance and avoiding the kind of 'eulogistic' interpretation of Freire which, for example, Kincheloe (1994, p. 216) has warned against.

Brazilian democratic socialism

In relation to the text *Education and Democracy*, O'Cadiz *et al*. clarify that the book is a

> critical examination and analysis of the ideas and performance of the educational administration headed by Paulo Freire, Secretary of Education of the municipality of São Paulo, Brazil between 1989–1991. Under Freire's leadership, the municipal Secretariat of Education [MSE] implemented a process of educational reform that reflected the democratic-socialist ideology and objectives of the Workers' Party [Partido dos Trabalhadores, PT] which won the municipal elections in 1989.
>
> (O'Cadiz *et al.*, 1998, p. 1)

Before looking at the actual policies and practice of Freire as Education Secretary in São Paulo between 1989 and 1991, it is therefore helpful to examine the underlying political ideology which grounds this educational project. As O'Cadiz *et al*. make clear, the Freirean educational reforms take their cue from 'the democratic-socialist ideology and objectives of the Workers' Party' and it is the latter's victory at the municipal elections in 1989 that provides the conditions conducive to Freire being made Education Secretary. We spoke above of how Freire was involved in the formation of the PT, although in exile and represented in Brazil by Gadotti. One of the interesting aspects of this analysis, therefore, will be to ascertain to what extent Freire's ideas changed from his earlier, more theoretical work in relation to the ideas generating the supposedly democratic socialism of the PT and the Secretariat. Another question we might ask here is precisely what is meant by 'democratic socialism', especially as the PT were elected in a parliamentary democracy which might be regarded as more of a social democracy than a democratic socialism. This problematic connects with the question we raised in Chapter 5 in terms of an interpretation of a 'Freirean turn' in politics from his early to his late work, where certain commentators (e.g. Quinn, 2010) see the later work as more reformist and less revolutionary.

In exploring the political ideology of the PT, we can see that there is a strong continuity in Freire's thinking from the early work onwards and the PT is, in many respects, a highly unusual political organization or party, insofar as it developed relatively late and represented a coming together of an extraordinarily differentiated series of political and ideological groupings. It also developed rapidly from a low base to become one of the strongest political parties in Brazil, right up until the present day. As Torres notes: 'Between 1980 and 1982 the PT grew from a few thousand to 212,000 members, being officially granted its provisional registration as a national political party on February 11, 1982' (Torres, 1994, p. xi). We can take account here of the aforementioned reading of successive phases of Latin American philosophy and politics by Cirigliano, and especially his conception of the period succeeding the military dictatorship, the phase where the PT was inaugurated, as a stage of 'the dis-time or time of asynchrony ... the time that affected all those who returned from exile during the long, dark night of the military regimes' (Andreola, 2004, p. xxxvii). Cirigliano also reads Freire's work (and especially *Pedagogy of Hope*) as 'breaking with dis-time' and of course *Pedagogy of Hope* was, in many respects, generated from out of these years of the late 1980s and 1990s, following Freire's return to Brazil. *Pedagogy of Hope* is a text which resonates with Freire's 'return to Brazil' and we can add, therefore, that Cirigliano's concept of a Freirean break with 'dis-time' (Andreola, 2004, p. xxxvii) was not simply philosophical but practical-philosophical. It may be seen not simply in Freire's texts but in his practical and political commitment at the Education Secretariat and with the Workers' Party. We might also note Freire's own attitude to his homecoming. Typically, for Freire, it is not as a demagogue that he returns but *as a philosopher*, unsure of which answers to give or what he wants to say to Brazil: 'in 1980, Freire returned to Brazil with the words; "I came to relearn Brazil and as long as I am in the process of relearning, reknowing Brazil; I do not have much to say; I have more to ask"' (quoted O'Cadiz, *et al.*, 1998, p. 102).

Returning to the issue of the Workers' Party, we might say that the PT is a very Brazilian phenomenon and this ties in with Freire's oft-quoted insistence on the peculiarity of the Brazilian political and educational context, what Torres refers to as 'a land of contrasts', a land of wonder and sorrow (Torres, 1994, p. ix). While there is constant mention of the specificity of Brazil, the emphasis on the principle of *particularity* (as opposed to universality) is not something unique to Brazil but is indicative of Freire's general methodology which we see, for example, in *The Letters to Guinea-Bissau* (Freire, 1978). This represents a development of the point made by Amilcar Cabral that one cannot simply import an ideology and methodology from a different context. The epigraph to the Guinea-Bissau text is taken from Cabral: 'I cannot pretend to organise a party or a struggle on the basis of my own ideas: *I have to do it starting from the reality of the country*' (Freire, 1978, p. i). The local context has always been crucial, indeed constitutive, for Freire, and here it is no different. This is an idea we see throughout his work, for example, even more vehemently in the early work in Chile, as described in *Extension or Communication* and also in *Cultural Action for Freedom*. There, he broadens out the analysis (these texts were written during his period in Harvard in the early 1970s), to cite a certain kind of imperialist mindset among the director societies, and it is clear that much of his invective in *Cultural Action for Freedom* is directed at his host country, America. Thus, the differentiated ideology of the Workers' Party may be seen as precisely a response to the singularity of the Brazilian problems. Let us now look at this ideological pluralism of the PT, a pluralism which can be connected to Freire's oft-cited philosophical 'eclecticism' (Elias, 1994), in more detail.

Ideological pluralism in the Workers' Party

The Workers' Party first arrived on the Brazilian political scene at the end of the 1970s, signalling the organization of significant opposition forces to the Brazilian military regime that had seized power in the 1964 *coup d'état*. In some respects, we might be surprised to hear of the importance of the Workers' Party in Brazil, given the onslaught of views which have proclaimed the death of socialism and the rise of neo-liberalism, especially in Latin America. However, as O'Cadiz *et al.* (1998, p. 25) comment,

> in terms of the party's ideological orientation, its intellectual leadership emphatically rejects the idea that socialism has been defeated, arguing for the reconstruction of a new socialist vision, moving away from the scientific socialism that buttressed the recently fallen communist bureaucratic authoritarian regimes of Eastern Europe and the Soviet Union.

Thus a clear distinction is made between the scientific socialism which has evidently failed but also a more authentic socialism that should not be seen in the same light. Consequently, the PT and Freirean argument is for the 'reconstruction' of a 'new socialist vision': in this measure, however, the PT or Workers' Party is not orthodox. Indeed, we can see the PT ideology as very much in line with the evolution of a 'New Left' understanding of politics, which we have traced in earlier chapters from the conflict over the notion of ideology and the debate concerning the base and superstructure, in successive Marxist thinkers from Gramsci and Lukács, to Althusser and Marcuse (Eagleton, 1994; Žižek, 1994). The original notion of *ideology* is itself complex and ambiguous in Marx (Balibar, 2007, p. 42ff.) but came to be understood by succeeding Marxism as based on the 'false consciousness' of the people under capitalism. This was then complicated by thinkers influential on Freire such as Georgs Lukács, *who moved the notion of falsity from consciousness to the situation*: 'the notion of ideology as thought true to a false situation' (Eagleton, 1994, p. 191), while Gramsci redirected the meaning again through his concept of *hegemony* (Eagleton, 1994, p. 197), which allowed for its sense to become more connected to 'lived, habitual social practice' (Eagleton, 1994, p. 197). Here, the situation itself under capitalism was no longer simply false but subject to contestation. It is the latter view that is most influential on Freire and we can see the direct influence here on the ideological pluralism of PT: if ideology is an ambiguous notion, always subject to contestation, it makes sense to eschew a formulaic or univocal understanding of politics. While hardly advocating a relativism, an ideological pluralism, under the general rubric of a leftist orientation in politics, develops a consistency between Freire's more elaborate theoretical engagements with leftism and his more political work with the PT and the Education Secretariat.

We can also see this problematic of ideology as key for Freire in his understanding of the teacher's role in education. Understood negatively, teachers and schooling may be seen as key elements in the 'reproduction' of the dominant ideology, as it is transmitted from educators to students and children. For O'Cadiz *et al.*, what is crucial to understand about Freire is *his faith in teachers and their ability and willingness to instigate change*: 'in some cases, educators are able to transgress the self-imposed limits of the particular school systems in which they are or feel embedded ... the basis [is] fundamental trust and faith in teachers' (O'Cadiz *et al.*, 1998, p. 3). However, it is precisely this faith that also allows Freire to diagnose and work against what he sees as the very hegemonic forces of social reproduction in schools: 'Paulo Freire has insisted in his many writings, lectures and dialogical books, that ideology plays a central role in the social reproduction of schooling' (O'Cadiz *et al.*, 1998, p. 3). *The critique of ideology* must therefore be kept at the forefront of teacher education and the education of children, according to Freire. At the same time, he vehemently rejects overly authoritarian or anti-popular conceptions of ideology in the Marxist tradition, which would outrule the agency of individuals (Althusser, 1994). None the less, while acknowledging the possibilities of individual and collective agency, Freire does not deny the power of the dominant ideology to 'reproduce' its norms and practices (Bourdieu and Eagleton, 1994). Schooling is a key site of such potential reproduction and the agency or otherwise of teachers is a very significant element in this process. As Freire, and O'Cadiz *et al.* see it, 'specifically, teachers are agents continuously negating their place among structures, rationales, norms, symbols and routines; the notion of the teacher, like the notion of democracy or the concept of the good life, is also a social construction' (O'Cadiz, *et al.*, 1998, p. 5). This is an important point: the notion of the teacher is a social construction: 'By the same token, the notion of what constitutes good teaching and the figure of the good teacher is constantly contested' (O'Cadiz *et al.*, p. 5).

Unlike many parties of the Left which often divide into smaller groups in myriad schisms, the Workers' Party continues to develop a much broader base of affiliated groups. What allows this, from a philosophical or ideological perspective, is that 'it is a party that allows a great deal of philosophical and ideological pluralism' (O'Cadiz et al., p. 23). Again, we might see this as a peculiarly Brazilian capacity. Because of this ideological pluralism, as O'Cadiz et al. describe it, its immediate aims are not the same as most revolutionary leftist groups; 'consequently, its principal [aim] is not to immediately dismantle the bourgeois capitalist state but to construct a *"popular democratic government"* that can begin to seek viable alternatives to the existing capitalist social formation and defunct models of anti-democratic socialism' (O'Cadiz et al., 1998, p. 25). This is significant, as it involves a two-pronged defence and project. On the one side, there is an acceptance of a parliamentary democracy which must work within capitalism to some extent, for the time being, although there is an attempt to seek viable alternatives to this capitalism, from the inside out, so to speak. On the other side, there is clear recognition that scientific socialism is dead and that what O'Cadiz et al. call 'defunct models' of anti-democratic socialism need to be overcome. The key term here is *democracy* and indeed Freire's vision and that of the PT generally of *popular democratic government* and a *popular public school* place exactly the emphasis on people's participation, which many of the so-called socialist states lost sight of. The key problem, then, has been the tension between democracy and socialism but we are also not talking here about a democracy linked to neo-liberal pragmatism but an authenticated democracy. So the PT and Freire are also calling for a redefinition or a reconceptualization of what we mean by democracy.

The PT has had significant electoral successes in Brazil: 'in 1988, its most significant electoral victory came in the form of the mayorship of the city of São Paulo' (O'Cadiz et al., 1998, p. 27). Since this period, the PT has become even more successful with successive Brazilian presidents, such as Lula, coming from within its party base and also maintaining very high levels of public approval through their leadership. In this earlier phase of the development, 'Paulo Freire was the logical choice for municipal Secretary of Education' and thus took over leadership for the first two years of its leadership, handing over to Moacir Gadotti (Gadotti, 1994) for the final two years, so as to return to his writing and teaching work. The years of the administration were thus 1989 to 1993, with Freire taking charge from 1989 to 1991 and Gadotti replacing him from 1991 to 1993. Let us now look at how the political ideology of the PT was developed into an educational philosophy which could ground revolutionary and far-reaching pedagogical policies, during Freire's time at the Secretariat. If Freire has always claimed that education is a political process through and through, the São Paulo period constitutes another fascinating example of the enactment of this vision, from Freire's later phase of work. We might say, however, that there remains a powerful continuity here with the transition made in Freire's earlier work, between Chapters 1 and 2 of *Pedagogy of the Oppressed* (Freire, 1996a): from politics to education, once more.

From politics to pedagogy once more: exploring the Freirean São Paulo Education Secretariat

In terms of the principles which founded the PT's approach and its connection to that of Freire's Education Secretariat most especially, O'Cadiz *et al.* foreground three principles: 'The PT's educational efforts were oriented by three principles: *participation, decentralisation* and *autonomy*; these principles were geared towards the party's goal of constructing a *Popular Public School*' (O'Cadiz *et al.*, 1998, p. 27). We can look at each of these principles in turn. Participation is clear-cut – there was a desire for the people to participate whether they were students, teachers or part of the general public. This was connected to the very idea of the popular public school but, as we know, for Freire, the school should not be seen in isolation from the wider society but must be seen as integral to the latter. This is a view which connects with Dewey's emphasis on the integration of school and community (Dewey, 1973), and was a key tenet of progressivism more generally (Darling and Nordenbo, 2003). The emphasis on the 'popular public school' also represents a break with the more orthodox Marxist critique of popular ideology (Althusser, 1994), and draws Freire close to Gramsci's concept of hegemony, as a constant popular struggle for democratic legitimation (Gramsci, 1988; Eagleton, 1994) and to the work of the Birmingham CCCS (Hall, 1996a). Second, in terms of decentralization, we can see this as a key strategy to move the main funding away from the more central and privileged schools towards the outlying schools, for example, in the *favelas* or shanty towns, which under the new Secretariat received a significant boost in funding and where teachers were sometimes paid 50 per cent extra to work in the schools, rather than in the centralized and more privileged schools. Once more, this demonstrates a tendency on behalf of the Secretariat (and the PT) *to work with the liberal-democratic (capitalist) system* rather than whole-heartedly against it: there is a dimension of accommodationism here, which would be highly criticized in some quarters, for example, by Alain's Badiou's more uncompromising leftism (Badiou, 2001).

Finally, in terms of school autonomy, as we shall see, this principle was strongly connected to Freire's principle of the whole curriculum where he wished to develop the curriculum out of the culture of the very specific school, under the principle which he made foundational of the *generative theme*. This extraordinarily ambitious project to rebuild the curriculum anew in each school, more or less, will be looked at below. But we should also take note that Brazil more generally, or indeed a significant number of the participants themselves, are not fully behind the PT, ideologically speaking. One of the issues here, which is raised by respondents in the analysis below, is that the direct link between the political ideology of the PT and the educational programme of the Secretariat led to accusations of political dogmatism. The positive or negative responses to the Secretariat from teachers and administrators thus often (although not always) split down party lines. We might see Freire's sense that pedagogy is never neutral as justifying this bias, but certainly it does raise concerns about a too-easy conflation of politics and education in Freire (this accusation is stronger when it concerns primary or elementary education). More generally, in addition, ideological differences and conflicts may be identified between the PT political-educational perspective and the influence in Brazil of the neo-liberal project, or what Freire sometimes called Brazilian 'corporatism' (Freire, 2005a), in its attempts to oppose the efforts of the democratic-socialist administration: 'the neoliberal project in Brazil which has countered the PT efforts in education and argued for a more commercialized understanding of education and schooling' (O'Cadiz et al., 1998, p. 29). This more commercialized understanding of education and schooling was, of course, anathema to Freire's understanding of an educational and pedagogic vision. It demonstrates the existence of similar forces at work in Brazilian education as Blake et al. outline as examples of more global trends in pedagogy, such as managerialism and instrumentalism (Blake et al., 2003b).

O'Cadiz et al. trace the geneaology of 'the ideal of the popular public school' (O'Cadiz et al.,1998, p. 23), which they say has emerged 'three decades after the emergence of the popular education movement in Brazil' (O'Cadiz et al., 1998, p. 23). The popular education movement was intrinsically Freirean and Freire had been appointed to a key position in 1963 in the Brazilian education department to oversee a national programme of literacy. It was this programme which generated the spleen of the established middle and upper classes in Brazil who feared their privilege was under threat. This was to lead to Freire's exile – as Gadotti puts it, 'the method which took Paulo Freire into exile' (Gadotti, 1994, p. 15). We will see a return of certain of these age-old divisions in Brazil in some of the school case studies below. For O'Cadiz et al., the emergence of the ideal of the popular public school 'is linked both historically and theoretically to Freire's initial arrival onto the educational scene in his country in the late 1950s' (O'Cadiz et al., 1998, p. 23). Once more, we see the extraordinary singularity and consistency of educational vision in Freire's work.

The interdisciplinary or inter-project

Throughout this book, we have emphasized the interdisciplinary nature of Freire's project and it is no surprise that this *interdisciplinarity* is central to Freire's practice in São Paulo. O'Cadiz et al. mention that 'The *Inter* project, along with other reforms implemented by the PT MSE, had far reaching effects on curriculum, instruction and teacher training, and as such, represents the primary effort of the secretariat to create one of its fundamental policy objectives' (O'Cadiz *et al.*,1998, p. 1). Here, we see some of the key areas of impact in educational policy and practice which took place in São Paulo: curriculum, instruction and teacher education. Thus, Freire's work at the Education Secretariat sought to revolutionize both elementary and primary education but also teacher education at third level through his notion of the *inter-project*.

There were *several distinct reform projects* that Freire and his Secretariat undertook, which, while distinct, none the less connected together in an overall vision of the inter-project. First, there was a '*movement for curricular reorientation*'. This was connected to Freire's concept of generative theme and was based on the vision that curriculum should not be something pre-established, but a pedagogy generated in the day-to-day expressive culture of the school. Moreover, curriculum should not be imposed from without, by educational 'experts', but should arise organically from a genuine dialogue between teachers and students. The intrinsic connections of this educational conception to Freire's paradigmatic problem-posing education, elaborated most dramatically in *Pedagogy of the Oppressed*, are unequivocal. Curricular reorientation is nothing other than problem-posing education being (radically and uncompromisingly) applied to the elementary school system of São Paulo in the 1990s. Given that teachers would need themselves to be educated into this radical practice of curricular reorientation, this approach also meant that a new policy must be applied to teacher education. The reorientation of the curriculum should take place at all levels of the education system, although, in the case of the Secretariat, the most significant emphasis was on the implementation of this approach in primary schools.

Interdisciplinarity was key to this pedagogical approach insofar as the new curriculum would be generated without strict adherence to the previously established distinct disciplinary areas of knowledge or enquiry. While this undoubtedly represented a very radical proposal for Brazilian primary schools, we should also note that, in many respects, it simply develops the logic of progressivist education, indeed even being compatible with the more moderate or revisionist progressivism outlined, for example, in Dewey's *Experience and Education* (Dewey, 1973). Having said this, the reform project to 'reorient' the curriculum was nothing less than a call to reinvent the notion and practice of curriculum, school by school, and day by day. A factor also guiding this concept of the need for radical curriculum renewal was the sense that many students in São Paulo remained completely alienated, as Freire saw it, from the curricula which teachers sought to impart to them. For Freire, one of the key obstacles to the overcoming of this *alienation* (the latter itself a key notion in Freire's early work, as we have seen, and deriving from Marx's understanding of human labour (Marx, 1992b)), was the fact that curricula paid no heed to extra-school knowledge or 'popular cultural understanding'. Thus, it is clear that ideologically this notion of curriculum reorientation also takes it's cue from

Gramsci's warning that popular cultural understanding must not be undestimated in its insights, despite the dangers of compliance with a dominating populism (Gramsci, 1988).

A second reform project, connected to the implementation of the first, concerned the development and maintenance of *continuing professional education groups* (for teachers, pedagogic coordinators and school directors) (O'Cadiz *et al.*,1998, p. 72), which was also formulated as the 'constitution of school site councils'. Thus, 'continuing professional education' did not just apply to adults but was also seen as a key factor in the political education of the young. The model for these professional groups related back to Freire's original vision of *culture circles*, which once more looked back to the original concept delineated in *Education as The Practice of Freedom*, of 'generative themes'. Such culture circles, therefore, could have no pre-established plan or programme but would rather follow the model of problem-posing education laid down in *Pedagogy of the Oppressed* most explicitly. There was to be a clear connection between the first two reform projects, insofar as the culture circles of the continuing professional groups would feed their renewed understanding into the first reform project of the 'reorientation of the curriculum'. Freire's vision imagined a loop effect between these two reform projects, each informing the other, and creating a community of dialogue (again, connecting back to a key notion of *Pedagogy of the Oppressed*).

Freire's Secretariat also sought to implement a less significant computer project known as Genesis but its fourth aspect was no less crucial than the first two projects: 'MOVA [the movement for youth and adult literacy]' (O'Cadiz *et al.*, 1998, p. 72). Connecting quite obviously to schooling, this fourth aspect also related to Freire's wider vision of *political literacy* and here the pedagogy of the São Paulo Secretariat came full circle – from education to politics and back to a politicized education. With regard to the PT's overall vision of education working through Freire as Secretary of Education, we may say that 'the political nature of Freire's notion of literacy is stressed rather than simply a linguistic or technicist understanding' (O'Cadiz *et al.*,1998, pp. 59–60). Here, with the question of literacy, we get some sense of the truly bewildering scale of Freire's educational project in São Paulo, as Torres (1993, p. 136) notes

> With his appointment in January 1989 as Secretary of Education of the City of São Paulo, Freire took charge of 662 schools with 772,000 students, from K8 (Kindergarten) to grade 8, in addition to heading adult education and literacy training in the City of São Paulo, which, with 11.4 million people, is one of the largest cities in Latin America.

A kernel of *three reform projects* thus provided the nexus of the *interprogramme* elaborated by Freire's Education Secretariat, itself guided by the 'ideological pluralism' of the leftist PT: *curriculum reorientation*, *professional education groups linked to school councils* and *MOVA*, or the movement for adult and youth literacy, understood as *critical and political literacy*. In each of these cases, key concepts developed from Freire's extensive philosophical work provide the theoretical elaboration of the practical reform vision: 'the central concepts of interdisciplinarity, generative themes, critical consciousness, and democratisation of education formed the foundation of this Freirean program for curriculum reform' (O'Cadiz *et al.*, 1998, p. 1). The notion of *'generative themes'* we have already seen developed by Freire, from his earliest work in the literacy programmes in Brazil and Chile, where the voice and experience of the rural proletariat must actually generate the terms and relevant words to be learnt and understood. It is present even in his 'first book', the seminal *Education as The Practice of Freedom. Critical consciousness* is similarly a key feature of the literacy and post-literacy programme, such that 'reading the word' is also 'reading the world'. Thus it can never be, for Freire, simply a matter of language acquisition but must involve a whole process of conscientization, a subjective evolution of personal and philosophical understanding, which also takes account of the socio-cultural and socio-political understanding of one's surroundings and society. Having been in enforced exile for 16 years, this project now gives Freire the opportunity to develop his philosophical ideas in the context from which they originated: 'Despite his fame and the global disssemination of his revolutionary philosophy of education, until 1989, Freire had not yet had the opportunity to extensively implement his ideas in a formal elementary school setting in his own country' (O'Cadiz *et al.*, 1998, p. 2).

'The São Paulo experience is, thus, first of all refreshing'

For Cadiz *et al.*, the São Paulo experience is, thus, first of all refreshing: 'the São Paulo experience, inclusive of the Inter project, is a refreshing perspective' (O'Cadiz *et al.*, 1998, p. 3), and we see this refreshing element in terms of two aspects. In the first case, we can speak of the more practical aspects of this change: 'innovative suggestions and concrete avenues for positive change' (O'Cadiz *et al.*, 1998, p. 3). These concrete avenues for change are fascinating in the context of Freire's prolonged effort to being about a symbiosis between theory and practice in his work from the most early days and texts onwards. Second, and just as crucially, for Cadiz et al, 'it advances the theoretical discussion on educational policy making and at the same time proposes a set of experiments to promote learning in schools that are full of imagination and hope' (O'Cadiz, *et al.*,1998, p. 3). Thus Freire also advances the theoretical discussion. Throughout their analysis of the project, O'Cadiz *et al.* outline a balanced and 'critical' perspective, exploring 'what seems to work and what could be improved in radical educational reforms ...

pinpointing some of the more significant successes and failures of the reform project' (O'Cadiz et al., 1998, p. 5).

The response of teachers and students to the inter-project

We should not lose sight of the key protagonists in this educational drama – the teachers and the students, both in terms of Freire's vision of the latter and their voice and response to the curricular changes being wrought. These responses must be viewed in the context of the situations of extreme deprivation in São Paulo, one of the poorest cities in Latin America, alongside weak standards of pedagogy in Brazilian initial teacher education. Given the latter context, the courage and ambition of the Freirean project is quite breathtaking (some might counter that it betokens naivete or misguided utopianism). However, we must foreground the people most directly affected by the proposals and implementations of change. O'Cadiz et al. make clear that while Freire's educational work and vision are at the heart of this project, their focus, in examining its implementation, will be very much on the views of the teachers and students who are seeking to put this vision into educational practice. 'More than indulging in the exaltation of politics and mystification of personalities, the analysis tries to understand how students and teachers were engaged in the process of curriculum change and democratisation of school governance' (O'Cadiz, et al.,1998, p. 2). This emphasis in Cadiz et al. on students and teachers is also perfectly appropriate and shows that, although Freire was seeking to implement significant policies, in many ways far more important than these were *the actual agents of change* themselves in schools, both *teachers and students*. The analysis of the views and practices of the students and teachers by O'Cadiz et al. therefore leads the emphasis away from simply Freire and Gadotti and their implementation of a highbrow philosophy of education. It is also perfectly in keeping with Freire's own constant emphasis on the need for the student voice to be heard, and indeed the teacher's voice. Again and again, Freire tells us that education can never be ideologically or politically neutral and of the intricate connections between politics and education. Here, O'Cadiz et al. tell us that we will be looking at precisely this political consciousness as it develops through the reform progammes in the São Paulo schools: 'we additionally expose the kind of political awareness emerging in the São Paulo schools and communities that participated in Freire's radical educational reform' (O'Cadiz et al., 1998, p. 2).

O'Cadiz et al. also seek to provide an empirical analysis to supplement the intra-theoretical and curriculum discussion. To this end, their examination of the São Paulo schools 'offers an ethnographic account of the reform experience through a case study analysis of four schools in São Paulo'

(O'Cadiz *et al.*, 1998, p. 12). Teachers' and students' views, experience and aspirations regarding educational reform and curriculum change are all explored. Different issues came to the fore here, including the aim of the project to create '*critical and active citizens*', both at teacher and student level respectively. Second, a more general emphasis on teaching and learning and epistemological outcomes was central to the evaluation of the project. 'A serious concern is whether teaching and learning actually improved in São Paulo municipal schools, during the Freirean experiment' (O'Cadiz *et al.*, 1998, p. 5). Third, there was an examination of the teachers' *theoretical knowledge* and its development through the project. Did the new policy orientation increase theoretical knowledge of the profession? This was seen as especially important given, first, Freire's continuous emphasis on the need for theory and the ideological dimension of the PT's involvement. Second, given the weakness of teacher education precisely from the theoretical point of view, it would be interesting to see if these deficiencies could be overcome through the 'reorientation' programme, especially with the second reform project of the professional working groups. O'Cadiz *et al.* make it clear that, in general, teachers are very willing to deal with and effect change, to become agents of change in a philosophical and educational sense. As they note, 'teachers more often than not, are energetic and willing to experiment. Encountering the right leadership and vision, they are able to create new horizons of pedagogical imagination and social realities in schools' (O'Cadiz *et al.*, 1998, p. 3). Evaluating the teacher's progress then would also be a matter of evaluating the quality of educational vision and leadership, a question which brought the accountability right back to Freire's own involvement and direction of the programme. As we will see, many teachers found the theoretical complexity of the project very hard to understand and there is evidence that many teachers did not fully understand or had a confused understanding of the philosophical foundations. Given the lack of professional development in teacher education which the Freirean administration faced, this is not surprising, but it does beg the question whether this was all too much, too soon.

Case studies of schools

I mentioned above the bewildering nature of the challenge facing Freire's Education Secretariat in the São Paulo municipal schools. It is worth stating again here: 'with his appointment in January 1989 as Secretary of Education of the City of São Paulo, Freire took charge of *662 schools with 772,000 students*, from K8 (Kindergarten to grade 8), in addition to heading adult education and literacy training in the City of São Paulo, which, with *11.4 million people*, is one of the largest cities in Latin America' (Torres, 1993, p. 136). Given the extraordinary complexity and breadth of the issues facing Freire, and the consequent complexity of the response and the implementation of the educational programme on the ground, any wholehearted assessment of the Education Secretariat is far beyond the remit of this chapter. I have drawn significantly on the work of O'Cadiz *et al.* in this chapter, but even their seven-year project on Freire's work is significantly weighted in favour of policy and philosophical critique than more ethnographic analysis. However, they do provide a selective ethnographic analysis of four schools involved in the project and I will refer to some of the detail of this analysis here. Again, my purpose is not in any way to claim that these responses are definitive but rather to explore some of the positive and negative aspects encountered in specific contexts of the project's implementation. My analysis will take its cue from what O'Cadiz *et al.* refer to as 'a summary of the project's impact at the site, as provided by teacher assessment of the project experience (including effects on teacher professional identity, educational philosophy and classroom practice, and changes in the institutional culture of the school and organization of the curriculum' (O'Cadiz *et al.*, 1998, p. 138). The responses of the teachers and students are thus primarily with regard to the first two reform projects of the Education Secretariat outlined above; that is, to *curriculum reorientation* and *professional education groups* linked to school councils. I will return to the relation between the impact of these two reform projects and the wider *MOVA*, or the movement for adult and youth literacy (understood as *critical and political literacy*), below.

Support, pedagogy, participation, dogmatism

In the first case study, at 'the Inter project at Sussumu school' (O'Cadiz *et al.*, 1998, p. 138), the characteristic features were of a very socio-economically deprived school on the outskirts of the *favela*. As one of the pilot schools in the project, this school initially had significant support from the central body of the Secretariat in terms of site visits. However, as the project became more mainstream in São Paulo, this central support decreased, and this led to a certain sense of disenchantment among the teachers. This was a school with very significant teacher turnover and unevenness in implementation, in terms of a mix of democratic and traditional pedagogies being used in the classrooms. In terms of the ethnographic analysis of the teachers in the school, O'Cadiz *et al.* clarify that 'different teachers' experience of the school was varied' (O'Cadiz *et al.*, 1998, pp. 159–160). A significant number of teachers were very positive, as there was increased creativity and better teaching produced, as well as a better discussion among the teachers. The issue of improved communication among teachers was cited in many instances as a great success of the Inter-project. However, in this case, the in-service was too theoretical, and many teachers did not understand, given the inadequacy of their professional development. From the student point of view at Sussumu, while initially negative, their perspectives became much more positive, and the increase in the participative culture of the school was cited as being especially important (O'Cadiz *et al.*,1998, pp. 159–60). From a more negative perspective, students often found that they had to work harder and some felt (on the basis of the *generative* theme principle) that there was too much emphasis on their own experience (O'Cadiz *et al.*, 1998, pp. 159–60).

In the second case study of the 'Habib School' (O'Cadiz *et al.*,1998, p. 168), the responses from both teachers and students were somewhat more negative than in the first instance. 'Some teachers discerned a politically dogmatic and educationally unsound element in the classroom practice and analysis' (O'Cadiz *et al.*,1998, pp. 174–175). One of the issues here is that the Reform project came under the rubric of the PT, the Workers' Party. If teachers were involved in some of the groups which came under this political umbrella, then they would be likely to follow the reforms. If not, they would be less inclined to do so. This raises the issue of the relation between education and politics, which has been a constant theme of the book. If education becomes too politicized, there is a danger of education being reduced to propaganda. If education pretends to be non-ideological, it often ends up simply reinforcing a hidden ideology. Freire has consistently argued that education needs to have a directive political vision but that this vision must remain genuinely open to dialogue and transformation – otherwise, one returns to the sectarianism which Freire spoke of in his Preface to *Pedagogy of the Oppressed* (Freire, 1996a).

However, all was not negative at the Habib School. There were very positive developments in terms of the teacher understanding and teacher dialogue. In addition, student participation was noted as significantly increasing. However, once again, we have the problem with the understanding of the philosophical or theoretical foundation of the educational project, 'although many teachers due to the lack of professional development still do not understand what was really going on' (O'Cadiz *et al.*, 1998, p. 190). Although the reason cited here is lack of professional development, there are also clearly issues in terms of the construction of the programme itself and its implementation. Given that the professional development of teachers was one of the reform programmes in itself, with regard to *professional education groups*, questions must be raised about the content and form of the Inter-project itself, whether, for example, it was realistically envisioned. It seems both unfair and wrong-headed to simply blame a previous lack of professional development for all of the above issues.

Finally, one of the principles which we identified as Deweyean in the project earlier was the notion of a more authentic link between community and the school. But was this properly achieved? Again, while some progress was made here, and one must also acknowledge the problematic socio-cultural context, the process at the Habib school encountered significant resistance: 'a lack of real success in bringing the communities into direct participation with the school' (O'Cadiz *et al.*, 1998, p. 190). Beyond the specifics of the Habib School, this issue of school and community dialogue was also noted as a more general problem throughout the Inter-project.

At the third school case study, Pracinhas School (O'Cadiz *et al.*, 1998, p. 193), we see perhaps the most positive result elicited with a true meaning attached to the Inter-project and a genuine understanding, achieved through dialogue, of what the foundational principles mean. O'Cadiz *et al.* tell us that 'an initial description of the school and community' (O'Cadiz *et al.*, 1998, p. 138) is significant, and this school and the final school analysed are in areas which are less socio-economically deprived than the first two. The school buildings and resources are significantly better; what this also signifies, of course, is the acute difficulties experienced by the first two schools in this sense of environment and the great challenges which these posed to the implementation of the Inter-project. Here, the relations between teachers and students seem significantly better. We get an interesting definition of the project from one of the teachers: 'Inter is a process of arriving at a particular theme; based on the student concerns and working on this theme with your group of teachers' (O'Cadiz *et al.*, 1998, p. 204). So interdisciplinarity begins with the student concerns. Student and teacher involvement at the Pracinhas School was exemplary and genuinely transformative for all concerned. What we also see here is the two reform projects working together in tandem – *curriculum reorientation* and *professional education groups* linked to school councils. This exactly exemplifies the original vision of Freire and Gadotti: there was to be a clear connection between the first two reform projects, insofar as the culture circles of the continuing professional groups would feed their renewed understanding into the first reform project of the 'reorientation of the curriculum'. Freire's vision imagined a symbiotic relationship between these two reform projects, each informing the other, and creating a community of dialogue (again, connecting back to a key notion of *Pedagogy of the Oppressed*).

The final example of the case study is very much in contrast with the previous one. This is the case study of 'Manoel de Paiva School'. O'Cadiz *et al.* subtitle this 'Conflict and Controversy' (O'Cadiz *et al.*, 1998, p. 213), for obvious reasons. This school is actually in a middle-class district of São Paulo, although it is also close to the *favela* and it is precisely the complexity of the social mix which causes conflicts within the school. Teachers talk of 'the changing nature of the social class status of the children' (O'Cadiz *et al.*, 1998, p. 226). This is especially brought out in the 'study of reality' (through the *generative theme*), where some of the teachers who seem convinced that they work in a middle-class school find that many of the children live in substandard conditions. This is also exemplary of a rigid teacher–student divide in terms of communication and understanding. Some teachers comment on an increasing 'privatization' in education where many of the children were moved to private school. However, due to the recession, many are returning and mixing with children from more working-class backgrounds. The teachers, however, all seem to come from more middle-class backgrounds (O'Cadiz *et al.*, 1998, p. 226). O'Cadiz *et al.* comment on a lot of parent and teacher conflict and tensions, as well as teacher-student conflict. The parents are described as accusing teachers of being inept and 'boring' practitioners (so as to explain their children's non-participation), while teachers accuse parents of not valuing education enough or not passing on this value of education to their children. But the most important problem was students' interest; students didn't seem to get involved or properly understand the Inter-project, although perhaps the more fundamental problem of teacher commitment and understanding was at the root of all this (O'Cadiz *et al.*, 1998, p. 226). Judged from outside, the Inter-project at the Manoel de Paiva School seems to have been almost a total failure. However, it is clear that many of the reasons for this failure lie in the culture of the school itself. None the less, the positive and negative aspects of each of the school's experiences raise issues about the value and practicality of the Inter-project per se. I will conclude this section with an exploration of some of the issues which these case studies have raised in relation to the vision of the Inter-project of the Education Secretariat, as well as in relation to Freire's wider philosophical project.

The struggle continues: Freire, Education and the Workers' Party

As Torres observed so clearly, Freire's Education Secretariat took on a pedagogical challenge that was, to all intents and purposes, impossible (Torres, 1993, p. 136). Overall, given the difficulties encountered and especially the extraordinary problems involved in trying to radically overhaul an educational system in Brazil and especially in São Paulo, we might see Freire's project as in many ways surprisingly successful. 'Student retention rate increased, especially in areas where there is great poverty' (O'Cadiz *et al.*, 1998, p. 234). However, huge problems also remained. One of the key elements in Freire's project is his conviction that teachers and students must drive the project, that teachers and students are the agents of change. However, this left a huge amount of autonomy not simply to the school but especially to the teachers themselves. In hindsight, we may wonder at whether this was successful but also whether there is a rather romanticized view of teachers in the Freirean philosophy, which doesn't necessarily bear out in terms of the realities of teacher education in the late twentieth and early twenty-first century. In several schools, teachers spoke of not properly understanding the concepts at the heart of the educational project. Again, we also have the issue of ideology and dogmatism. Given the political involvement of the PT underlying the education project, teachers commented on what amounted to them as a sectarian bias in the implementation of the programme. Given Freire's consistent indictments of sectarianism, this seems an especially tragic outcome.

However, this was an extraordinarily expansive programme which related not simply to the first two reform projects concentrated on the schools (already 772,000 students) but also to Freire's heading up of adult education and literacy training in the City of São Paulo, with *11.4 million people*. The project is thus mind-boggling in its breadth and depth. What has been explored here then is simply one very micro-interpretation of the project, itself reliant on the work of O'Cadiz *et al.*, (1998). What we should not lose sight of here, however, is *the interconnectedness between the three reform projects outlined under the rubric of the Inter-project and Freire's lifetime's work*, both theoretical and practical. Gadotti outlines evocatively how Freire's literacy project began in Rio Grande do Norte in 1963, with Freire and his team going to live in Angicos for a month: 'A month later, three hundred formerly illiterate pupils were reading and writing' (Gadotti, 1994, p. 32). However, the expansion of this extraordinary pedagogy into a national programme was short-lived: 'The military coup, however, interrupted the work right at the beginning and cancelled all the work that had already been done' (Gadotti, 1994, p. 15). Freire's return to Brazil in 1980 and his involvement with the origin and development of the PT, and his evolution of the Inter-project with the Education Secretariat, thus signals his victory over what Gadotti calles 'the meaning of the 1964 coup' (Gadotti, 1994, p. 38). That is, the military's attempt to stifle social and political change and to reinforce the domination of the middle classes and of foreign, capitalist vested interests. The Education Secretariat in São Paulo should be seen as another powerful and symbolic example of the victory of not simply Freire over the coup, but of the victory of the PT, and of all those Brazilian people who seek a more equal and fair society. The Inter-project, extraordinary in its daring and its vastness (but also, as we have seen, flawed and imperfect) must be viewed as one more phase of this continuing process of change in Brazil, as motored by Freire, Gadotti and the PT. The continuing political success of the PT in Brazil following Freire's death, through Lula and others, signals that this struggle goes on into the present. For Freire, summing up his own work after the project was completed, there is only positivity and the sense of a militancy which we have described above: 'democracy demands structures that democratise' (quoted O'Cadiz *et al.*, 1998, pp. 249–250).

Concluding remarks: on the later Freire

It is clear that we can designate a change in emphasis in Freire's later work, beginning with *Pedagogy of Hope* (Freire,1992), as Ana Maria Araújo Freire notes (cited in Freire, 2004, p. 26). Although the latter text itself is primarily concerned with 'reliving' the genealogy and development of *Pedagogy of the Oppressed*, it does indicate certain new key concepts to be elaborated, and Freire's later work takes up this challenge in more detail. One such notion is of a Freirean 'progressive postmodernism' and we have seen how Freire has indeed foregrounded this notion, in his work with the PT and at the Education Secretariat. With the latter, this progressive postmodernism may be most clearly seen in relation to his commitment to the 'ideological pluralism' (which I have connected to a new leftism) in the PT. Undoubtedly, the PT's extraordinary success in Brazil, both at political and educational levels, may be seen as, in many ways, determined by their willingness to adopt a more nuanced approach to the issues of ideology and power than some of the more traditionalist left-wing parties. I have also traced how this should not be seen as simply an issue of practical politics but how it takes its cue from a complex debate within Marxism concerning a number of key questions, such as ideology, the relation between base and superstructure, and the relation between parliamentary democracy and the quest for a more socialist and egalitarian society. The key intellectual figure here in Marxism has been Gramsci (Gramsci, 1988) but in the Brazilian context, Freire's refinement and development of the Gramscian position (through his own complex, eclectic philosophy) has been hugely influential. The issue of whether Freire's later work represents a paradigm shift from his earlier emphases in this regard remains a moot question (Quinn, 2010).

Moreover, we also traced in this chapter how the ideological pluralism of the PT sought to develop its insights into the educational sphere, following the success of the municipal elections of 1989. As Education Secretary, Freire took on a Herculean task but his pedagogical proposals and policies derived whole-heartedly and consistently from his theoretical work, looking right back to his 'first text' *Education as the Practice of Freedom*. That text also warned about the specificity of the Brazilian context, as well as the lingering problems with both the ghosts of colonialism and a neo-liberalism (or 'corporatism'), which was growing in strength. In Freire's implementation of the Inter-project through the Secretariat, focused on the key reform projects of *curriculum reorientation, professional education groups linked to school councils* and *MOVA*, or the movement for adult and youth literacy, significant difficulties emerged which were articulated in O'Cadiz *et al.*'s detailed analysis. None the less, significant positives can also be taken from this experience, especially in relation to the issue of 'popular participation', which has been a constantly reiterated goal of Freire's philosophy. This indeed, as Gadotti has articulated, strikes at the very heart of 'the meaning of the 1964 coup' (Gadotti, 1994), helping the Brazilian people to move beyond this impasse. The continuing evolution and success of the PT at popular level in Brazil testifies to the ongoing nature of this work, of this progressivism in education and politics.

CHAPTER SEVEN

Postmodernist tension and creativity in Paulo Freire's educational legacy

From critical pedagogy to the Birmingham Centre for Contemporary Cultural Studies

Introduction – the pluralist legacies of Paulo Freire

Any authentic development of Freire's work must strive to avoid a sycophantic discipleship or literalism; as Nietzsche observed in *Zarathustra*, it is a poor disciple who simply repeats the lessons of the master. None the less, there are significant issues with regard to extending Freire's work in the twenty-first century, and substantially diverse approaches to this legacy have evolved. As suggested in the Introduction, the increased receptivity to Freire's texts in more mainstream philosophy of education in recent years has been due to what may be described as a *paradigm shift* in the latter discipline's self-understanding. Having previously been dominated by a specific interpretation of neo-Kantian thought, grounded in an 'analytic' approach to education and philosophy (Hirst and Peters, 1970), more recent philosophy of education has developed a more 'continentalist' approach, which emphasizes the 'socio-political' contexts of pedagogy (Blake *et al.*, 2003b). The work of, for example, Derrida (Derrida, 1978) and Foucault (Foucault, 1998) has become increasingly influential in education discussion. The previously dominant analyticity and neo-Kantianism no longer seems so relevant in the context of an increasingly powerful politicization of education.

This insight, under the guise of the 'critical pedagogy' movement, is being developed influentially in the USA. This movement, led by figures such as Peter McLaren (McLaren, 1994), bell hooks (hooks, 1994) and Henry Giroux (Giroux, 2000), acknowledges Freire's work as pivotal in its self-understanding and seeks to apply neo-Freirean approaches to problems in contemporary education and society. However, we have seen throughout this book that Freire's influence and range of thinking extends globally. We have been especially concerned with his connections to a Third Worldist context, or specifically a Latin American situation, both politically and pedagogically. However, in this chapter, I will look rather at how his work has been developed by critical pedagogy in the United States and also at how his work may be seen as integrally connected, in a more UK-based context, to the work of the Birmingham Centre for Contemporary Cultural Studies (CCCS), originally founded in the 1970s. The thinkers originally connected with the CCCS have now become individual thinkers in their own right (Hall, 1996a; Willis, 1981) but their connection to the original ethos of the CCCS remains significant. These respective developments of Freire's work share significant affinities but also manifest tensions with regard to their interpretations of Freire.

Both the critical pedagogy school of thinking and the Birmingham CCCS may be seen as simultaneously working *with* and *against* certain aspects of Freire's thinking, but Freire has always acknowledged the need for such a challenge to his approach. As we shall see, the relation between modernity and postmodernity, which has become such a paradigmatic theme for Freire in his later work, from *Pedagogy of Hope* (Freire, 1992) onwards, becomes quite significant in our reading of Freire's relationship to these two traditions of thinking. In addition, the concept of an educational progressivism, which Freire has advocated consistently in his later work (but with a specific understanding of the latter) also becomes a site of contestation. The questions of youth culture and media culture, and their impact on human agency, also figure predominantly in these analyses.

In the first half of this chapter I will explore how the critical pedagogy educational movement maintains a powerful but complicated relationship to Freire's work. I will analyse specific aspects of how Henry Giroux (Giroux, 2000), Peter McLaren (McLaren, 1994) and bell hooks (hooks, 1994) have evolved the problematic of Freire's work in more recent times, both respecting and developing his legacy.

Henry Giroux: film, hedonism and the limits of progressivism

The example I will foreground from Henry Giroux relates to the discussion of 'contemporary youth culture' in critical pedagogy, most especially as these are represented through film and media. In his book *Breaking In To The Movies* (Giroux, 2000), Henry Giroux puts forward a critique of several examples of contemporary film and media. Giroux makes clear from the beginning of his book that he sees films as a source of knowledge. Film is not simply entertainment, and Giroux stresses the political nature of cinema as ideological. To ensure a substantive democracy, he says, we must make sure that films and cinema play a pedagogical and political role in shaping identities. He observes:

> central to this issue is whether educators are dealing with a new kind of student forged within organizing principles shaped by the intersection of the electronic image, popular culture, and a dire sense of indeterminacy … educators are increasingly faced with the challenge of addressing how different identities among youth are being produced in spheres generally ignored by schools.
>
> (Giroux, 2000, p. 1)

For Giroux, media and visual arts constitute the most powerful educational tools of the contemporary era: 'Films do more than entertain, they offer up subject positions, mobilise desires, influence us unconsciously, and help to construct the landscape of American culture' (Giroux, 2000, p. 3). Second, in constructing such culture, media demonstrates its paradigmatic power in the contemporary context and its shaping of educational discourse itself: 'they also deploy power through the important role they play connecting the production of pleasure and meaning with the mechanisms and practices of powerful teaching machines; put simply, films both entertain and educate' (Giroux, 2000, p. 3).

This emphasis on the significance of 'popular culture' from the point of view of pedagogy is something shared by critical pedagogy and the CCCS (Hall, 1996a). As Giroux observes,

> popular culture, including film, now plays pedagogically and politically in shaping the identities, values, and broader social practices that characterise the increasingly postmodern culture in which the electronic media and visual forms constitute the most powerful educational tools.
>
> (Giroux, 2000, p. 10)

This centrality of popular culture and film creates several difficulties for pedagogy but one of the most significant relates to the theoretical or philosophical poverty in actually interpreting these movements. According to Giroux, the tools used by film and media theory lack the requisite critical insight and socio-political insight: 'missing from [film theory analyses] are the ways in which films are located along a circuit of power that connects the political economy and regulation of films with how they function as representational systems implicated in processes of identity formation and consumption' (Giroux, 2000, p. 12). Giroux castigates film directors such as Quentin Tarantino (*Pulp Fiction*), Gus Van Sant (*My Own Private Idaho*) and Richard Linklater (*Slacker*) for *their failure to provide a moral vision to counter what he sees as an increasingly indulgent but also self-destructive youth subculture*. He reserves his especial ire for the work of controversial photographer and film-maker Larry Clark (the photographic work *Tulsa* and the film *Kids*) (Clark, 1995), and the work of Quentin Tarantino, both of whom Giroux accuses of voyeurism and the exploitation of youth. In two essays in *Breaking In To The Movies* (Giroux, 2000), Giroux tackles what he sees as the pedagogical and moral dangers of their work, in Chapter 9, entitled 'Media Panics and the War Against *Kids*: Larry Clark and the Politics of Diminished Hopes', and Chapter 10, 'Racism and the Aesthetic of Hyper-Real Violence: *Pulp Fiction* and Other Visual Tragedies'. Here my main focus will be on the analysis of Clark's photography and filmwork.

The degradation of youth: Larry Clark

For Giroux, a new form of 'representational politics' has evolved in America centred on media culture: 'fueled by degrading visual depictions of youth as criminal, sexually decadent, drug crazed, and illiterate; in short, youth are viewed as a growing threat to public order; young people are no longer seen as a symptom of a wider social dilemma; they are the problem' (Giroux, 2000, p. 174). Giroux's analysis here is original as he posits a previously unnoticed connection between conservatism and transgressive art:

> I want to illuminate how Larry Clark's *Kids* functions pedagogically within a broader discourse about youth, focusing specifically on how such reproductions resonate with specific conservative attacks on related issues of sexuality, race and gender. Central to this analysis is a critique of transgressive art that serves to deploy teenage sexuality as decadent and predatory.
>
> (Giroux, 2000, p. 178)

While recognizing the distinctiveness of both transgressive art on the one side and conservatism on the other, Giroux none the less points to a surprising complicity between the two, if not in terms of their intention, at least in terms of their effects: 'such critics often legitimate rather than challenge the current conservative agenda for dispensing with those youth they view as disposable, if not dangerous, to the imperatives of the free market and global economy' (Giroux, 2000, p. 178). Giroux reads the specifics of Clark's aesthetic approaches into this critique. First, Clark's aesthetic approach is one of the male 'gaze' which objectifies the bodies of young girls, for example, in *Kids*. Second, the offshoot of this aesthetic approach is a consequent dimunition in agency: 'passivity and helplessness become the privileged modes of behaviour' (Giroux, 2000, p. 181). Consequently, Giroux interprets an 'ideological conservatism which under-girds *Kids*' (Giroux, 2000, p. 181), despite all the claims to transgressive radicality. Clark's is a 'viewpoint marked by the absence of a reflective moral perspective' (Giroux, 2000, p. 181). Giroux even goes so far as to accuse such transgressive art and criticism of 'perversion', for example, in the case of 'Amy Taubin' (Giroux, 2000, p. 184), an affirmative interpreter of Clark's work.

Grounding Giroux's analysis here is a critique of progressivism and a hidden complicity between such progressivism and conservatism. This is reminiscent of John Dewey's arguments about traditionalism and progressivism made in *Experience and Education* (Dewey, 1973). Giroux makes this point clear in the following paragraph:

> While it is important for progressives to continue to argue for freedom of expression in defending films or other cultural forms that they might find offensive ... they also need to take up what it means to provide an ethical discourse from which to criticise those images, discourses, and representations that might be destructive to the psychological health of children, or serve to undermine the normative foundations of a viable democracy.
> (Giroux, 2000, p. 188)

Needless to say, Giroux's reading of youth culture runs the risk of feeding the 'moral panic' his work is set up to address. On his own reading, critical pedagogy is less about condemning youth culture and more about delineating specific patterns of negativity which seem to have developed both in education and in society. For artists such as Tarantino or Clark, however, the critical pedagogy response is too 'moralizing' (Clark, 2008). It seeks to adapt and normalize the expressiveness of youth culture to a pre-ordained emancipatory ideal. As Tarantino says, if you don't like his film, 'don't watch it, man' (quoted Giroux, 2000, p. 188). Similarly, Clark is unabashed in his confidence that his representation of youth culture is a truer and more authentic version than any moral critique from Giroux or his like. For Clark, there is also a clear sense that any genuine transformation of youth can only come from within youth culture itself. Critical Pedagogy runs the risk, on this reading, of imposing a solution from without, an external panacea. To paraphrase Freire, transformation must be *by youth, with youth but not for youth* (Freire, 1996a). Which ever perspective one takes, it is clear that the Giroux/Clark debate foregrounds the importance of contemporary media and film in the construction of youth identity and youth ethics, and their relation to education. Giroux is an example of how critical pedagogy has faced this challenge head-on, bringing Freire's work to bear on more contemporary developments within education and culture. Here, they may be seen to be employing, above all, Freire's key insight that *culture is always political*. I will return to the question of how faithful their reading of Clark and transgressive art is to Freire's thought below. Suffice it to say here that there seem to be both affinities and tensions with Freire's own work. On the one side, there are affinities with regard to the undeniably political nature of culture and the danger of false consciousness of the 'oppressed'. On the other side, there is disaffinity, or at least tension, in perhaps an overly simplified or one-dimensional reading of popular culture and youth dissent.

Peter McLaren: a critique of 'ludic postmodernism'

A second example of how critical pedagogy has developed Freire's legacy is in the example of the work of Peter McLaren (McLaren, 1994). Influenced by Giroux in his early work, McLaren's work is especially characterized by an attempt to come to terms with the challenges and opportunities of 'postmodernist' thought. As with Giroux, McLaren pays explicit debts to Freire's thought throughout his work. Here, I want to focus on a seminal (but debatable) distinction which McLaren makes between two kinds of postmodernism (McLaren, 1994, p. 212). McLaren begins with a very relevant quotation from Freire's *The Politics of Education* (Freire, 1985), which bears on the question of the relation between aesthetics and politics, which we have seen as so central to Giroux's analysis of Larry Clark and transgressive art:

> For me, education is simultaneously an act of knowing, a political act and an artistic event. I no longer speak about a political dimension of education, I no longer speak about a knowing dimension of education. As well, I don't speak about education through art. On the contrary, I say education is politics, art and knowing.
>
> (Freire, 1985, p. 193)

Of course, this still begs the question, *which politics and which art?* For Giroux, much postmodern art is not art in the proper sense, that is, art which conforms to a specific ethical and political understanding of transformation and critique. In his essay, McLaren goes on to develop a distinction between two kinds of postmodernism, a 'reactionary postmodernism' (McLaren, 1994, p. 212) and a 'postmodernism of resistance' (McLaren, 1994, p. 212).

The problem with much postmodern social theory, as McLaren understands it, is that it 'has excluded from its practice the ability to think in utopian terms' (McLaren, 1994, p. 195). McLaren favourably quotes Richard Bernstein:

> Sometimes it seems as if we are living through a rage against modernity, a total disenchantment with the hopes and aspirations of what is best in our own democratic heritage, and with the type of fallibilistic humanism that Dewey advocated. But perhaps, after the dialectic of fashionable forms of relativism and domesticated nihilism work themselves out, we may return to the spirit of Dewey.
>
> (quoted McLaren, 1994, p. 196)

This highlights a strong connection between Dewey and Freire which McLaren has often cited, and McLaren has been critical of some forms of critical pedagogy and critical theory for eschewing the Deweyian influence as too modernist or 'liberal reformist' (McLaren, 1989).

For McLaren, then, the opposition is between what he terms 'ludic postmodernism' (McLaren, 1994, p. 205) [also known as 'sceptical' and 'spectral' postmodernism] and what has been referred to as 'oppositional postmodernism', 'radical critique all theory', 'postmodern education', 'resistance postmodernism', and 'critical postmodernism'. Developing the work of Teresa Ebert, McLaren proposes a transformative politics based on what he calls a 'resistance postmodernism' as a way of forcefully contesting ludic postmodernism. Ebert has described the latter approach as a 'cognitivism and an immanent critique that reduces politics to rhetoric and history to textuality and in the end cannot provide the basis for a transformative social practice' (quoted McLaren, 1994, p. 206). In contrast,

> resistance postmodernism is geared to understanding totalising systems of power such a patriarchy and capitalism as well as global structural relations of domination and the systematicity of regimes and exploitation. In this way, it redresses some of the shortcomings that result from the emphasis ludic postmodernism places on detotalising, Foucauldian micropolitics'.
>
> (McLaren, 1994, p. 206)

In conclusion, however, McLaren significantly cites the need to embrace a certain postmodernism on behalf of critical pedagogy. It would seem as if the way back to a pure modernism is forever blocked: 'as we search for a politics of liberation outside of the modernist constraints of consensus and epistemological certainty, for a politics inclusive of the multiple experiences and voices of groups oppressed within and outside of the developed world, Freire's work can continue to be instructive' (McLaren, 1994, p. 211). For McLaren, such a position (which is undeniably postmodern, albeit on his terms oppositional postmodernist) would enable new forms of liberation struggle against multiple forms of oppression while, at the same time, facilitating the disruption of essentialist identities of oppressed groups. It is to these new articulatory practices that Freire's work holds out its promise of possibility in these 'new' times.

(McLaren, 1994, p. 211)

bell hooks: 'we cannot enter the struggle as objects in order later to become subjects'

One final critical pedagogy theorist whom I would like refer to here is bell hooks (hooks, 1994). Her work is perhaps less explicitly associated with critical pedagogy than the others, although she is certainly claimed by, among others, McLaren. Her work brings an unusually critical analysis to bear on Freire's work, citing significant problems with his relation to feminism, for example, while none the less acknowledging his crucial influence on her own work. In an unusually formatted essay, 'bell hooks speaking about Paulo Freire: the man his work' (hooks, 1994, p. 146) where she interviews herself (in two voices), hooks refers to the empowering philosophy of Freire's *Pedagogy of the Oppressed* (Freire, 1996a) for her as an African-American southern woman. 'I had learned so much from his work – learned new ways of thinking about social reality that were liberatory. Paulo was one of the thinkers whose work gave me a language; he made me think deeply about the construction of an identity in resistance' (hooks, 1994, p. 146). Here, hooks sees one particular insight of Freire's as indispensable: 'there was this one sentence of Freire's that became a revolutionary mantra for me, "we cannot enter the struggle as objects in order later to become subjects"' (hooks, 1994, p. 147). Indeed, hooks' own method of writing here (as indeed her style of confessional writing generally) may be seen to instantiate or operationalize the Freirean method itself in practice. 'Gloria Watkins talking with bell hooks, her writing voice, a paradigmatic example of how the Freirean method works, a playful dialogue with myself' (hooks, 1994, p. 147). 'I wanted to speak about Paulo and his work in this way for it afforded me an intimacy –a familiarity – I do not find it possible to achieve in the essay, and here I have found a way to share the sweetness – the solidarity I talk about' (hooks, 1994, p. 147). But this solidarity is also couched in a cautious but necessary critique and distance:

There has never been a moment when reading Freire that I have not remained aware of not only the sexism of the language but the way he (like other progressive third world leaders, intellectuals, critical thinkers such as Fanon, Memmi etc) constructs a phallocentric paradigm of liberation – wherein freedom and the experience of patriarchal manhood are always linked as though they are one and the same.

(hooks, 1994, p. 148)

hooks feels it is important not to shy away from this problem, and here she is perhaps more courageous than her counterparts in critical pedagogy, who often opt for the more eulogistic style.

Here, hooks steers a middle ground between, on the one side, those in critical pedagogy who more or less refuse to criticize Freire (except very mildly or incidentally) and those, for example, in the ranks of American feminism, who would completely reject Freire's philosophy and pedagogy on the basis of the sexism of his language (which they see as amounting to a statement of fundamental misogyny): 'for me this is always a source of anguish for it represents a blind spot in the vision of one who has profound insight, and yet I never wish to see a critique of this blindspot overshadowing anyone's [and feminists in particular] capacity to learn from the insights' (hooks, 1994, p. 152). For hooks, the danger of such an approach is that we miss the immense insight of Freire, but also importantly we miss the ongoing nature of Freire's work, his self-critique and the openmindedness of his work: 'in so much of Paulo's work there is a generous spirit, a quality of open-mindedness that I feel is often missing from intellectual and academic arenas in US society, and feminist circles have not been an exception' (hooks, 1994, p. 152). Having looked at the connections and affinities between Freire's original work and its genealogy and the evolution of what has become known as critical pedagogy in America (especially the work of Giroux, McLaren and hooks), I want now to look at how there are also disaffinities or tensions which are significant in this legacy.

Tensions in the critical pedagogy analysis

Critical pedagogy very explicitly pays its debts to Freire and there is homage paid to him by the key critical pedagogy thinkers, such as Henry Giroux, bell hooks and Peter McLaren. However, not all commentators agree on the positivity of such connections, with some sceptical of critical pedagogy's developments of Freire and others critical of the assumptions of both critical pedagogy and Freire's own original work. One important example of such criticism is that of Nigel Blake and Jan Masschelein, which they put forward of critical pedagogy in their essay 'Critical Theory and Critical Pedagogy' (Blake and Masschelein, 2003). They argue that critical theory plays only a marginal role at best in the development of critical pedagogy, seeing the project as determined largely by Freire's *Pedagogy of the Oppressed* (Freire, 1996a) and the so-called new sociology of education (which included Bourdieu and Bernstein) (Bourdieu and Eagleton, 1994).

For these commentators, critical pedagogy remains attached to a strongly instrumental and functional concept of educational practice, because it has not questioned the very concept of educational *praxis* itself, but conceived it as an instrument for liberation or repression. Educational practice still receives its meaning from the goal or end at which it should aim, here conceived as a utopia. Education then becomes the realization or execution of this programme; it is thus fundamentally a 'technological project'. Its first step, according to Blake and Masschelein, is the formulation of an ideal or utopia, which it uncritically supposes both possible and necessary. It thus remains subject to the same instrumental logic which it itself deplores at the heart of the capitalist system. As Blake and Masschelein polemically observe, 'the deeper failure [of critical pedagogy] has been to overlook the most serious motive behind Critical Theory, its negative aspect and messianic impulse, transforming it into a positivistic form of ideology critique and program building' (Blake and Masschelein, 2003, p. 53).

Tensions between Clark and Giroux

Aside from the issue of the relation between critical theory and critical pedagogy, we can also highlight analogous ideological tensions if we return to the discussion between Giroux and Clark. If films and media constitute a new form of public pedagogy, then this brings the responsibility of value and character formation with it. One question here is to what extent, for example, Giroux's model of interpretation depends upon a neo-Marxist conception of false consciousness among youth. That is, on this view, youth cannot see reality which is obscured by processes of negative socialization and ideological manipulation by the capitalist system. Much current educational theory works under similar presuppositions concerning the emancipation of the underclass (i.e. capitalism is wholly bad and the delinquency of youth is due to external factors).

This so-called 'emancipatory' perspective may be questioned from a number of points of view but a film-maker and photographer such as Clark (Clark, 1995), through his diverse and challenging artistic work, particularly makes us question the hierarchical power dynamic at work between educators and youth, in such a supposedly emancipatory ethic. As Freire outlines in *Pedagogy of the Oppressed*: 'liberation of the oppressed, by the oppressed themselves, with the oppressed but never for the oppressed' (Freire, 1996a). Otherwise, power and especially the power of decision and autonomy is never transferred to the oppressed; what one gets is simply the substitution of one oppression for another. Clark's work steers clear of such concepts of emancipation and, in so doing, although he doesn't bring about emancipation himself or seek to do so, he leaves open the possibility of an authentic and autonomous self-development and transformation of youth.

Giroux's reading of Clark is, however, wholly negative. Giroux accuses Clark of 'irresponsibility' and of the absence of any moral framework for judging or encouraging youth (Giroux, 2000, p. 178). However, it is clear that Giroux and Clark share one perspective in common: neither see film or media as primarily a form of entertainment. Clark's films break all the rules of conventional entertainment – the characters are barely drawn, nothing much happens, what does is rather gruesome, and a general air of helplessness and ennui pervades his scenes. His characters refuse to be entertaining and his choice of real children, as opposed to actors, for the roles is another example of his conscious effort to distance his work from the industry. This is hardly surprising; his photographic work from *Tulsa* (Clark, 1980) onwards is rooted in community, in subcultures of the underclass, and pointedly avoids the professionalism of much mainstream and fashion photography. It is *self-consciously amateur* and, to this extent, Clark would seem to be making a pedagogical point about youth not dissimilar to that of Giroux: the commodification of culture and, most especially in this context, youth and childhood, should be resisted. Here, we can see why Clark is so interested in subcultural youth. At this micro-level, there is the real possibility of overcoming the stereotypical generalities of contemporary youth; 'youth as such' or contemporary youth or 'young people today'. Rather, in all its tawdry disharmony, we get a picture of this individual group of youths, at this particular time, in this particular place, whether it is Tulsa or New York. I think Giroux is wrong when he accuses Clark of unequivocally glorying in fatalism and circularity. Much of Clark's work seems intent on demonstrating the horrific effects of such nihilism – death, murder, disease and the degeneration of human relationships to instrumental utility. However, it is true that, at times, Clark seems to suggest that there may be a positive kind of deviancy in this nihilism, as if, through its very apocalyptic destructiveness, youth was offering some kind of counter-ideology to normal society. These moments are none the less rare. I think the crucial difference between Giroux and Clark lies rather in their pedagogical approach to youth and its implications for an ethics and politics of childhood and youth.

One of the methodological problems one might associate with the kind of moral position taken by Giroux (i.e. youth must be emancipated from their capitalist predicament) is that it is perhaps excessively general. There is one answer for all youth and it's a simple answer of emancipation. Clark's art seems to point us in a different direction. If there is a moral answer to the dilemmas of youth, it can only evolve from within the specific context itself. Clark's powerful depiction of the particularities of each problem situation seems to suggest that solutions as well as problems need to be particular. The resolution for Clark of the predicament of youth cannot come from above, but can only develop from the most base, bottom level. In this, Clark may be showing himself more faithful to an emancipatory ethos than is Giroux's excessively top-down methodology. The current dominant pedagogical approach to youth, then, needs, it seems to me, a serious *rethink*.

One way to understand what is going on here is to make a distinction between two kinds of leftist thinking: on the one side, that developing from Althusser and Marcuse's *One-Dimensional Man* and its pessimistic definition of consumption as sheer passivity within a mechanism of domination (Althusser, 1994; Marcuse, 2002). This is a tradition from which critical pedagogy takes a significant degree of its perspective. On the other, one has a notion of consumption as a form of production that comes to disrupt the established order. Here, we have the leftist thinking of Henri Lefebvre (Lefebvre, 2002), as well as the development into the work of the Birmingham CCCS (Hall, 1996a; Willis, 1981), which I would like to look at in more detail below. Developing this point, we can certainly see how this analysis might be applied to the critique of popular culture and postmodernism which Giroux and McLaren most especially put forward. What is wrong with 'ludic postmodernism', we might ask? Certainly we can critique the legitimacy of this latter category in itself but we can also look to tensions between critical pedagogy and the evolution of Freire's own thought. Is the latter more subtle in his analysis of culture and education (and their problematic intersection) than the former?

Here we return to some of the issues which we addressed earlier in our discussion of the evolution of Freire's thought. As Freire delineates, what he calls the problem of 'sectarianism' is paradigmatic for the possibilities of any emancipatory ethic. Might this problematic be relevant in terms of a reading of Giroux's work and its analysis of art and culture, especially youth and film culture? Might it also be applicable to McLaren's perhaps rather over-hasty distinction between ludic and resistance postmodernism (McLaren, 1994)? To use Freire's own term, do both Giroux and McLaren here run the risk of becoming caught up in a 'circle of certainty'? As Freire puts it, the sectarian (because they are caught within a 'circle of certainty') cannot perceive what Freire terms the 'dynamic' of reality. Freire has acknowledged that his earlier work runs the risk of becoming the very sectarianism it sets out to critique. Here, we might ask whether the legacy of his philosophical work developed through critical pedagogy might run a similar (or even intensified) risk. For Freire, the dividing line between 'popular knowledge' and the expert is fatal for the educator, or at least the one who wishes to be radical rather than sectarian. This was a paradigmatic theme of Freire's work even before *Pedagogy of the Oppressed* (Freire, 1996a). In his early text *Extension or Communication* (Freire, 2005a), he demystifies all aid or helping relationships. He sees an implicit ideology of paternalism, social control and nonreciprocity between experts and 'helpees' and refers to the oppressive character of all nonreciprocal relationships (Freire, 1996a). We might also ask a related point about McLaren's distinction between a 'ludic' and a 'resistance' postmodernism (McLaren, 1994). Freire refers to a 'new saying': is McLaren's distinction not too much of an 'old saying'? Is it not too binary to be authentically Freirean and indeed perhaps too orthodox? Freire wrote *Pedagogy of the Oppressed* (Freire, 1996a) in 1967/1968. In 1992, he seeks to look at it again, 'rethink it, restate it; and to do some new saying as well; by speaking of hope' (Freire, 1992). For Freire, this is a permanent process of search which requires patience and humility. It is also a fraught process, and we have seen some of its tensions in our analysis of critical pedagogy.

While critical pedagogy has taken up the Freirean legacy most explicitly in America, it has often been argued that Freire's legacy does not bear, for example, on the British context. However, an interesting counter-example, which I now want to look at, is the example of the so-called Birmingham CCCS, which began its work in the 1970s but whose work has also evolved through the later decades, most especially in the work of Stuart Hall (Hall, 1996a) and Paul Willis (Willis, 1981) respectively.

Understanding the analysis of the Birmingham CCCS

In this section, I want to look at the work of the Birmingham CCCS in more detail. My rationale here is that, as with critical pedagogy, we can see the Birmingham CCCS developing the legacy of Freire's original work in newer, postmodern times. As with critical pedagogy, the CCCS's relation to Freire is not simple or unequivocal. However, an analysis of the respective affinities and disaffinities will, I think, be instructive for us here, most notably because the tensions manifested between the CCCS and Freire are related but significantly different from those of critical pedagogy. Here, I will concentrate on the work of two figures, although the work of the school is obviously more wide-ranging and arguably conflictual than this. I will look at the work of Stuart Hall and of Paul Willis (Hall *et al.*, 1993; Hall, 1996a–c; Willis, 1981, 2004). Again, my analysis here will be very selective, only bearing on their relevance for my topic.

It is arguable that Freire's work, on my terms, has been more faithfully developed by thinkers such as Stuart Hall and the Birmingham School of Cultural Studies (CCCS), who are more subtle in their analysis of the complexity of popular culture and subcultures than critical pedagogy, without losing sight of the need for clear political commitments and action. As Hall has put it,

How a politics can be constructed which works with and through difference, which is able to build those forms of solidarity and identifi-cation which make common struggle and resistance possible but without suppressing the real heterogeneity of interests and identities, and which

can effectively draw the political boundary lines without which political contestation is impossible, without fixing those boundaries for eternity?
(Hall, 1996a, p. 273)

It is the immense challenge of this 'politics of difference' (Charles Taylor's term) that I believe Freire's work genuinely confronts.

If the initial work of the Birmingham CCCS from 1975, in *Resistance through Rituals* (Hall *et al.*, 1993), is very much focused on youth subcultures in postwar Britain, it soon develops into a more generalized analysis of the way hegemony is maintained, structurally and historically. The work of Stuart Hall especially may be seen as deepening the Gramscian insight (Gramsci, 1988) that cultural or superstructural elements play a constitutive and not just a derivative or reflexive role in the constitution of social and political life. Two of Hall's essays are paradigmatic in this context: 'The Problem of Ideology: Marxism Without Guarantees' (Hall, 1996c) and 'Cultural Studies and its Theoretical Legacies' (Hall, 1996a). The latter essay is important in this context because it is one of the clearest statements of the rationale behind the connection between cultural studies and education from the 1970s onwards. Initially, this stemmed from the origins of the Cultural Studies movement in the Adult Education movement in Britain in the 1950s and 1960s. Figures such as Raymond Williams and Richard Hoggart explored the issue of 'culture and education' from the perspective of those groups or individuals who had been marginalized by the centralized education system and mainstream culture. In the essay 'The Problem of Ideology; Marxism Without Guarantees' (Hall, 1996c), Hall points to certain problems in the more traditional concept of Marxist ideology, and he proposes a work of reconstruction which is not predetermined by ritual orthodoxy. That is, Hall posits a move away from an abstract theory of ideology and towards the more concrete analysis of how, in particular historical situations, ideas organize human masses, and create the terrain on which human beings move, acquire consciousness of their position, struggle, etc., which makes the work of Gramsci a figure of seminal importance.

Laclau, according to Hall (Hall, 1996c), has demonstrated definitively the untenable nature of the proposition that classes, as such, are the subjects of fixed and subscribed class ideologies. He has also dismantled the proposition that particular ideas and concepts belong exclusively to one particular class; ideas and concepts do not occur in language or thought in that single isolated way with their content and reference irremovably fixed. Hall's essay 'Cultural Studies and its Theoretical Legacies' (Hall, 1996a) thus establishes the open horizon of Marxist theorizing, the development and refinement of new concepts which alone is the sign of a living body of thought, capable still of engaging with and grasping something of the truth about new historical realities.

Alternative versions of culture, especially working-class culture, and education, especially adult education, were explored as a means of questioning the assumed principles of the centralized education system. Evolving out of this work in the 1970s, The Birmingham Cultural Studies Centre (CCCS) extended this new focus of attention to so-called 'youth culture'. According to theorists such as Hall, Phil Cohen (Cohen, 1999) and Angela Mc Robbie, the explosive changes being wrought in society were creating an acute gap between two sets of groups, between adult and youth culture, each understood in a general sense. Second, within youth culture, between more mainstream youth and more marginalized, disaffected youth, who expressed their alienation through the formation of subcultures (Hall *et al.*, 1993). The pedagogical significance of these subcultures and the relationship between youth alienation and education or schooling was a central concern of the Birmingham group from the beginning. The importance of cultural studies may be seen as its refining of a Left Marxist perspective into the 1980s and 1990s, through a new emphasis on the interconnectedness of race, gender, sexuality and youth issues. This is intellectual work 'as a practice which always thinks about its intervention in a world in which it would make some difference, in which it would have some effect' (Hall, 1996a, p. 273).

The work of Paul Willis: no more duped youth

Paul Willis (originally a doctoral student at the CCCS) develops Hall's eclectic and radically democratic approach to the relationship between education, culture and society, while also maintaining a strong connecting spirit to the work of Paulo Freire, most especially in his seminal first text, *Learning to Labour* (Willis, 1981). In particular, the emphasis on agency (or subjectivity), on the importance of creativity and on the continuing relevance of class (although now complexified and mediated by culture) is emphasized. Willis continues to evolve this analysis in his later works, such as *The Ethnographic Imagination* (Willis, 2000). An important recent collection of essays on Willis, *Learning to Labour in New Times* (Dolby *et al.*, 2004), with essays by significant thinkers such as Michael Apple (Apple, 2004), demonstrates the continuing influence and legacy of Willis. Two contributions of his own to the volume (an essay and an interview) are significant here, as Willis seeks to recontextualize *Learning to Labour* in the light of his subsequent intellectual development (Willis, 2004). In these texts, there is a clear *rapprochement* between Willis and Freire's work.

In *Learning to Labour in New Times* (Dolby *et al.*, 2004), Dolby *et al.* speak of the 'oppositional working-class culture' foregrounded by Willis and its misapprehension by much contemporary educational and political discourse (especially of a Leftist kind). Willis teaches us that 'what youth do is important; they are political actors and not simply dupes. ... Reproduction is never total' (Willis, 2004). Developing the notion of an irreducibility of human experience to class or ethnicity, Willis allows us to see moments of creativity or new possibilities within social and political situations, which many other commentators view as fatalistic. He also allows educational discourse to 'decentre school' and to develop policy from below. For Michael Apple, Willis puts forward not a representative model but a 'disclosure model' (Apple, 2004). He develops an innovative reading of the 'complex social field of power' and eschews (*contra* Althusser, Bourdieu and others) a 'reductive and economistic reading of class' (Apple, 2004). Willis allows us to focus on an anti-essentializing problematic, where a class analysis needs to return, but as a 'project' (Apple, 2004). Again, the connections and affinities to Freire's work are striking.

Connecting Freire and the CCCS

The importance of cultural studies may be seen as its refining of a Left Marxist perspective into the 1980s and 1990s, through a new emphasis on the interconnectedness of race, gender, sexuality and youth issues. It is possible to argue that it is precisely this ideological dimension of the work of the Birmingham school which has had the greatest impact on the rise of critical pedagogy as an attempt to analyse this same problematic in a more contemporary setting, and with more specific reference not simply to youth culture, but to youth in educational and school settings. However, as central figures in critical pedagogy continue to emphasize, we must not lose sight of the genealogy of these issues in discourse and in the evolution of culture and society – otherwise, we risk tackling the present in an historical vacuum. Just as the Birmingham school looked back to figures such as Antonio Gramsci to develop their conception of the 'organic intellectual' who sought to connect academic research with the 'real world', so too the more recent work looks back to the example of Hall *et al.* as paradigms of what intellectual work can achieve when it maintains a strong link to political and educational practice.

The work of the Birmingham Centre for Contemporary Cultural Studies (CCCS) bequeathed a number of important unresolved questions to the analysts who followed. To what extent is 'youth culture' a symptom of underlying intergenerational tension and difficulties? Can we distinguish between better and worse versions of youth culture or youth subcultures (i.e. those that are more or less attuned to their participants' well-being)? What is the relation between this well-being of youth, or its lack, and the institutional educational contexts in which youth find themselves day-to-day (i.e. how does school and education impact on the well-being or otherwise of youth)? These issues were indicated and developed by the earlier CCCS but never resolved. The development of critical pedagogy in the United States in the 1980s and 1990s was an attempt to address these issues more directly and this movement was especially concerned with addressing what it saw as the intrinsic connection between education and the well-being of youth. Critical pedagogy, therefore, as its name suggests, was concerned to focus the insights of cultural studies on the school and the youth of the school. Alongside the influence of the CCCS, the work of Paulo Freire was crucial in the evolution of critical pedagogy, and here we see somewhat of a missing link – that between Freire and the Birmingham CCCS. From his initially most important text *Pedagogy of the Oppressed* (Freire, 1996a) right through to his work in the 1980s and early 1990s, such as *Pedagogy of Hope* (Freire, 1992), Freire was convinced of the interconnectedness of school and culture, education and society. Moreover, in a manner similar to the feminists' work in the CCCS, Freire worked out from the fundamental principle that the political is the personal – or *the pedagogical is the personal*.

Developing insights from earlier existentialist thinkers such as Sartre (Sartre, 2007), Freire focused on how the evolution of contemporary society and education produced a culture of 'sadism' (Freire, 1996a), where the individual self becomes enculturated into treating all others as objects for its own use. The corollary of this sadism, however, is an underlying 'masochism' (Freire, 1996a), a failure of the self to understand him/herself and to properly relate to others in an authentic manner. Interpersonal relations become stultified in what Freire refers to powerfully as a culture of 'necrophily', or death. At the root of this problem, for Freire, is a system of education which has developed into a pure instrumentalism – what he refers to as a 'banking system'. Both Freire and the CCCS are working out of a broadly defined neo-Marxist perspective, sensitive to cultural change and youth, and critical of the negative impact of an instrumental educational and societal system which seems to alienate youth and subtract from their well-being. At the same time, the vision of both schools of thought is fundamentally optimistic and transformative, arguing for the responsibility and potential of each individual to enact change and progress in their particular situation. While cognizant of the macro-dimension and its restrictions on individual agency, both Freire and the CCCS ultimately theorize from the micro-level of individual practices and individual temporalities or 'history from below' (Hall, 1996a).

The futures of critical pedagogy: where to now?

We have thus explored in some detail the connections between Freire and the movements of critical pedagogy and the Birmingham CCCS respectively. In conclusion to this chapter and the book, I want to explore what we might term the 'possible futures' of Freire's thinking. I begin by referring to two key readings of a meta-level problem of interpretation. This latter problematic is especially concerned with the tensions between modernist and postmodernist elements in Freire's work, and the manner in which those tensions are also manifest in the work of those who have developed his legacy, through either critical pedagogy, or, as another example, through the Birmingham CCCS. The first interpretation is that of the late Joe L. Kincheloe (Kincheloe, 1994), given in an Afterword to an anthology of essays on Freire (from a critical pedagogy perspective). The second reading comes from Freire himself and is given in his Preface to a different but related anthology of work, published the year before (Freire, 1993a).

In his Afterword to an anthology of essays on Freire (from a critical pedagogy perspective), Joe L. Kincheloe contextualizes the significance of the relationship between Freire's original work and more 'postmodernist' approaches to his legacy. As he observes, 'what an interesting development this volume heralds; radical pedagogy and social theory can no longer be contemplated outside the parameters of postmodernism' (Kincheloe, 1994, p. 216). Kincheloe calls for a reconsideration of Freire's work, but not in a negative sense. Rather, for Kincheloe, the very emphasis on reconsideration is a 'barometer of democracy' and a sign that 'the critical educational tradition is flourishing' (Kincheloe, 1994, p. 216). Kincheloe contrasts this *open-ended and more heterodox approach* to Freire's legacy with a tendency 'to deify Freire and in the process destroy the living vibrancy of the work' (Kincheloe, 1994, p. 216). Rather than this sycophantic approach, a more authentic alternative is to see Freire's work as a call to become more fully human, which will always involve 'critique' from the perspective of more contemporary developments in culture and society (many of which Freire could not, or at least did not, anticipate). Kincheloe ends his analysis with a call for the formulation of a 'critical [post-] epistemology for a radical pedagogy' that will enable us to 'ethically ground a postmodern education' (Kincheloe, 1994, p. 217).

But this view of the necessity of a radical interrogation of Freire's work is not simply an externalist view. In many respects, it mirrors a call for such reconstruction and critique that comes from within Freire's own work. This is especially clear when one reads Freire's (Freire, 1993a) Foreword to another anthology on his work, entitled *Paulo Freire: A Critical Encounter* (McLaren and Leonard, 1993a). Written some 20 or more years after *Pedagogy of the Oppressed*, this Foreword gives us a very significant insight into Freire's own meta-assessment of the evolution of his thought. Freire begins by clarifying that this anthology is more than simply a homage or 'testament' to his original work. Rather, there is more importantly an attempt to 'refine and develop a critical pedagogy attentive to the changing face of social, cultural, gender and global relations' (Freire, 1993a, p. ix). Freire explicitly mentions several key issues here, such as the nature of subjectivity and its relation to language, the connection between interpretation and practice, and the problematic of authority, most especially as it relates to feminist pedagogy (this last point relates back to our earlier discussion of bell hooks) (hooks, 1994)).

Freire also explicitly thematizes the difficult relationship between 'modernist' and 'postmodernist' themes in his work, especially as this relates to the development of his work in critical pedagogy. In this anthology, many of the authors address the issue of the problematic of postmodernism head-on. Significantly, they choose not to simply reject the latter per se but rather to interrogate its potential for transformation and critical insight. As Freire notes, 'a number of these authors have attempted to bring my work into conversation with European thinkers who represent what has come to be called "modernist" and "postmodernist" strains of thought' (Freire, 1993a, p. ix). Freire acknowledges that his own early work often does not directly address these issues, but he speaks of an appreciation of 'how much has been accomplished by what Giroux describes as "critical postmodernist thought"' (Freire, 1993a, p. ix). The chapters in the book by Giroux, Da Silva and hooks, for example, attempt according to Freire, to

> Illustrate the ways in which my readings of subjectivity, experience and power bear some relation to certain strains of poststructuralist thought. In addition, they attempt to reveal how some aspects of my work can be appropriated into and extended by critical postmodern educational practice, without sacrificing some of modernity's laudable goals.
>
> (Freire, 1993a, p. ix)

This is a fascinating statement from two perspectives. In the first case, it is interesting, since it emblematizes Freire's own relation to poststructuralist (or 'postmodernist') thinking, a connection which is often underestimated. On the other side, Freire is also demonstrating a certain complicity between modernism and postmodernism, where modernity's 'laudable goals' might paradoxically be better achieved, in some instances, by postmodernism. However, Freire ends with a note of warning, which demonstrates that he is hardly naïve when it comes to the wider politics of this encounter.

> I agree with Giroux and McLaren when they caution educators that excursions into the discourse of postmodern social theory are often purchased at the price of sacrificing narratives of freedom underwritten by an ethical imagination. I share their concern that current epistemological and ontological shifts taking place in social theory must be firmly grounded in human narratives of emancipation and social justice.
>
> (Freire, 1993a, p. x)

So we have seen how there are significant affinities between Freire and the critical pedagogy evolution of his thought, while there are also disaffinities and tensions. I have especially paid heed to one of the key nodes of postmodern culture, the question of how to interpret media and popular cultural developments. Since Gramsci, this has been a key question for the leftist thinker. Questions remain as to how this problematic will evolve into the future and as to how Freire's legacy might develop in relation to such a problematic.

Last thoughts

My claim in this book has been that Freire's work leaves a complex legacy which must be adapted to new times and to new challenges. Critical pedagogy is very explicit in its debts to Freire and, as we have seen, it develops an internally differentiated approach which varies from Giroux's focus on youth culture, to McLaren's interest in 'resistance postmodernism', to hook's emphasis on feminism and a residual problem of patriarchal language in Freire. Certainly, there are tensions here, both with Freire's own thought and among the thinkers themselves, but against the aforementioned reading of Blake and Masschelein (Blake and Masschelein, 2003) which accused critical pedagogy of instrumentalism and positivism, it would seem that such internal differentiation points to an openmindedness and theoretical (and practical-political) flexibility, which is wholly in keeping with Freire's original approach to pedagogy and culture. Freire's own advocation and affirmation of this critical pedagogy approach should also be seen as a significant factor in understanding the relationship between his original thought and the theory which seeks to develop his legacy. In effect, critical pedagogy is to be credited with keeping a vibrant Freirean tradition alive and well, kicking and screaming into a postmodernist epoch. That said, there remains a residual tendency towards binarism within critical pedagogy, most especially in the work of Giroux and McLaren. Whether this itself relates to a binarism in Freire's own work is open to debate. But, going forward, it would seem that the channels of communication to youth culture, transgressive art and ludic postmodernism should perhaps be kept more open than heretofore. The example of the wider implications for leftist thinking are instructive here, most especially if we contrast a tendency towards emphases on 'domination' and 'creativity/production' (admittedly this itself runs the risk of binarism, and all the while we see the significance of Freire's original distinction between sectarianism and radicalization in *Pedagogy of the Oppressed*).

On the other side, we are faced with a less explicit rendering of the Freirean legacy in the British context, through the work of the CCCS. On one level, there is much connection between critical pedagogy and the CCCS, and the former refer continually to the influence of the latter on the development of their work (especially Giroux and McLaren). However, the problems here are somewhat different from those of critical pedagogy. While beginning with a quite radical understanding of Gramscian politics, it is arguable that the CCSS, and most especially the work of the later Hall, develops in a strongly postmodernist dimension (under the influence of Derrida, among others). Here, in contrast to the problem of critical pedagogy being too rigid, it might be argued that the CCCS betrays its Gramscian and Freirean roots, becoming too assimilated into a postmodern discourse. By the same token, the CCSS perhaps demonstrates the importance of new ways of seeing and new ways of saying, Freire's 'new saying'. In its very radicality towards culture and postmodernism, it perhaps provokes critical pedagogy to become less rigidified and moralistic. Conversely, critical pedagogy challenges the CCCS to become less culturalist, perhaps less 'ludicly' postmodernist, on McLaren's terms. It would seem to be in this very dialogical encounter between the CCCS and critical pedagogy that Freire's legacy is both eminently manifested and put repeatedly to the test of the most insistent demands of the contemporary epoch.

BIBLIOGRAPHY

Primary sources

Freire, P. (1977), *Cultural Action for Freedom*. Translated by J. da Veiga Coutinho. London: Nicholls.

—(1978), *Pedagogy in Process: The Letters To Guinea-Bissau*. New York: Writers and Readers Co-operative.

—(1985), *The Politics of Education: Culture, Power and Liberation*. Boston, MA: Bergen and Garvey.

—(1992), *Pedagogy of Hope: Reliving Pedagogy of the Oppressed*. Translated by R. Barr. London: Continuum.

—(1993), 'Foreword' to *Paulo Freire: A Critical Encounter* edited by P. McLaren and P. Leonard. London: Routledge, pp. ix–xii.

—(1995a), 'Some Issues: Neutrality, Respect for the Students, Epistemological Curiosity, and International Financial Aid', in M. de Figueiredo-Cowen and D. Gastaldo ed. *Paulo Freire at the Institute*. London: Institute of Education.

—(1995b), 'The Progressive Teacher', in M. de Figueiredo-Cowen and D. Gastaldo ed. *Paulo Freire at the Institute*. London: Institute of Education.

—(1995c), 'Reply to Discussants', in M. de Figueiredo-Cowen and D. Gastaldo ed. *Paulo Freire at the Institute*. London: Institute of Education.

—(1996a), *Pedagogy of the Oppressed*. London: Continuum.

—(1996b), *Letters to Cristina: Reflections on My Life and Work*. Translated by D. Macedo, Q. Macedo and A. Oliveira. London: Routledge.

—(1998), *Pedagogy of Freedom: Ethics, Democracy and Civic Courage*. Oxford: Rowman & Littlefield.

—(2004), *Pedagogy of Indignation*. London: Paradigm.

—(2005a), *Education as the Practice of Freedom*, in P. Freire, *Education For Critical Consciousness*. London: Continuum.

—(2005b), *Extension or Communication* in P. Freire, *Education For Critical Consciousness*. London: Continuum.

—(2005c), *Education for Critical Consciousness*. Translated by M. Ramos, L. Bigwood and M. Marshall. London: Continuum.

—(2005d), *Teachers as Cultural Workers: Letters to Those Who Dare Teach*. Expanded edition translated by D. Macedo, D. Koike and A. Oliveira. Cambridge, MA: Westview Press.

—(2006), *Pedagogy of the Heart*. Translated by D. Macedo and A. Oliveira. London: Continuum.

Freire, P. with Escobar, M., Fernández, S. and Guevara-Niebla, G. (1994), *Paulo*

Freire on Higher Education: A Dialogue at the National University of Mexico.
New York: State University of New York.

Freire, P. and Faundez, A. (1989), *Learning to Question: A Pedagogy of Liberation.*
Translated by T. Coates. Geneva: WCC.

Freire, P. and Macedo, D. (1993), 'A Dialogue with Paulo Freire', in P. McLaren
and P. Leonard. ed. *Paulo Freire: A Critical Encounter.* London: Routledge,
pp. 169–76.

Freire, P. and Torres, C. A. (1994), 'Twenty Years After Pedagogy of the Oppressed:
Paulo Freire in Conversation with Carlos Alberto Torres' in P. McLaren and
C. Lankshear, ed. *Politics of Liberation: Paths from Freire.* London:
Routledge.

Selected secondary texts

Althusser, L. (1994), 'Ideology and Ideological State Apparatuses (Notes Towards
an Investigation)', in S. Žižek ed. *Mapping Ideology.* London: Verso, pp. 35–47.

—(2001), *Lenin and Philosophy and Other Essays.* Monthly Review Press: New
York.

Andreola, B. A. (2004), 'Letter to Paulo Freire', in P. Freire *Pedagogy of
Indignation.* London: Paradigm.

Appiah, K. A. (2006), 'Identity, Authenticity, Survival: Multicultural Societies
and Social Reproduction', in L. Thomassen *The Derrida-Habermas Reader.*
Edinburgh: Edinburgh University Press.

Apple, M. (2004), 'Between Good Sense and Bad Sense: Race, Class, and Learning
from Learning to Labour', in N. Dolby *et al.* (with Paul Willis) *Learning to
Labour in New Times.* London: RoutledgeFarmer, pp. 61–82.

Araújo Freire, A. M. (1992), 'Notes', in P. Freire *Pedagogy of Hope: Reliving
Pedagogy of the Oppressed.* Translated by R. Barr. London: Continuum.

—(2004), 'Prologue', in P. Freire *Pedagogy of Indignation.* London: Paradigm, pp.
iv–xii.

Araújo Freire, A. M. and Macedo, D. ed. (1998), *The Paulo Freire Reader.* New
York: Teacher's College.

—(2005), 'Preface', in P. Freire *Teachers as Cultural Workers: Letters to Those
Who Dare Teach.* Expanded edition translated by D. Macedo, D. Koike and A.
Oliveira. Cambridge, MA: Westview Press, pp. vii–xxvii.

Badiou, A. (2001), *Ethics.* Verso: London.

Bakunin, M. (1883), 'What is Authority?', in G. Woodcock ed. (1977), *The
Anarchist Reader.* Glasgow: Fontana, pp. 210–12.

—(1910), 'Perils of the Marxist State', in G. Woodcock ed. (1977), *The Anarchist
Reader.* Glasgow: Fontana, pp. 215–18.

Balibar, E. (2007), *The Philosophy of Marx.* London: Verso.

Bataille, G. (1988), *Visions of Excess: Selected Early Writings.* Translated by
A. Stoekl. Minnesota: University of Minnesota Press.

Baugh, B. (2003), *French Hegel: From Surrealism to Postmodernism.* New York:
Routledge.

Bell, D. (1973), *The Coming of Post-Industrial Society.* New York: Basic Books.

Bernasconi, R. ed. (2004), *Race.* Routledge: London.

Bhabha, H. (1986), 'Foreword: Remembering Fanon: Self, Psyche and the Colonial Condition', in F. Fanon, *Black Skin, White Masks*. London: Pluto.

Black, B. (1997), *Anarchy After Leftism*. Birmingham: CAL Press.

Blake, N. and Masschelein, J. (2003), 'Critical Theory and Critical Pedagogy', in N. Blake, P. Smeyers, R. Smith and P. Standish (eds) *The Blackwell Guide to the Philosophy of Education*. Oxford: Blackwell, pp. 38–57.

Blake, N., Smeyers, P., Smith, R. and Standish, P. (2003b), 'Introduction', in *The Blackwell Guide to the Philosophy of Education*. Oxford: Blackwell, pp. 1–18.

Bookchin, M. (1974), 'Paris, 1968', in G. Woodcock ed. (1977) *The Anarchist Reader*. Glasgow: Fontana, pp. 316–21.

Bourdieu, P. and Eagleton. T. (1994), 'Doxa and Common Life: An Interview'. in S. Žižek (ed.) *Mapping Ideology*. London: Verso, pp. 265–77.

Brown, C. (1975), *Literacy in 30 Hours: Paulo Freire's Process in North East Brazil*. London: Open Learning and Teaching.

Buber, M. (2002), *Between Man and Man* London: Routledge and Kegan Paul.

Burke, A. (2007), 'Cross-Competencies in the Competencies/Standards Debate in Teaching and Teacher Education', *North-South* AB 5, June.

—(2009), 'The B.Ed. Degree: Still Under Review', *Oideas*, September, pp. 1–43.

Callan, E. and White, J. (2003), 'Liberalism and Communitarianism', in N. Blake, P. Smeyers, R. Smith, and P. Standish (eds) *The Blackwell Guide to the Philosophy of Education*. Blackwell: Oxford, pp. 95–111.

Carr, W. ed. (2005a), *The RoutledgeFalmer Reader in Philosophy of Education*. London: Routledge.

—(2005b), 'Introduction: What is the Philosophy of Education', in W. Carr ed. *The RoutledgeFalmer Reader in Philosophy of Education*. London: Routledge, pp. 1–15.

Carr-Hill, R. (1995), 'Empowerment for the Individual or the State', in M. de Figueiredo-Cowen and D. Gastaldo ed. *Paulo Freire at the Institute*. London: Institute of Education, pp. 56–60.

Chew, J. (1995), 'Literacy Among Surrey Sixth Formers', in M. de Figueiredo-Cowen and D. Gastaldo ed. *Paulo Freire at the Institute*. London: Institute of Education, pp. 51–5.

Chonchol, J. (2005), 'Preface to *Extension or Communication*', P. Freire, *Education for Critical Consciousness*. Translated by M. Ramos, L. Bigwood and M. Marshall. London: Continuum, pp. 79–84.

Clark, L. (1980), *Tulsa*. New York: Virago.

—(1995), *Kids* (screenplay). New York: Grove Press.

—(2008), 'Interview: I'm Just Telling It Like It Is' with Sean O'Hagan In the *Guardian* newspaper. London: 17 February.

Cohen, P. (1999), *Rethinking the Youth Question: Education, Labour and Cultural Studies*. Durham, NC: Duke University Press.

Coutinho, J. Da Veiga (1977), 'Preface', in P. Freire, *Cultural Action for Freedom*. London: Nicholls, pp. 7–12.

Cowen, R. (1995), 'Afterword', in M. de Figueiredo-Cowen and D. Gastaldo ed. *Paulo Freire at the Institute*. London: Institute of Education, pp. 76–8.

Da Silva, T. T. and McLaren, P. (1993), 'Knowledge Under Siege: The Brazilian Debate', in P. McLaren and P. Leonard ed. *Paulo Freire: A Critical Encounter*. London: Routledge, pp. 47–89.

Darder, A. (2002), *Reinventing Paulo Freire: A Pedagogy of Love*. New York: Westview Press.

Darling, J. and Nordenbo, S. E. (2003), 'Progressivism', in N. Blake *et al*. *The Blackwell Guide to Philosophy of Education*. Oxford: Blackwell, pp. 288–308.

De Figueiredo-Cowen, M. and Gastaldo, D. (1995), 'Paulo Freire in the Nineties: Life Experience and Progressive Education', in M. de Figueiredo-Cowen and D. Gastaldo ed. *Paulo Freire at the Institute*. London: Institute of Education, pp. 1–16.

Debord, G. (1990), *Comments on the Society of the Spectacle*. London: Verso.

—(2000), *Society of the Spectacle*. London: Rebel Press.

Derrida, J. (1977), *Margins of Philosophy*. Translated by Alan Bass. Chicago, IL: University of Chicago Press.

—(1978), *Writing and Difference*. Translated by Alan Bass. Chicago, IL: University of Chicago Press.

—(1982), 'The Ends of Man', in *Margins of Philosophy*. Translated by Alan Bass. Chicago, IL: University of Chicago Press, pp. 109–36.

—(2000), *Le Toucher, Jean-Luc Nancy*. Paris: Éditions Galilée.

Dewey, J. (1973), *Experience and Education*. New York: Collier Books.

Dhillon, P. A. and Standish, P. ed. *Lyotard: Just Education*. London: Routledge.

Dolby, N. and Dimitriadis, G. (2004), 'Learning to Labour in New Times: An Introduction', in N. Dolby *et al*. (with Paul Willis) *Learning to Labour in New Times*. London: RoutledgeFarmer, pp. 1–16.

Dolby, N. *et al*. (with P. Willis) ed. (2004), *Learning to Labour in New Times*. London: RoutledgeFarmer.

Drolet, M. (2004), *The Postmodernism Reader: Foundational Texts*. London: Routledge.

Dunne, J. (1997), *Back to the Rough Ground: Practical Judgement and the Lure of Technique*. Notre Dame, IN: University of Notre Dame Press.

Dunne, J. and Hogan, P. (2004), *Education and Practice: Upholding the Integrity of Teaching and Learning*. London: Blackwell.

Dunne, J. *et al*. ed. (2000), *Questioning Ireland: Debates in Political Philosophy and Public Policy*. Dublin: IPA.

Eagleton, T. (1994), 'Ideology and its Vicissitudes in Western Marxism', in S. Žižek ed. *Mapping Ideology*. London: Verso, pp. 179–226.

Elden, S. (2004), *Understanding Henri Lefebvre*. London: Routledge.

Elias, J. (1994), *Paulo Freire: Pedagogue of Liberation*. New York: Teacher's College Press.

Fanon, F. (1986a), *Black Skin, White Masks*. London: Pluto.

—(1986b), *The Wretched of the Earth*. London: Penguin.

Flahault, F. (2003), *Malice*. London: Verso.

Flanagan, F. (2003), *The Greatest Educators Ever*. London: Continuum.

Foucault, M. (1998), 'A Preface to Transgression', in J. D. Faubion ed. *Aesthetics – Essential Works of Foucault 1954–1984* Volume 2. London: Penguin.

—(2004), 'Foreword', in G. Deleuze and F. Guattari. *Anti-Oedipus*. London: Continuum.

Franks, B. (2006), *Rebel Alliances: The Means and Ends of Contemporary Anarchisms*. Edinburgh: AK Press.

Fromm, E. (2001), *The Fear of Freedom*. London: Routledge.

Gadotti, M. (1994), *Reading Paulo Freire: His Life and Work*. New York: State University of New York Press.

Garcia, T. (2011), *Hate: A Romance*. London: Faber and Faber.

Gardiner, P. (2002), *Kierkegaard: A Very Short Introduction*. Oxford: Oxford University Press.

Garrison, J. and Neiman, A. (2003), 'Pragmatism and Education', in N. Blake *et al. The Blackwell Guide to Philosophy of Education*. Oxford: Blackwell, pp. 21–37.

Giroux, H. (1993), 'Paulo Freire and the Politics of Postcolonialism', in P. McLaren and P. Leonard ed. *Paulo Freire: A Critical Encounter*. London: Routledge, pp. 177–88.

—(2000), *Breaking In To The Movies*. New York: Routledge.

Giroux, H. and Aronowitz, S. (1992), *Postmodern Education*. London: Routledge.

Goulet, D. (2005), 'Introduction', in P. Freire *Education for Critical Consciousness*. Translated by M. Ramos, L. Bigwood and M. Marshall. London: Continuum, pp. vii–xiii.

Gramsci, A. (1988), *The Antonio Gramsci Reader: Selected Writings 1916–1935*, edited by D. Forgacs. London: Lawrence & Wishart.

Gutierrez, G. (2001), *A Theology of Liberation*. New York: SCM Press.

Gutmann, A. ed. (1994), *Multiculturalism: Examining the Politics of Recognition*. Princeton, NJ: Princeton University Press.

Habermas, J. (1986), *Toward a Rational Society: Student Protest, Science and Politics*. London: Polity Press.

Hall, S. (1996a), 'Cultural Studies and its Theoretical Legacies', in D. Morley and K. H. Chen ed. *Stuart Hall: Critical Dialogues in Cultural Studies*. London: Routledge, pp. 262–75.

—(1996b), 'Gramsci's Relevance for the Study of Race and Ethnicity', in D. Morley and K. H. Chen ed. *Stuart Hall: Critical Dialogues in Cultural Studies*. London: Routledge, pp. 411–40.

—(1996c), 'The Problem of Ideology: Marxism Without Guarantees', in D. Morley and K. H. Chen ed. *Stuart Hall: Critical Dialogues in Cultural Studies*. London: Routledge, pp. 25–46.

Hall, S. *et al.* ed. (1993), *Resistance through Rituals: Youth Subcultures in Post-War Britain*. London: Routledge.

Hegel, G. W. F. (1979), *Phenomenology of Spirit*. Translated by A. V. Miller. OUP. Oxford: Oxford University Press.

Heidegger, M. (1991), *Nietzsche: The Will to Power as Art v. 1* (Nietzsche, Vols I and II). Translated by David Farrell Krell. Australia: HarperCollins.

Held, D. (1989), *Introduction to Critical Theory: From Horkheimer to Habermas*. London: Routledge.

Hirst, P. and Peters, R. (1970), *The Logic of Education*. London: Routledge & Kegan Paul.

hooks, b. (1994), *Teaching to Transgress: Education as The Practice of Freedom*. London: Routledge.

Huxley, A. (1970), *Ends and Means*. London: Virago.

Illich, I. (1971), *Deschooling Society*. New York: Marion Boyars.

—(1996), 'Foreword', in M. Hern ed. *Deschooling Our Lives*. Canada: New Society, pp. i–vi.

Irwin, J. (2010a), *Derrida and the Writing of the Body*. Ashgate: Surrey.

—(2010b), 'Re-Politicising Education – Interpreting Jean-François Lyotard's *The Postmodern Condition* in a Contemporary Context', in C. Mc Donnell ed. *Yearbook of the Irish Philosophical Society*. Dublin: Mullin Print.

—(2010c), 'A Well-Being Out of Nihilism – Nietzsche, Anarchism and Postmodern Thought', in B. Franks ed. *Anarchism and Moral Philosophy*. London: Palgrave and Macmillan, pp. 208–25.

—(2011), 'A Postmodernist Rendering of Freire's Educational Vision? – Some Reflections on the Birmingham CCCS', in M. O'Brien and A. O'Shea ed. *Pedagogy, Oppression and Transformation in a 'Post-Critical' Climate: The Return to Freirean Thinking*. London: Continuum.

Jameson, F. (2001), 'Introduction', in L. Althusser *Lenin and Philosophy and Other Essays*. New York: Monthly Review Press, pp. vii–xiv.

Jaspers, K. (1971), *Philosophy of Existence*. Pennsylvania, PA: Pennsylvania Press.

Kearney, R. (1986), *Modern Movements in European Philosophy*. Manchester: Manchester University Press.

—(1988), *The Wake of the Imagination*. London: Routledge.

Kierkegaard, S. (1992), *Either/Or: A Fragment of Life*. Translated by A. Hannay. London: Penguin.

Kincheloe, J. L. (1994), 'Afterword', in P. McLaren and C. Lankshear ed. *Politics of Liberation: Paths from Freire*. London: Routledge, pp. 216–218.

—(2005), 'Introduction' in P. Freire *Teachers as Cultural Workers: Letters to Those Who Dare Teach*. Expanded edition translated by D. Macedo, D. Koike and A. Oliveira. Cambridge, MA: Westview Press, pp. xli–xlix.

Kojève, A. (1980), *Introduction to the Reading of Hegel: Lectures on the Phenomenology of Spirit*. New York: Cornell University Press.

Kozol, J. (1978), 'Foreword' in P. Freire *Pedagogy in Process: The Letters To Guinea-Bissau*. New York: Writers and Readers Co-operative.

Kress, G. (1995), 'Representation as Transformation, in M. de Figueiredo-Cowen and D. Gastaldo ed. *Paulo Freire at the Institute*. London: Institute of Education, pp. 38–50.

Lacey, D. (2000), *Fanon: A Life*. London, Granta: London.

Lefebvre, H. (2000), *The Production of Space*. London: Blackwell.

—(2002), *Critique of Everyday Life: Foundations for a Sociology of the Everyday Volume 2*. London: Verso.

—(2003), *Key Writings*, edited by S. Elden *et al.* London: Continuum.

Long, F. (2008), 'Protocols of Silence in Educational Discourse', *Irish Educational Studies*, 27 (2), pp. 5–17.

Lyotard, J. F. (1986), *The Postmodern Condition: A Report on Knowledge*. Translated by G. Bennington and B. Massumi. Manchester: Manchester University Press.

—(1993), *Political Writings*. Translated by B. Readings and K. P. Geiman. Minneapolis: University of Minnesota Press.

Macedo, D. (1994), 'Preface', in P. McLaren and C. Lankshear ed. *Politics of Liberation: Paths from Freire*. London: Routledge, pp. xiii–xix.

Maritain, J. (1943), *Education at the Crossroads*. New Haven, CT: Connect.

Marcuse, H. (2002), *One-Dimensional Man: Studies in the Ideology of Advanced Industrial Society*. London: Routledge.

Marx, K. (1992a), 'The Theses on Feuerbach', in K. Marx *Early Writings*. Translated by R. Livingstone and G. Benton. London: Penguin, pp. 421–23.

—(1992b), 'Economic and Philosophical Manuscripts (1844)', in K. Marx *Early Writings*. Translated by R. Livingstone and G. Benton. London: Penguin, pp. 279–400.

—(1998), *The German Ideology: Including Theses on Feuerbach and an Introduction to the Critique of Political Economy*. London: Prometheus Books.

—(2008), *The Communist Manifesto*. Oxford: Oxford University Press.

May, T. (1994), *The Political Philosophy of Poststructuralist Anarchism*. Philadelphia, PA: Pennsylvania University Press.

McDonough, T. (2004), *Guy Debord and the Situationist International*. Texts and documents edited by T. McDonough. Cambridge, MA: MIT Press.

McLaren, P. (1989), *Life in Schools*. New York: Routledge.

—(2005), 'Preface: A Pedagogy for Life', in P. Freire *Teachers as Cultural Workers: Letters to Those Who Dare Teach*. Expanded edition translated by D. Macedo, D. Koike and A. Oliveira. Cambridge, MA: Westview Press, pp. xxvii–xli.

McLaren. P. and Lankshear, C. (1994a), 'Introduction', in P. McLaren and C. Lankshear ed. *Politics of Liberation: Paths from Freire*. London: Routledge, pp. 1–11.

McLaren, P. and Leonard, P. (1993a), ed. *Paulo Freire: A Critical Encounter*. London: Routledge.

—(1993b), 'Editor's Introduction: Paulo Freire and the Dangerous Memories of Liberation', in P. McLaren and P. Leonard ed. *Paulo Freire: A Critical Encounter*. London: Routledge, pp. 1–7.

Memmi, A. (1975), *The Colonizer and the Colonized*. London: Virago.

Morley, D. and Chen, K. H. ed. (1996), *Stuart Hall: Critical Dialogue in Cultural Studies*. London: Routledge.

Morrow, R.A. and C. A. Torres (2002), *Reading Freire and Habermas: Critical Pedagogy and Transformative Social Change*. New York: Teachers' College Press.

Moseley, A. (2008), *An Introduction to Political Philosophy*. London: Continuum.

Mouffe, C. (2005), *The Return of the Political*. London: Verso.

NCCA Ireland (1999), Irish Primary School Curriculum. Dublin: NCCA.

Newman, S. (2001), *From Bakunin to Lacan: Anti-Authoritarianism and the Dislocation of Power*. Plymouth, MA: Lexington Books.

Newsam, P. (1995), 'Foreword' in M. de Figueiredo-Cowen and D. Gastaldo (eds) *Paulo Freire at the Institute* ed. London: Institute of Education, pp. v–vii.

Nietzsche, F. (1998), *On the Genealogy of Morals*. Translated by R. J. Hollingdale. London: Penguin.

—(2004), *On the Future of Our Educational Institutions*. Indiana: St Augustine's Press.

O'Cadiz, M. del Pilar, Lindquist Wong, P. and Torres, C. A. (1998), *Education and Democracy: Paulo Freire, Social Movements and Educational Reform in São Paulo*. Oxford: Westview Press.

O'Sullivan, D. (2005), *Cultural Politics and Irish Education since the 1950s: Policy, Paradigms and Power*. Dublin: IPA.

Osborne, P. (2000), *Philosophy in Cultural Theory*. London: Routledge.

Peters, M. and Wilson, K. (2003), 'Postmodernism/Post-structuralism', in N. Blake *et al. The Blackwell Guide to Philosophy of Education*. Oxford: Blackwell, pp. 57–72.

Plato (1961), *The Collected Dialogues of Plato*, rdited by E. Hamilton and H. Cairns. New York: Pantheon.

Pring, R. (2010), *John Dewey*. London: Continuum.

Quinn, P. (2010), 'Paulo Freire's Theory of Education as Political Transformation', in C. McDonnell ed. *Yearbook of the Irish Philosophical Society*. Dublin: Mullin Print.

Rancière, J. (1991), *The Ignorant Schoolmaster: Five Lessons in Intellectual Emancipation*. Translated with an introduction by Kristin Ross. Stanford, CA: Stanford University Press.

Readings, B. (1996), *The University in Ruins*. Cambridge, MA: Harvard University Press.

Rojek, C. (2003), *Stuart Hall*. Oxford: Polity Press.

Ross, K. (1991), 'Translator's Introduction' in Rancière *The Ignorant Schoolmaster: Five Lessons in Intellectual Emancipation*. Stanford, CA: Stanford University Press, pp. i–xx.

—(2004), *May '68 and its Afterlives*. Chicago, IL: University of Chicago Press.

Sartre, J. P. (1986), 'Preface to *The Wretched of the Earth*: Black Orpheus', in F. Fanon. *The Wretched of the Earth*. London: Penguin.

—(2003), *Being and Nothingness*. London: Routledge.

—(2007), *Existentialism and Humanism*. London: Methuen.

Schaull, R. (1996), 'Foreword', in P. Freire *Pedagogy of the Oppressed*. London: Continuum, pp. i–viii.

Seery, A. (2008), 'Slavoj Žižek's Dialectics of Ideology and the Discourses of Irish Education', *Irish Educational Studies*, 27(2), pp. 25–37.

Singer, P. (2000), *Marx: A Short Introduction*. Oxford: Oxford University Press.

Smeyers, P., R. Smith, and P. Standish ed. *The Blackwell Guide to the Philosophy of Education*. Oxford: Blackwell, pp. 38–57.

Sugrue, C. ed. (2004), *Curriculum and Ideology: Irish Experiences, International Perspectives*. Dublin: The Liffey Press.

Tarantino, Q. (1994), *Pulp Fiction* (film).

Taylor, P. (1994), *The Texts of Paulo Freire*. New York: Virago.

Thomassen, L. ed. (2006), *The Derrida-Habermas Reader*. Edinburgh: Edinburgh University Press.

Tormey, R. and Haran, N. (2002), *Celebrating Difference, Promoting Equality – Towards a Framework for Intercultural Education in Irish Classrooms*. Limerick: CEDR/CDU MIC.

Torres, C. A. (1993), 'From the Pedagogy of the Oppressed to A Luta Continua; The Political Pedagogy of Paulo Freire', in P. McLaren and P. Leonard ed. *Paulo Freire: A Critical Encounter*. London: Routledge, pp. 119–145.

—(1994), 'Foreword' in M. Gadotti *Reading Paulo Freire: His Life and Work*. New York: State University of New York Press, pp. ix–xiii.

Torres, C. A. and Freire, P. (1994), 'Twenty Years after Pedagogy of the Oppressed: Paulo Freire in Conversation with Carlos Alberto Torres', in P. McLaren and C. Lankshear ed. *Politics of Liberation: Paths from Freire*. London: Routledge, pp. 100–107.

Toscano, A. (2010), *Fanaticism: On the Uses of an Idea*. London: Verso.

Trebitsch, M, (1991), 'Preface', in H. Lefebvre *Critique of Everyday Life*, Volume 1. London: Verso, pp. i–xxi.

West, C. (1993), 'Preface', in P. McLaren and P. Leonard ed. *Paulo Freire: A Critical Encounter*. London: Routledge.

Willis, P. (1981), *Learning to Labour*. New York: Columbia University Press.

—(2000), *The Ethnographic Imagination*. London: Polity Press.

—(2004), 'Interview' in N. Dolby *et al.* (with P. Willis) *Learning to Labour in New Times*. London: RoutledgeFalmer, pp. 197–226.

Woodcock, G. (1977b), 'Anarchism: A Historical Introduction', in G. Woodcock ed. *The Anarchist Reader*. Glasgow: Fontana.

Woodcock, W. ed. (1977a), *The Anarchist Reader*. Glasgow: Fontana.

Žižek, S. ed. (1994a), *Mapping Ideology*. London: Verso.

—(1994b), 'Introduction: The Spectre of Ideology', in S. Žižek ed. *Mapping Ideology*. London: Verso, pp. 1–33.

—(2006), *Lacan*. London: Granta.

INDEX